THE HALLOWEEN LECTURES
FIFTEEN FIENDISH YEARS OF
VAMPIRES, WEREWOLVES, WITCHES, WIZARDS,
MONSTERS, MOVIES, TUDORS, TRICKS AND TREATS
2001-2015

William B. Robison

Happy Pigg Publishing 2015

This is dedicated to my collaborators, enablers, and dearest loved ones–
Bibbet, Matt, Sara, Zoë, and Molly

AN ADMONITION TO PERUSERS

Is this serious history? If you have gone as far as opening the cover to check out the preface, table of contents, or some other indicator of what is in a book enticingly entitled *The Halloween Lectures*, then surely you have asked that question already. But your inquiry poses a dilemma for me. If I answer "yes," half of you will put the book back on the shelf. If I answer "no," the other half of you will put it back. So, I am going to answer "sort of," after which I hope that all of you will hang on to the book and read it instead of all of you putting it back. If you pay for it instead of stealing it, that will be even better.

Not satisfied with that answer? Then here is a further explanation. The essays in this volume are based on a series of lectures (more below), which in turn are based on serious historical scholarship, a fair amount of it my own. I am a serious historian, that is, I make a living teaching and writing history. At the same time, I am not an overly "serious" serious historian, which is to say that while I take the proper practice of the historical discipline very seriously indeed, I do not take myself very seriously at all. One of the main reasons I do history for a living—probably the most important—is that it is fun. I also like teaching history, and I am willing to do just about anything to get my students to both take it seriously and enjoy themselves while learning it. Students who have fun learning keep doing it. Students who keep learning history make better citizens and more critical thinkers. And, if I am lucky, they laugh at my jokes.

Now, what about those lectures and the essays based thereon in this book? In 1986 my institution, Southeastern Louisiana University, inaugurated an annual, month-long celebration of the arts, humanities, and social sciences held each October called Fanfare. From the first, the Department of History and Political Science—of which I am a faculty member—participated in the festivities. However, in 2001—a couple of years after I became Department Head—we established the annual Then and Now Fanfare History and Politics Lecture Series with the purpose of providing educational, but simultaneously entertaining, lectures about history and politics suitable for a general audience of faculty, staff, students, and community people. That year, on Halloween, I gave a lecture called "Bad History Goes to the Movies."

Though this initially was intended to be a one-off event, "History Goes to the Movies" became a regular feature of the series, with a different faculty member taking on films and television about his/her field of expertise each year. The next year, in 2002, I gave another presentation at the end of the month, which I labeled the "More-or-Less Annual Halloween Lecture." As it has turned out, "more" is the pertinent modifier—there has been a Halloween lecture every year (at least so far). Usually, though not always, the subject is related in some way to All Hallows Eve and/or the popular cultural phenomena associated with it: vampires, werewolves, witches, wizards, Nostradamus, monster movies, Frankenstein, the Puritan war on traditional Christian holidays. Otherwise, it is about the Tudors or Stuarts in England, my actual area of scholarly expertise, though I find some way to relate even that to the occasion, for example, by discussing the Gunpowder Plot of 1605, which led to Guy Fawkes Day (November 5) becoming a more popular mid-autumn holiday in England than Halloween.

Of course doing an annual lecture on Halloween has consequences. First of all, it requires that there be tricks. Therefore, each year there is a prequel to the lecture, i.e., some sort of gimmick, stunt, or other tomfoolery. Since the prequels are an integral part of the program, I have included relics of them here in the form of scripts and links to https://myspace.com/headongoolah/videos, where readers may find audio and/or video for all but the first year (2001). The second requisite thing is treats. Therefore, at the end of each lecture I throw candy to the audience, though no remnants of that aspect of the program have survived. The principle artifacts extant are the lectures themselves, some in the form of notes and some on video that has been shown on cable television by the Southeastern Channel. I have reproduced them as accurately as possible in the essays here. They were fun the first time around—for me and, I think, the audience (maybe it was just the candy)—and I hope that they will be both educational and entertaining again. Each of these lectures also has what might be considered a moral at the end. Just consider all of this my contribution to good citizenship and critical thinking. The only question now is whether I will win the Nobel Prize for Literature or Peace. Maybe both.

Another thing—perceptive readers will notice right away that Happy Pigg Publishing is not a well-known scholarly press. As a matter of fact, it is an entity that I created to publish—via CreateSpace—these lectures and whatever else I might decide in the future to publish outside the traditional machinery of scholarly publishing. I created these lectures primarily to be educational and entertaining, and going the scholarly press route would simply delay publication and make them too expensive. I want to make them available and affordable.

I would like to acknowledge (or share the blame with) numerous people. A series of university presidents have refrained from attempting to revoke my tenure: Sally Clausen, Randy Moffett, and John Crain. A series of Deans of the College of Arts and Sciences and, more recently, the College of Arts, Humanities, and Social Sciences have provided valuable support for Fanfare and to me: John Miller, Albert Doucette, Tammy Bourg, Bryan Depoy, and Karen Fontenot. Fanfare has had a series of brilliant and dedicated directors: Harriet Vogt, Donna Gay Anderson, Kenneth Boulton, and Roy Blackwood. The staff in the Department of History and Political Science—especially Jai'me Barrilleaux, Antoinette Brabham, Cheryl Cannon, and Joyce White—provided me with incredible assistance and support. David Evenson, Kenneth Boulton, and Dale Newkirk—successive Heads of the Department of Music or now the Department of Fine and Performing Arts—have allowed us the use each year of Pottle Auditorium, and Pottle stagecraft wizards Ellen Lipkos and Amanda Klipsch have provided stunning technical assistance, including pyrotechnics for *It's A Live Onstage Reanimation.* Gerard Blanchard, Head of the Department of Chemistry and Physics, loaned me a Van der Graaf generator, chemist Bill Parkinson let me borrow his tie-dyed lab coat, and Barbara Moffett, Head of the Department of Nursing, provided a gurney for the same production. My colleague Barbara Forrest made a hilarious cameo appearance is *There's a War . . . A War on Christmas,* and several of my colleagues' pictures appeared in *Who Killed the Great Pumpkin?* Actor Wade Heaton appeared onstage as Satan in *A Wizard, a Witch, an Apple, and the Devil* and as Mr. McTogaman in (the regrettably un-filmed) *Mr. Robison's Spooky Neighborhood,* as well as on film as Orson Welles in *Preposterodamus the Forgotten Seer,* which also featured former graduate student Chuck Dellert as Weenus of Wallachia. Actor George Sanchez appeared onstage as Dr. Frankenstein's monster (George is my father-in-law—make of that what you will), along with Donna Gay Anderson as the "flower girl." My brother Tucker Robison composed two "Renaissance Dances" for *Preposterodamus* and appeared in that film as the simple-minded Fantod, as did my sister-in-law Natasha Sanchez in multiple roles. My son Matt was in the same film, and my daughters Zoe and Molly have appeared on film and onstage on multiple occasions. My wife Bibbet (Elizabeth) has commented on my scripts, directed, filmed, edited, and provided special effects for my prequel movies, as well as appearing onstage. She and my children also have given me much encouragement, perhaps against their own better judgment. My colleagues, friends, and fellow carpoolers Charles Elliott and Harry Laver have provided me with frequent feedback and humorous inspiration since the early days of the lecture series. My colleagues, friends, and fellow musicians in the band Impaired Faculties—Joe Burns, Dan McCarthy, Randy Settoon, and Ralph Wood—have helped me maintain a positive creative attitude and a sense of fun since 2013. Finally, I am grateful to all the faculty, staff, students, and community folk who have come to my lectures over the years.

TABLE OF CONTENTS

Table of Contents

Table of Contents

2001 PREQUEL
THE LIGHT-UP HALLOWEEN HAT

This was the lamest prequel ever because I did not know that I was establishing a tradition of beginning each presentation with a gimmick, nor did I realize that I was inaugurating a series of Halloween lectures—this was just a lecture that took place on Halloween. So, I wore a baseball cap with an orange flashing light-up ghost. With a coat and tie. People chuckled a little.

Alas, the hat has disappeared. But the prequels get better.

2001 LECTURE
BAD HISTORY GOES TO THE MOVIES

Please allow me to begin with a disclaimer. I am not an expert on film and history, nor am I an expert on movies in general. I am just a historian who watches movies with a historian's sensibility. As a result I am a pariah in own home—my family refuses to watch history movies with me unless I promise to keep quiet. Moreover, it is not just talking that they have banned. I am prohibited from making faces, rolling my eyes, sighing, grunting, groaning, coughing in a suspicious manner, or in any other way expressing disbelief, disgust, or dismay. Therefore, I am taking it out on you!

Okay, the truth is that I actually like most of the movies I am addressing here. Many of them are good movies that happen to include a fair amount of bad history. What I would like to do, therefore, is offer some general observations about how movies handle history and why, provide some examples from my period of expertise—late medieval and early modern England, and suggest some conclusions about why the way movies portray history matters.

Hollywood loves history—the epic stories, the costumes, the pageantry, the battle scenes, and, of course, the Oscars that history movies win. For many years all a studio had to do to guarantee success was to cast Charlton Heston (the pre-*Planet of the Apes* Charlton Heston). As I tell my students, there is really no Western Civilization without Charlton Heston. He has played Moses, El Cid, Michelangelo, Thomas More, Cardinal Richelieu, Charles George Gordon, and more. Then the movie industry stopped making Heston-esque epics, and the next thing you knew he was selling Bud Lite. The closest thing we have to a new Heston is Russell Crowe, who is very good indeed. However, Heston and Crowe's films—like most history movies—are frequently inaccurate. *Gladiator* (2000), for example, is a good film, but it contains its share of inventions. One is that while Marcus Aurelius and Commodus were real historical figures, Crowe's Maximus was not.

Hollywood loves history because it loves money, and despite the myth that history is boring or that at least people find it that way, history flicks sell. But Hollywood is not noted for original thinking—it routinely gets stuck on formulas. The modern formula for movie success says you must have sex and car chases. For most of history, however, car chases are not an option (though occasionally chariots appears as stand-ins). That leaves only sex, which often leads to problems with bogus romantic subplots. So, for instance, the popular and very entertaining movie *Enemy at the Gates* (2001)—based on William Craig's nonfiction book of the same name about the Battle of Stalingrad—recounts a real duel between two World War II snipers, the German Erwin König (Ed Harris) and the Soviet Vasily Grigoryevich Zaitsev (Jude Law), but it introduces a fictional love triangle involving Zaitsev, Soviet political commissar Danilov (Joseph Fiennes), and local female militia volunteer Tania (Rachel Weisz).

Another problem is recycling formulas that worked the first time. So, for example, Mel Gibson as William Wallace in *Braveheart* (1995) becomes Mel Gibson as Benjamin Martin in *The Patriot* (2000), though he did not moon the British in the latter. Of course we are used to Mel Gibson being recycled, but we expect Danny Glover and Joe Pesci to show up when that happens. One of the most egregious recent examples is this: *Saving Private Ryan* (1998) was a huge critical success and *Titanic* (1997) made lots of money while reducing millions of teenage girls to tears; therefore, someone figured: World War II is hot right now, so let's remake *Titanic* during WWII. Thus, we got another movie featuring two hours of a sappy, irrelevant love story followed by 45 minutes of great special battle effects—*Pearl Harbor* (2001). There was so little real history that not only did veterans complain, even the critics did so. Sadly another formula when making history movies is that the screenwriter must improve on the actual story. The notion that truth is not only stranger, but also frequently more interesting, than fiction has not penetrated the consciousness of many screenwriters.

There are three broad categories of "history" movies: (1) movies based on myths or legends, (2) "true-to-life" fiction set against a historical background, and (3) movies about actual historical figures and events—all three of which may include movies with a message. Some people might question why myth and legend are included here at all. But, in fact, many moviegoers do not know the difference between myths and legends on one hand and actual history on the other. And the former often look like history movies.

A case in point is Arthur—the mythical medieval monarch, not the drunken Dudley Moore. Somehow, again and again, a sixth-century Celtic warrior king, defending his realm against sixth-century Saxons, ends up in thirteenth-century armor, as in *Excalibur*. Worse than that, of course, is that there was no Arthur in the first place. The character who appears in Geoffrey of Monmouth's eleventh-century *History of the Kings of Britain*, Sir Thomas Malory's fifteenth-century *Le Morte d'Arthur*, the dozens of knock-off novels, and the many Arthur movies is at best an amalgam of several actual rulers or, more likely, a complete legend. Another example is Robin Hood, who apparently was from Kansas in his most recent incarnation. [This refers to Kevin Costner's non-English accent in the 1991 *Robin Hood: Prince of Thieves*; this lecture preceded Russell Crowe's 2010 *Robin Hood*, which has some significant historical problems of its own, like making Robin Hood's father the author of the Magna Carta and having the French land at Dover in what are essentially D-Day Higgins boats.] Though medieval English forests had their share of poachers and thieves, there was no Robin Hood. Yet another example is Hercules, the most abused mythical figure in movie history, but there was no Hercules either. On the other hand, there really was a Dracula, but he was a fifteenth-century prince of Wallachia (where he ruled off and on between 1448 and 1477), not a vampire.

Regrettably Arthur, Robin Hood, and Hercules bring up another unpleasant subject—cartoon movies. These not only botch up mythology but also real history. There are lots of examples. Everybody is mad at Disney about something, and I am no different. I do not care about the sexual preference of their amusement park employees or the allegedly phallic minarets in *Aladdin* (1992—here is a hint: all towers are phallic). What I cannot forgive is *Pocahontas* (1995). Of course an accurate movie about Pocahontas really would get Disney in trouble with the Puritans, and I do not mean the ones from seventeenth-century New England. Instead of giving much-deserved equal time to Native Americans, this movie turns Pocahontas into a kind of new age wood sprite with a lite-rock sound track and a supporting cast of stereotyped evil European imperialists and anthropomorphic animals. Why am I so vehement about this? It is because my children own the movie and watch it over and over and over!

True-to-life fictional movies set against a historical background sometimes are better at giving viewers a sense of history than those that purport to be about real historical people and events. Costume dramas like the Merchant-Ivory films provide a pretty good "feel" for the times. The first half-hour of *Saving Private Ryan* contains the most realistic war footage ever, according to World War II veterans. *Platoon* (1986) is not bad either. Though it offended some Vietnam veterans (and understandably so—not all soldiers in Southeast Asia were "My Lai massacre" types), the battle scenes—some of which will make your skin craw—were a useful antidote to the Rambo movies.

Movies about actual historical figures and events usually are problematic. Some areas of history suffer particularly badly, for example, the American Civil War. Bruce Chadwick, in *The Reel Civil War*, discusses more than 800, most of which he identifies as bad history. In the first half of the twentieth century, Civil War movies were mostly of the "moonlight and magnolias" variety. By far the most noteworthy is *Gone With The Wind* (1939), a great movie but one that is based on a novel, not on historical research. It is populated with plantation aristocrats and happy darkies but no plain folk of the sort that my colleague Sam Hyde discusses in his work. In the second half of the twentieth century movie Southerners appear to comprise Colonel Sanders, the supporting cast of *Deliverance* (1972), and a bunch of guys that look like Ernest T. Bass.

Speaking of formulaic portrayals also brings up Westerns— everybody out West was a cowboy or an Indian. So, for example, in the 1950s TV series *The Adventures of Kit Carson*, the explorer and trapper became a six-gun totin', rootin', tootin', shoot-'em-up avatar of justice (Bill Williams) with a Mexican sidekick named El Toro (Don Diamond). Pirate movies are similar. Most cinema buccaneers are not much more realistic than Captain Hook. Thus, it is entirely appropriate that Charles Laughton appeared in 1945 in *Captain Kidd*, a largely fictional movie about a real historical figure, and then in 1952 in *Abbott and Costello Meet Captain Kidd*, which obviously was not supposed to be real.

One problem is that as soon as you start writing a screenplay, fiction creeps in. Movies dealing with periods prior to the twentieth century have to invent lot of dialogue and business. They frequently resort to time compression or expansion. Cecil B. De Mille's 1956 Biblical epic *The Ten Commandments* (1956), now an annual television event, is three hours and forty minutes long but contains at most half an hour's worth of material based on actual scripture. That movie is almost half a century old, and the technology used at the time means it looks like a movie. But films now look much more "realistic," which makes them harder to doubt (though modern war movies are never realistic enough for military detail fanatics).

As my colleague and movie historian Bill Parrill notes, movies often tell us more about the period in which they were made than the period about which they were made. Here Westerns again are relevant. In the 1950s everybody looked like Gary Cooper—tall, clean cut, and handsome. By the late 1960s they began looking more like the Grateful Dead, and the 1970s they all looked like Clint Eastwood because mostly they all *were* Clint Eastwood. The message changed, too, as the fresh-scrubbed, white-hat-wearing hero gave way to the scruffy anti-hero and good-guys-versus-bad-guys to moral ambiguity.

Another example of presentism in cinema is Joan of Arc, the subject of two recent movies—*Joan of Arc* (TV 1999) and *The Messenger: The*

Story of Joan of Arc (1999)—both of which make her an early hero of feminism. But Joan was most certainly not a feminist, a completely anachronistic concept in the fifteenth century. She was a peasant girl, almost certainly illiterate, who began hearing what she believed to be the voices of saints, telling her that she should help the French King Charles VII take back his throne from the English in the latter stages of the Hundred Years War. She persuaded a local worthy named Robert Baudricourt to introduce her to Charles, who believed her mad but allowed her to ride into battle with his soldiers, who thought her to be divinely inspired. Eventually she was captured by England's ally, the Duke of Burgundy. After Charles refused to ransom her, Burgundy turned her over to the English, who burned her as a witch (there—I had to get in a least one Halloween reference). The same sort of retroactive attribution of feminism to a powerful female figure occurs with Elizabeth I of England, but more on that later.

And then there is Oliver Stone, all of whose movies are about Vietnam in one way or another. There is now a whole book on his treatment of "history," *Oliver Stone's USA: Film, History, and Controversy*, edited by Robert Brent Toplin and featuring an article on the film *JFK* (1991) by my colleague and Kennedy assassination expert Michael Kurtz. As he notes, it is a great movie—the editing of modern film and contemporary video is particularly brilliant—but it is terrible history.

Now I would like to look at my own period in history, late medieval and early modern Britain. First, let us turn to Scotland. Two recent movies about Scots national heroes, *Braveheart* (1995) and *Rob Roy* (1995) are more about late twentieth century Scottish nationalism than about the actual historical figures. *Braveheart*, set in the late thirteenth and early fourteenth centuries, is about a real Scotsman, William Wallace, who helped lead a revolt against the English King Edward I and wreaked considerable havoc in northern England before being captured, convicted of treason, and hanged, drawn, and quartered. The major primary source for Wallace is the writing of the poet Blind Harry, who is rather sketchy and imprecise about details. Most of the supporting cast for Mel Gibson's Wallace are invented out of whole cloth. While Wallace did have a wife who was murdered, it did not happen as in the movie. The bogus love story between Wallace and the French Princess Isabella, wife of the English Prince Edward (later Edward II) is entirely implausible—Wallace died in 1305, at which time Isabella was about ten years old, unmarried, and still living in France.

Edward I, though really nicknamed "Longshanks," is otherwise a caricature—the one-dimensional villain bears little resemblance to reality. Though capable of brutality and no friend of the Scots, he also was a reformer known for increasing the role of parliament in England, expanding the scope of the common law, and imposing greater law and order through his various statutes. The movie also misrepresents Prince Edward, whom it portrays as a foppish homosexual—though the prince was bisexual, he was hardly the feckless character of the movie, and at no point did the king throw one of his male lovers out of a window. On the Scottish side, Robert the Bruce becomes a turncoat, and for some reason his father appears to be rotting (with an undefined wasting disease) throughout the film. The Battle of Sterling (Bridge) mysteriously occurs without the famous span over the River Forth, even though the bridge was the critical tactical element in the Scots' victory. At the subsequent Battle of Falkirk, it was the Welsh who deserted Wallace, not the Irish as in the movie. Finally, Edward I was not on his deathbed when Wallace was captured, and the depiction of hanging, drawing, and quartering is inaccurate.

Another major Scottish movie, which came out the same year as Gladiator, is *Rob Roy*, starring Liam Neeson in the title role. Like Wallace, Rob Roy MacGregor was a real historical character, though one much romanticized onscreen—of course part of the blame for that goes back to the nineteenth century novelist, Sir Walter Scot, whose 1817 novel did much to create the modern legend. The real Rob Roy participated as an eighteen-year-old in the failed 1689 Jacobite rising against William III led by the Viscount Dundee and as an adult was an outlaw who made his living rustling cattle. In the movie Rob Roy is the hero. The fictional character Archibald Cunningham (Tim Roth) steals £1,000 that the Duke of Montrose has loaned Rob Roy, but in reality one of Rob Roy's own men was the likely thief. Although the movie is set in the 1710s, it does not mention the 1715 Jacobite Rebellion or James Edward the Old Pretender.

Two excellent medieval England movies focus on the reign of Henry II in the twelfth century, with Peter O'Toole as the king—*Becket* (1964) and *The Lion in Winter* (1968). Both convey an accurate sense of the problems that Henry faced—first with the recalcitrant Archbishop of Canterbury Thomas Becket (Richard Burton) and then with his own wife Eleanor of Aquitaine (Katherine Hepburn) and their sons Richard (Anthony Hopkins), Geoffrey (John Castle), and John (Nigel Terry)—even if they compress time and make factual errors—there are numerous anachronisms in both; Becket was a Norman, not a Saxon; the alleged homosexual relationship between Richard and Philip II is a myth. The latter movie features debuts by both Hopkins and Timothy Burton as Philip. An amusing, if irrelevant, discovery I made while ordering a copy of *Becket* recently [in 2001] is that if you type in "Becket" on Amazon.com's search engine, you get hits for both "Live Nude Girls" and "Sister Wendy" (the art critic nun).

Now let us turn to the Tudors [this lecture preceded a number of Tudor movies that appeared in the first decade of the 21st century, as well as the Showtime series about Henry VIII]. The first sound film about Henry VIII, *The Private Lives of Henry VIII* (1933) featured Charles Laughton as the king, whom he played as a gluttonous buffoon—a big fat idiot with a drumstick. More recent and much better in terms of cinematic art is *A Man for All Season* (1966), for which Paul Scofield won a Best Actor Oscar for his role as Sir Thomas More. Although the film gets right the broad outlines of More's struggle with his conscience over Henry's divorce from Catherine of Aragon and his break with Rome, it is too black and white, exaggerating More's saintliness and ignoring his own persecution of heretics while he was Lord Chancellor. Robert Shaw's Henry is a bit over the top, though Orson Welles is excellent as the corpulent and corrupt Cardinal Thomas Wolsey and Leo McKern as the cunning, conniving Cromwell; nevertheless, they and everyone else in the film are made—inaccurately—to seem entirely venal in comparison with More. *Anne of the Thousand Days* (1969)—with Richard Burton as Henry, Irene Papas as Catherine, Genevieve Bujold as Anne Boleyn, Anthony Quayle as Wolsey, and John Colicos as Cromwell—is actually more accurate, though it also has factual problems. The BBC television mini-series, *The Six Wives of Henry VIII* (1970)—with Keith Mitchell as Henry—is on the whole the best portrayal, though it is a bit uneven because it gives equal time to all six wives.

If I were making a movie about Henry VIII, my choice of actor to play the king would be somewhat unorthodox—I would choose Billy Bob Thornton. Now that might seem odd, but here is why. I believe that Henry VIII was actually the prototype for the Southern male in America. Does that sound stupid? Go ahead, laugh. But then think about it. He had a good Southern-sounding name, Henry Tudor. Like many Southerners, he was part Anglo-Saxon and part Celtic. He composed and played music like that still heard in Appalachia. He honored the code of chivalry. He liked to wrestle. It was never in doubt that he would rather hunt than work. And check out that beard.

But of course Henry is best known for his tumultuous marital history. So consider this. If your brother (Arthur) dies and you marry his widow (Catherine of Aragon); if you cheat on her while she is pregnant with a woman (Elizabeth Blount) who gives you a bastard son that you acknowledge and name after yourself (Henry Fitzroy); if you take another mistress (Mary Boleyn), then abandon her, divorce your wife, and marry your ex-girlfriend's sister (Anne Boleyn); if you accuse her of adultery with three of your buddies (William Brereton, Henry Norris, Francis Weston), her music teacher (Mark Smeaton), and her brother (George Boleyn); if you have her beheaded and marry her serving woman (Jane Seymour), who dies after giving birth to your sickly and religiously fanatical son (Edward VI), who himself dies tragically young; if you marry again to an alcoholic with poor hygiene (Anne of Cleves) and accuse her of lying about her virginity; if you divorce her and marry a woman half your age (Catherine Howard), who sleeps with at least one of your courtiers (Thomas Culpeper); if you have her killed and then take up with a twice-widowed woman (Catherine Parr) who is infatuated with your brother-in-law (Thomas Seymour), who in turn fools around with your teenaged daughter (Elizabeth) after you die . . . well, then you just might be a redneck!

Another Tudor movie that is rather problematic is *Lady Jane* (1986), with Helena Bonham Carter as Lady Jane Grey, the tragic "nine days queen" who briefly came to the throne between the reigns of Edward VI and Mary I. This film focuses on a bogus romance. Hoping to prevent the Catholic Mary from taking the throne, the Protestant Duke of Northumberland really did force Jane to marry his son Guilford Dudley (played by Cary Elwes of *The Princess Bride*—so where is Andre the Giant?). However, in the movie she then falls madly in love with him, tries to exclude Northumberland from power, and embarks on a program of radical social reform—none of which actually happened—before losing her throne and being executed for treason.

Elizabeth I is better served by another BBC mini-series, *Elizabeth R* (1971), in which Glenda Jackson "replaces" Bette Davis as the "classic" Elizabeth. It is relatively accurate, well written, and features excellent acting throughout. Regrettably, Jackson then reprised her role in the movie *Mary Queen of Scots* (1971), which featured Vanessa Redgrave as Mary and contains a number of inaccuracies, the worst of which is a meeting between Elizabeth and Mary that never really occurred. Far worse, though, in terms of ignoring the facts is Shekhar Kapur's *Elizabeth* (1998). Cate Blanchett is brilliant as Elizabeth, but the role the movie assigns to her bears only a slight resemblance to the queen's reign. Mary Tudor (Kathy Burke) is reasonably accurate, though perhaps she is a bit more "evil" than necessary. There are some real howlers in this one—the Duke of Norfolk

(Christopher Eccleston) is an amalgam of the very old 3rd Duke and his grandson, the 4th; Bishop Stephen Gardiner, who died in 1555, survives into Elizabeth's reign to make trouble for her; William Cecil (Richard Attenborough), born 1521, and Francis Walsingham (Geoffrey Rush), born 1532, are elderly while Robert Dudley (Joseph Fiennes), also born 1532, is extremely young; Walsingham has an affair with and then murders Marie of Guise (Fanny Ardant), Regent of Scotland; and one of Elizabeth's maids is murdered with a poison dress intended for her.

The timing of this movie was rather confusing because it came out the same year as *Shakespeare in Love*, in which Shakespeare at least is Shakespeare but not much else is accurate. The confusion arises because Fiennes and Rush are in both films. When Fiennes as Dudley is in bed with Elizabeth (which did not happen), you wonder—what is Fiennes as Shakespeare doing having sex with the Queen when he is having a fling with Gwyneth Paltrow, a girl dressed as a boy so she can play a girl in Shakespeare's play. And when Rush shows up, is that Walsingham or Philip Henslow or possibly David Helfgott? [Rush played pianist Helfgott in the 1996 movie *Shine*.] And then Judi Dench turns up as Elizabeth in *Shakespeare in Love*, and you are thinking—my God, Liz, what has happened to you? Speaking of Dench, she is pretty accurate in *Mrs. Brown* (1997) as Victoria, a queen more suited to her body type.

But seriously, folks, there are lots of inaccuracies in both. Not the least is that *Elizabeth* has the queen, still young, cutting off her hair and covering herself with pale white makeup in order to consciously emulate the Virgin Mary. Here again there is an attempt to invest her reign with anachronistic feminism. What is ironic about all this is that the Tudor era was full of real women who are enormously interesting in their own right and without dubious inventions—Margaret Beaufort, the mother of Henry VII and the real founder of the Tudor dynasty; Elizabeth of York, the wife of Henry VII and mother of Henry VIII; all six of Henry VIII's wives; Mary Tudor; and Elizabeth herself; not to mention non-English figures like Marguerite of Navarre, Mary of Guise, Mary Queen of Scots, and Catherine de Medici.

Why does any of this matter? First of all, the study of history, like all forms of academic inquiry, is a search for truth, and there is historical truth to be found, contrary to the arguments of Hayden White and other post-modernists. Second, understanding history is part of being a good citizen. History and language are what give a nation its sense of identity. This is especially important for Americans because we are such a diverse nation. Non-American history is also important because America is part of

Western Civilization, and understanding it is critical to making sense of our own history. It is unfortunate, but true, that during the last election [2000] voters got more news from late night comedians than the actual news media. Similarly, people often get their "history" from movies. Consider this: threats to democracy usually are based on lies about history. Fascism has given us Leni Riefenstahl's *Triumph of the Will* (1934), communism the inaccurately labeled "socialist realism," and now terrorists lie about our civilization and distort the history of their own religion.

Now, will democracy fail because of bad movies? No. But movies that accurately portray history could be a great teaching tool. Regrettably, that probably will not happen, but at least we can watch them intelligently and make sure that we get real history somewhere. There are lots of good books on film and history that help make that possible. On the other hand, there are some things we should not rush. It has been less than two months since the September 11 attacks [2001], and there already is talk of movies. I hope that will not happen too soon. I am not ready for a romantic comedy set against the backdrop of the World Trade Center attacks or a movie called *Young Osama* about an earnest desert lad seduced by the dark side. I also hope that there will be no bioterrorism movies that promote panic (we have CNN for that). Movies about the current war in Afghanistan need to be handled with care. We are not ready for a fairy tale about an aging Rambo wiping out the entire Afghan nation, but we also are not ready for a movie that makes Americans bad guys. Finally, history reminds us that despite the adversity we now face, we are the luckiest generation in history. We may not all get to be heroes, but all of us can do something to help. You can know your history, act with pride and responsibility, fly the flag, donate blood, donate money, pray for peace, and pray for victory. When the movie does get made, it needs to have a happy ending based in reality.

Suggestions for Further Reading

Bruce Chadwick, *The Reel Civil War: Mythmaking in American Film* (2002); William Craig, *Enemy at the Gates: The Battle for Stalingrad* (2001); Susan Doran and Thomas Freeman, eds, *Tudors and Stuarts on Film: Historical Perspectives* (2008); George MacDonald Fraser, *The Hollywood History of the World* (1989); Kevin J. Harty, *The Reel Middle Ages: American, Western and Eastern European, Middle Eastern and Asian Films About Medieval Europe* (2006); Charlton Heston and Jean-Pierre Isbouts, *Charlton Heston's Hollywood: 50 Years in American Film* (1998); N.J. Higham, *King Arthur: Myth-Making and History* (2008); J. C. Holt, *Robin Hood* (1989); Samuel C. Hyde, ed., *Plain Folk of the South Revisited* (1997); Trevor McCrisken and Andrew Pepper, *American History and Contemporary Hollywood Film* (2005); Doris Milberg, *World War II on the Big Screen: 450+ Films 1938-2008* (2010); Sue Parrill and William B. Robison, *The Tudors on Film and Television* (2013); William B. Robison, ed., *History, Fiction, and 'The Tudors': Sex, Politics, Power, and the Showtime Television Series* (2016); Peter C. Rollins and John E. O'Connor, *Hollywood's West: The American Frontier in Film, Television, and History* (2009) and *Why We Fought: America's Wars in Film and History* (2008); Jon Solomon, *The Ancient World in the Cinema*, revised edition (2001); Robert Brent Toplin, *History by Hollywood*, 2nd edition (2010), *Oliver Stone's USA: Film, History, and Controversy* (2003), and *Reel History: In Defense of History* (2002); Brian Steel Wills, *Gone with the Glory: The History of the Civil War in Cinema* (2006); Martin W. Winkler, ed., *Gladiator: Film and History* (2004).

2002 PREQUEL
A WIZARD, A WITCH, AN APPLE, AND THE DEVIL

This is the beginning of the more theatrical prequels. It survives on video filmed by the Southeastern Channel. There is not much of a plot. This is largely an opportunity to use special effects to set an appropriate Halloween mood. There are several gravestones onstage. When the doors to Pottle Auditorium open to allow the audience to come in, the house lights are down, and the only illumination in the theatre comes from the colored lights on the headstones. Spooky music is playing. After a passage from Mussorgsky's "Night on Bald Mountain," my colleague Dr. Judith Fai-Podlipnik reads the following introduction:

> Good afternoon. Welcome to today's installment of Then and Now, the Fanfare History and Politics Lecture Series, sponsored by the Department of History and Political Science. I am Dr. Judith Fai-Podlipnik, Associate Professor of History. I was asked to introduce today's speaker because I am Hungarian, and—as everybody knows—until the end of World War I, Hungary included Transylvania. Our speaker today, Dr. Robison, has been delayed slightly. He had to stop at the University Police Station to get a parking hangtag for his broom. Also, since we have just had a full moon, it took him a lot longer than usual to shave. Finally, he refused to come out of his darkened dressing room until university officials assured him that there are no mirrors or garlic in the Pottle Music Building. Dr. Robison and his wife Bibbet have a son, two daughters, two golden retrievers, a beagle, and an indeterminate herd of cats. So far as he knows, none of the cats are witch's familiars; however, there is strong circumstantial evidence that the beagle is possessed by the Devil. Dr. Robison will speak today on "Vampires, Werewolves, Witches, and Wizards: Popular Superstition in Late Medieval and Early Modern Europe."

Then the room goes completely dark, and the sound of wind can be heard over the PA system. After half a minute music suddenly starts— Van der Graaf Generator's organ-heavy rendition of "Theme One," composed for the BBC by George Martin of Beatles fame and recorded by VDGG for their 1971 album *Pawn Hearts*. It is loud and sounds eerie. The

13

lights come up to show "fog" billowing onstage from a smoke machine. And now a word about my trip to San Antonio.

Earlier in the month I had attended a conference there. One night while dining on the River Walk, my family and I spotted a vendor selling some magnetic "earrings" with flashing lights in them. Of course we had to have some. I later discovered that I could make them stick to my glasses. One thing lead to another, and pretty soon I had a black warlock's robe with a cowl covering my face, so that all you could see was what looked like two red eyes flashing. I wore it again while walking around the neighborhood with my kids on Halloween night, and it scared the daylights out of a couple of miniature Spider-Men, who had a furious metaphysical debate about my nature. One kept repeating, "That's a man," while the other shook his head in horrified doubt. I was quite pleased.

Anyway, I emerge from behind the back curtain at center stage in the fog wearing the robe with eyes flashing, brandish my broom (my putative mode of transportation) at the sky, and lightning flashes. I then go over to the left side of the stage and conjure "fire" out of an artificial firepot, after which I do the same on the right. At this point a witch (my wife Bibbet) comes out from stage right and offers me an apple (a veiled Biblical reference for anyone who is really paying attention). As I take it, the Devil (Wade Heaton)—who has emerged from stage left, taps me on the shoulder and wags his finger in a "no" gesture. I give back the apple. At this point the witch instead offers me a mortarboard, which I put on. The Devil holds up a "Publish or Perish" tee shirt for the audience to see, then hands it to me. I then wave both the Devil and the witch away, go over to the podium, set my broom on top of it, and hang an official University Police temporary guest parking tag around it. I then throw candy to the audience (the only time I have done that before the lecture instead of after).

Okay, so it is not Shakespeare. I had no idea what it meant then, and I have no idea now. But it got some laughs, and people were paying attention when I started the lecture. Inevitably, I suppose, a handful of sourpusses disapproved, maintaining that I was compromising the dignity of the professoriate. Everybody else seemed to enjoy it, and that was all the encouragement I needed to determine that I would have to do more the following year.

Watch the video at https://myspace.com/headongoolah/videos.

2002 LECTURE
VAMPIRES, WEREWOLVES, WITCHES, AND WIZARDS: POPULAR SUPERSTITION IN LATE MEDIEVAL AND EARLY MODERN EUROPE

Given the nature of my subject and the melodramatic introductory segment you have just witnessed [*A Wizard, a Witch, an Apple, and the Devil*], please allow me to begin with some disclaimers. First of all, I am not a vampire. I am a historian, so I do study dead people, but I am only interested in what they did while they were alive, not thereafter. Second, I am not a werewolf. I cannot even grow a full beard. I was once in a band that played "Little Red Riding Hood" by Sam the Sham and the Pharaohs (also known for "Woolly Bully" and "Ring-Dang-Do"), and I could do a respectable wolf howl at appropriate points in the song, but that does not really qualify. Third, I am not a witch in any of the senses in which that term is used. I spent a lot of time in my youth pushing a broom in my father's hardware store, but I have never ridden one. I did fall off the garage in our back yard one time (a local journalist reported that I was playing Tarzan) but that was flying only in a very limited sense—it was a short trip with an abrupt landing that resulted in a concussion. Fourth, I am not a wizard, unfortunately, or I would have the same parking place every day, but I have read all of the *Harry Potter* books, and I can tell you that they will not hurt you or your kids—there is no profanity, no sex, no graphic violence, the good guys win, and they get kids to read books [incredibly, the books actually were controversial at this time]. They are no more harmful to the current generation of kids than *The Wizard of Oz* or *The Lord of Rings* were to us. My kids have read them all, and they have shown no inclination to stop going to church or to start worshipping the Devil. Instead of worrying about Harry Potter, we need to focus our attention on real evil—there is plenty of that. Fifth, while I certainly do believe in the reality of evil, I do not actually believe in vampires, werewolves, witches, and wizards as those terms were understood in late medieval and early modern Europe. That might seem obvious, but recent surveys show that about 25% of Americans do believe in vampires and witches. Sixth, I want to note before I begin that my topic overlaps with the history of religion, so I will discuss that as necessary, but I have absolutely no intention of disparaging anyone's religious beliefs. In fact, part of my own interest in this topic arises from my larger interest in religion and religious history.

Having offered this long list of disclaimers, what is my motive for this lecture? First, my area of scholarly specialization is Tudor England—in the sixteenth century—the period of Henry VIII and Elizabeth, of the Protestant Reformation and the Catholic Reformation. Some of my work extends back into the fifteenth century and forward into the seventeenth century. That overlaps with the great witch craze, c.1450-1650, which is an important part of that period of history. Beliefs about vampires, werewolves, and wizards in turn were connected to those about witches. A second motive is that I am interested in demythologizing this subject. Debunking myths and misconceptions is a recurrent theme in this year's "Then and Now" Fanfare History and Politics Lecture series, in my own Fanfare lectures in years past, and (I hope) in my teaching and writing generally. I want to show what people actually believed in late medieval and early modern Europe. Third, I hope it will be fun. Today is the day before Halloween, after all, and a big part of my mission as a historian is to show students that learning history *is* fun when taught and written properly and when you approach it with some degree of imagination and some sense of adventure.

Let me now address some myths and misconceptions and tell you where some of these arise. As you might suspect, one of the principal culprits is popular culture: fiction, movies, and television. We have had a hundred years of vampires in fiction from Bram Stoker to Anne Rice, in the cinema from Nosferatu to Dracula to Lestat. Dracula alone has been played by the incomparable Bela Lugosi, by Christopher Lee (who currently can be seen as the good-wizard-gone-bad Saruman in *The Fellowship of the Ring*), by Frank Langella, by—believe it or not—Jack Palance (try imagining that if you have seen him with Billy Crystal), by Gary Oldman, and the list goes on. Tom Cruise has done Lestat in *Interview With A Vampire*. And that is not to mention the Count on *Sesame Street*, with whom many of you grew up, and Count Chocula, whose cereal many of you ate while you watched *Sesame Street*.

We have had werewolves from the Chaney dynasty (not Dick and Lynne but Lon Chaney and Lon Chaney Jr.) down to Michael J. Fox in *Teen Wolf* to Warren Zevon with "Werewolves of London" and all those *Craven* movies. We have had witches from Shakespeare's *Macbeth* to Broomhilda in the Bugs Bunny cartoons, from *The Wizard of Oz* to *The Blair Witch Project*, on television from Samantha to Tabitha to Sabrina to Martha Stewart. We have had wizards from Merlin to Gandalf to Mickey Mouse in *The Sorcerer's Apprentice* to the little kid with the broken glasses and the lightning bolt scar on his head. That has formed a lot of people's images of what earlier folk believed in late medieval and early modern Europe, but it does not bear much resemblance to actual belief in that period.

Another problem is that the contemporary sources are biased by definition. There were written by people in authority, who—for one thing—believed quite explicitly in vampires, werewolves, witches, and wizards, and who also expected to find them—that is why they were looking. On the other hand, it is only fair to point out that they were very, very careful—within the limits of the rules with which they operated—not to accuse someone falsely.

Another source of a good deal of confusion is the ongoing debate carried on largely outside of academia but all over popular culture between various groups who describe themselves as neo-pagans and certain groups of fundamentalist Christians. The neo-pagans include a broad range of people, some of whom call themselves witches (e.g., Wiccans), some of whom call themselves Druids, and so on. What they tend to have in common is worship of a goddess, often identified with one of the goddesses of the ancient world—Diana the Roman goddess of the hunt is a particularly good example, but there are others. What they argue is that there is continuity from the worship of ancient goddesses back among the Romans and even earlier and all the way down through the Middle Ages, into the early modern period, and so to the present, and that consequently those who were persecuted during the witch craze were followers of Diana or of a nature or fertility cult. They are understandably rather hostile to those who allegedly persecuted them. But there is not much evidence in the historical sources for such continuity. For one thing, in the ancient world there were lots of goddesses just as there were lots of gods, but there was never one goddess worshipped everywhere by everybody. A lot of people worshipped the moon, often personified as female, and a lot of people worshipped the sun, usually personified as male, for the fairly obvious reason that if you do not have electricity those are the two most impressive things in the sky. But there is not a single goddess or a single nature cult that has survived unbroken all the way down to the present. This is a misconception that is based largely on the fairly weak scholarship of a woman named Margaret Murray. Now, that does not mean that if you follow one of these particular groups, you have to give up your own particular beliefs, but they do not have much relevance to late medieval and early modern Europe.

On the other hand there have been some groups of Christian fundamentalists who have accepted the contemporary definition from late medieval and early modern Europe of witches as diabolical, i.e., in a league with the Devil, and therefore have drawn the conclusion that anyone who calls himself or herself a witch now must be a worshipper of Satan. That is not really true either. One of the problems is that neither of these previous groups, based on the work that I have read by both of them, pay much attention to current scholarship done by historians who actually have looked at the sources from the Inquisition and other places. This is not to deny that there are important theological divisions between neo-pagans and fundamentalist Christians—or Christians of any kind. I am simply saying that a lot of the argument that is going on is an argument about something that does not exist.

Another thing that has skewed our picture is the rise in the academic community of women's history and of the feminist interpretation of history. By no means do I intend to cast aspersions on that whole approach to history—it has been very valuable in a lot of ways. But what has happened in some cases is that historians have interpreted the whole witch issue as something that is basically male versus female and misogynist, focusing on gender to the exclusion of other factors that in some cases are a lot more important, e.g., poverty (as we will see momentarily).

Another problem is that there are people right now in our society who do describe themselves as Satanists—as Satan-worshippers—and some of them are. Why? I do not know. Others are basically people who do not believe in anything—Anton LaVey comes to mind—people who are essentially hedonists and use that whole Devil imagery as a way of playing that up. Then, of course, there are people who do it as a showbiz gimmick, whether in movies or onstage. We have had from time to time the backward masking debate about whether certain rock and roll records have Satanic messages in them if you play them backwards. I tried this with my Led Zeppelin albums, and I could not get anything except backwards Led Zeppelin. Just to be ecumenical about it, I played some New Age records backwards, and they sounded the same.

Another thing that has often skewed our perception of the history of witches is abuse of the term "witch hunt." Nowadays every time any group becomes the target of any group (like, say, the government), immediately the cry goes up of "witch hunt." Two classic examples of that are during the Red Scare in the 1950s and more recently in the case of terrorism. There is a difference, though. There were some communists in America in the 1950s—maybe not as many as Joe McCarthy said, but he was not making it up from scratch. There have been some terrorists in America in recent years. There were not, as far as I am concerned, any actual witches during the real witch-hunt.

Another thing has been bogus comparisons, e.g., comparing the witch persecutions to the Holocaust or to Stalin's famine purges, which killed millions of people. Now, as far as I am concerned, if one single person is killed unjustly on the basis of an accusation of being a witch, that is one too many. But we are not talking about anything remotely on the scale of what Hitler or Stalin did or, for that matter, Mao, Pol Pot, Idi Amin, or pick your dictator.

To get at the reality of late medieval and early modern belief, we must look at background. Beliefs about vampires, werewolves, witches, wizards are widespread and at least as old as civilization, probably older. Astrology, sorcery, and prophecy were part of many ancient religions and are part of some modern ones. But the witch persecutions happened in Europe between about 1450 and 1650, and we have to ask—why? The witch craze occurred at the time of a vastly different worldview from the one that we have now. Although it took place at a time contemporary with the Age of Discovery and Renaissance, it came before most Europeans had absorbed the meaning of either and before Europe felt the full impact of the Scientific Revolution of the seventeenth century and the Enlightenment of the eighteenth. It also occurred contemporaneously with the Reformation, and in that case there is a very important connection.

During the period we are discussing, before the Scientific Revolution became well established in the minds of even educated people, even the most learned people accepted a geocentric cosmology—based on the Greek philosopher Aristotle and the Hellenistic astronomer Ptolemy—which argued that the earth is at the center of the universe. They thought of heaven and hell as physical locations—hell below us and heaven above—rather than different states of existence. They organized all matter, living and non-living, into a Great Chain of Being that has nothing to do with biology, chemistry, or geology as we practice those sciences now. They lived in a world where there were only four elements—earth, air, fire, and water (not really elements at all), which were believed to act in conjunction in heat, cold, dryness, and wetness to affect health, wealth, events, and so on. Medicine was still based on the humoral theory of the ancient medical doctor Galen, which argued that the human body is made of four humors—black bile, yellow bile, phlegm, and blood—and that what makes us sick is an imbalance of those humors. This is what educated people believed. So, if you got sick, they bled you, or they used a leech to do it if you were a little squeamish about the knife (personally I think I would prefer the knife to the leech). The beauty of this is that it is self-fulfilling. If you bleed somebody, and he gets better, obviously the cure worked. If he dies, you say that you got to him too late, which is the same thing they tell you now. The use of leeches led to doctors being referred to as "leeches." In some cases that still happens, too, although for somewhat different reasons.

This was also a period in which everybody believed in magic, and I do not mean "magic" in the sense of pulling a rabbit out of a hat or David Blaine burying himself alive for eight days. I mean magic in the sense of being able to harness supernatural forces. For example, one of the most educated people in Elizabethan England—a man with perhaps the largest library in the world at that time—was a guy named John Dee. Besides being a scientist, a historian, and a politician, he was also a magician and an astrologer. This was a period when everyone believed in astrology. I do not mean astrology in the limited sense where you look at your horoscope and see that you are a person with a lot of energy and are going to meet a tall dark stranger. I am talking about an extraordinarily complicated system based on observation of celestial objects like stars, planets, sun, moon, comets, meteors, and looking at these in conjunction with the elements and the humors to predict the future. If you look, for example, at Anthony Grafton's recent book on the Italian astrologer Girolamo Cardano, you will see that he spent years learning this stuff—it was all wrong, but it was still quite an intellectual achievement. In addition, people in this period still tried very hard to do prophecy. We do that, too—we just have people called economists, meteorologists, and sports handicappers.

Europe was slow to catch up to advances in science in this period. Galileo invented the world's first telescope that was useful for astronomical purposes and discovered that the moon's geology looks a lot like the Earth's and that Jupiter has four moons (or at least four that he could see). He got in a lot of trouble for that—he was accused of being a heretic. When he offered to let the Inquisition look through his telescope, their response was no, thank you, the telescope is an instrument of the Devil. Galileo, by the way, has been rehabilitated. Pope John Paul II issued a statement that Galileo was right, that the telescope is not an instrument of the Devil, and Jupiter does have those moons.

But even the scientific pioneers had one foot in the past. If you think about science in the seventeenth century, the first person who comes to mind is Sir Isaac Newton, the man who was the Einstein of his day and who virtually invented modern physics and calculus. But while he was doing that, he also practiced alchemy, trying to turn lead into gold, and he practiced astrology, trying to predict the future—so, one foot in the future, one foot in the past.

People often ask how this could be going on during the Renaissance and the First Scientific Revolution. But in one sense the Renaissance may have made things worse because it involved a systematization of information and a revival of ancient knowledge—some of which is wrong—and inaccurate "knowledge" became more concretized as a result. Furthermore, even though during the Renaissance neo-Platonism to some extent replaced Aristotelianism—which had been used to buttress belief in supernatural magic—neo-Platonism was never as widespread, plus neo-Platonists believed in magic—just natural magic—and in the physical reality of the Devil, so it did not really change things that much. Finally, this was an era when democracy, individual rights, and religious toleration—things we take for granted—were still radical ideas, and it was an age when people fought wars over religion. Thus, there are many reasons why this period was ripe for the witch craze.

There are some common myths and misconceptions about witches and witch persecutions. Many people assume that witch persecutions were largely a medieval affair, and there are a few examples from the Middle Ages. But by and large, witch persecutions happened between 1450 and 1650, not earlier. There are notable exceptions like Joan of Arc, but that was in the 1430s. Another misconception is that the Inquisition's main business was witch hunting. But its main focus was on pursuing heretics. Witches might be considered a particular kind of heretic, but it was other kinds of heretics who occupied most of the Inquisition's attention in the Middle Ages. Pope Gregory IX founded the Roman Inquisition in 1231 to combat the Cathars (Albigensians) and Waldensians (primarily in southern France) and also to harass the Holy Roman Emperors, who were the papacy's rivals. It was not until 1468 that Sixtus IV founded the more notorious Spanish Inquisition at the behest of Ferdinand of Aragon and Isabella of Castile, the patrons of Christopher Columbus, and the popes never controlled it. The Spanish Inquisition was a tool of the monarchy from day one, and while it was used against witches occasionally, its prime targets were Jews and Muslims in Spain who had converted to Christianity and then relapsed. The Inquisition did not bother Jews and Muslims who remained in their original faith, but it considered those who converted to Christianity and then back to their original faith to be heretics. Paul III refounded the Roman Inquisition in 1541 to counter Protestantism, but it never extended throughout Europe. The Inquisition never had authority in England.

Another myth is that the Inquisition was pervasive, that it was rounding up witches everywhere. Actually, though beliefs about vampires, werewolves, witches, and wizards were pervasive, persecutions were not. Most communities never had a single case of a witch persecution. Still another misconception is that all accused witches were women. It is true that most people accused of witchcraft were women, but about 25% overall were men, sometimes known as warlocks or wizards. In some areas—e.g., Alsace and Lorraine—more men were prosecuted than women, so it is not entirely gender specific. Closely associated with this idea is the notion that witch persecution is a misogynist enterprise, and there is no question that that is part of it. But actually a lot of the accusations were those that one woman brought against another or, in some cases, one man against another, so it is not just another battle in the war of the sexes. There also is the misconception that millions of people died in the witch persecutions, and that is just not true. You can find this in print, but historians who have combed the records have only been able to find about 50,000. That is 50,000 too many, but if you spread 50,000 over two centuries, that is far fewer people than died in persecutions for heresy or in the religious wars. Then there is the misconception that witches turned Eric Idle into a newt—well, no, actually that did not happen.

What, then, were actual beliefs that people had in the late medieval and early modern years? One element that was always present is the idea that witches practiced what is known as the *maleficium*. This is a Latin word that means performing an evil act. The term we would use today is "black magic." It is undoubtedly true that there were people alive at the time who would have done this if they could have, and there were others—deluded though they might be—who thought that they actually were capable of *maleficia* and tried to perform them. But that was not what really got you into trouble. What did that was diabolism, that is, having made a pact with the Devil. If you look at the records of both the Inquisition and more secular authorities, people frequently confessed to the *maleficium* without any pressure on them at all, but they never confessed to making a deal with the Devil until they were tortured. If you torture somebody long enough, he or she will confess to anything, so confessions made under torture are very suspect. In any case, the deal with the Devil supposedly was a bargain whereby the witch got the power to perform black magic. *Maleficia* included a variety of acts—murder, injury, damage to crops, causing a cow to dry up, and more. Just about anything bad might be ascribed to a witch.

Another essential element was the idea of the sabbat, that is, the witches' sabbath, which is a mockery of the Judeo-Christian Sabbath. Witches supposedly attended sabbats, encountered the Devil, and performed various unspeakable acts with him or his demons. Yet another essential element—and here you really have to apply some 21st century rationality—is the belief that witches could fly from their houses to sabbats on brooms or some other form of transport enchanted by some sort of cream, a spell, or the like. There was also a belief that some witches were capable of metamorphosis, that is, of changing themselves into animals. Here is where the belief in werewolves became tied to witchcraft. In medieval folklore werewolves generally were considered to be beneficent creatures who protected humans from danger in the forest. However, the Inquisition typically attributed any supernatural powers not derived from the Church to be diabolical, and werewolves thus came to be regarded as evil. The same thing happened in the region of Italy known as the Friuli, where the benandante—good witches who protected the local crops from bad witches—also became targets of the Inquisition.

Although most Inquisitors followed the rules for prosecuting witches carefully—indeed their meticulous recordkeeping accounts for most of our knowledge about continental prosecutions—the deck was stacked against the accused. The Inquisition could arrest a suspect on the basis of testimony by only two witnesses, the accused had no right to know the identity of his accusers or to counsel, the alleged witch could be tortured until he or she confessed and then further to force him or her to reveal the names of other witches, and the courts gave credence to considerable tendentious evidence. A mole, wart, or other skin irregularity might be assumed to be an extra nipple from which the Devil or his familiars sucked the witch's blood. Almost any animal could be assumed to be a witch's familiar—not just black dogs or cats but even insects! There were even manuals for witch finders, like the notorious *Malleus Maleficarum*.

Where do vampires fit into all of this? The stock image is of Count Dracula, a tall, pale, aristocratic Transylvanian who sleeps in coffin on his back; travels at night by transforming himself into a bat; bites the necks of victims and sucks their blood, thereby turning them into vampires; has an aversion to crosses, mirrors, garlic and sunlight; is immortal and can be killed only with a stake through his heart. [That remains true of most fictional vampires right down to those in the *Buffy the Vampire Slayer* movie and television series, though not those in the *Twilight* novels and movies.]

Actual beliefs about vampires from late medieval and early modern Europe are quite different. Vampires were short, fat, ruddy, and poor; usually buried without coffins; did not transform into bats; typically bit their victims near the heart, which killed them; and had no aversion to mirrors. The precise origin of vampire beliefs is impossible to know. But what almost certainly kept such beliefs alive was the way in which people of this period handled the dead. Graves often were not very deep, and corpses often "emerged" from them when dogs or wild animals dug them up. If the grave were especially shallow, the constriction of the corpse's muscles might actually cause it to "sit up" (gravestones were placed over the head to prevent this). If vampire hunters found a corpse and drove a stake through the chest, a buildup of gases in the abdomen from decomposition might cause the corpse to gasp or exhale, creating the impression that it had just "died again." People used a variety of apotropaics to prevent vampires from returning to life and to keep away those who did—the most famous example being garlic. Ironically, the real "Dracula"—Vlad Tsepes the Impaler, Prince of Wallachia—was never the subject of vampire myths, nor did he live in Transylvania in the castle associated with his legend, though he was a sufficiently horrifying sadist in his own right.

Here are a few additional points about wizards. The line between a male witch and an astrologer-magician like John Dee or the notorious Nostradamus was a thin one. Much of the modern imagery of the wizard owes more to astrology than black magic. The pointed hat and beard actually go back to the ancient Etruscans, from whom the Romans learned the practice of divination—telling the future by examining the entrails of animals. The moon and stars that adorn a wizard's clothing are obviously related to an astrologer's primary focus of study.

Finally, what connects vampires, werewolves, witches, and wizards to Halloween? The answer is, in truth, very little. Halloween is, in fact, a Christian holiday properly known as All Hallows Eve. It falls around the same time as the old Celtic holiday known as Samhain, which was at times associated with the dead, but there is no direct connection between the two. Much of the modern association of Halloween and witches is a relatively recent development inspired by commercial considerations. But that is another lecture for another year. Right now it is candy time, and thus everyone in the audience needs to utter those magic words, "trick or treat."

Suggestions for Further Reading

Bengt Ankarloo and Stuart Clark, *Witchcraft and Magic in Europe*, 6 vols. (1999-2002); Paul Barber, *Vampires, Burial, and Death: Folklore and Reality* (1990); Norman Cohn, *Europe's Inner Demons: The Demonization of Christians in Medieval Europe* (1977); John Demos, *The Enemy Within: 2,000 Years of Witch-hunting in the Western World* (2008) and *Entertaining Satan: Witchcraft and the Culture of Early New England* (2004); Radu Florescu and Raymond

McNally, *Dracula, Prince of Many Faces: His Life and His Times* (1990); Carlo Ginzburg, *The Night Battles: Witchcraft & Agrarian Cults in the Sixteenth and Seventeenth Centuries* (1992); Ronald Hutton, *The Rise and Fall of Merry England: The Ritual Year 1400-1700* (1994) and *The Triumph of the Moon: A History of Modern Pagan Witchcraft* (2001); Henry Kamen, *The Spanish Inquisition: A Historical Revision* (1999); Malcolm Lambert, *Medieval Heresy: Popular Movements from the Gregorian Reform to the Reformation* (2002); Brian Levack, *The Witch-Hunt in Early Modern Europe*, 3rd edition (2006); Diane Purkiss, *The Witch in History: Early Modern and Twentieth-Century Representations* (1996); James Randi, *The Mask of Nostradamus: The Prophecies of the World's Most Famous Seer* (1993); Lyndal Roper, *Witch Craze: Terror and Fantasy in Baroque Germany* (2006); Jeffrey Burton Russell, *Mephistopheles: The Devil in the Modern World* (1990) and *Witchcraft in the Middle Ages* (1984); Montague Summers, *The Malleus Maleficarum of Heinrich Kramer and James Sprenger* (1971); Keith Thomas, *Religion and the Decline of Magic: Studies of Popular Beliefs in Sixteenth and Seventeenth Century England* (1971); Benjamin Woolley, *The Queen's Conjurer: The Science and Magic of Dr. John Dee, Adviser to Queen Elizabeth I* (2002).

2003 PREQUEL
PREPOSTERODAMUS THE FORGOTTEN SEER

This is my first foray into filmmaking. The premise of the "documentary" based on the script below is that Nostradamus had an illegitimate half-brother named Preposterodamus who also was a gifted seer but has now been forgotten. The rationale is that the widespread popular belief in Nostradamus in the present day is so preposterous that the only way to do something more ridiculous is by inventing for the phony prophet a phony brother or, if you will, a phony phony prophet. This sets up an introduction to the lecture on Nostradamus whereby I point out that as ridiculous as the Preposterodamus film might be, it is only marginally more so than the things people believe about the real Michel Notredame. This "documentary" is a parody of Orson Welles' "documentary" about Nostradamus, *The Man Who Saw Tomorrow* (1981).

Watch the video and an edited-for-television version of the lecture at https://myspace.com/headongoolah/videos, purchase a DVD for a nominal fee (or get it free when buying this book), and listen to the soundtrack on the CD *Show Tunes* by Headongoolah (which is me before Impaired Faculties). Parts of the script below were omitted from the final film version because of length. You also can hear the two Renaissance Dances that my brother Tucker Robison composed for the film at https://soundcloud.com/trobison_1 and learn more about his music and related services with Robison Productions at his business website, http://www.robisonpro.com/.

SCREEN	A lit jack-o-lantern
VOICE	Ladies and gentlemen, welcome to the More-or-Less Annual Halloween Lecture. Today's lecture is the final installment of the 2003 "Then and Now" Fanfare History and Politics Lecture Series sponsored by the Department of History and Political Science at Southeastern Louisiana University. Today's lecturer is Dr. William B. Robison, Department Head and Professor of History. His presentation, Nostradamus: Poet, Prophet, Pharmacist, Phraud, will begin as soon as the attendants remove the strait jacket. Meanwhile, please watch the following video about Nostradamus' long forgotten brother, whom historians only recently have rediscovered.

SCREEN   EEN [large letters appear]
                Extrasensory Ectoplasm Network

VOICE   E . . . E . . . N

SCREEN   [scrolling]
                Funding Provided By
                False Fleeting Friends o' Fanfare
                HIPS Institute for Higher Consciousness
                Murphy Wallace Foundation

VOICE   The following program is made possible by a grant of thirteen dollars and seven cents from the False Fleeting Friends o' Fanfare, the HIPS Institute for Higher Consciousness, and the Murphy Wallace Foundation.

SCREEN   TUV [large letters]
                Totally Unprofessional Video Presents

VOICE   Totally Unprofessional Video Presents . . .

SCREEN   Not Just Another Factual Biography

VOICE   . . . Not Just Another Factual Biography this week featuring . . .

SCREEN   Preposterodamus the Forgotten Seer

VOICE   . . . Preposterodamus the Forgotten Seer . . .

SCREEN   With host Orson Welles

VOICE   . . . with your host, cinema legend Orson Welles!

SCREEN   An unctuously smiling Orson seated at a desk with a large bottle of Paul Masson. In the background are posters from the Mercury Theater and Citizen Kane.
                [Caption: Orson Welles, Actor/Director/Vendor o' Vino]

ORSON   Hello and welcome to Not Just Another Factual Biography. Tonight's program is further underwritten by Paul Masson, where we will serve no wine before its time. And I do believe it's time!
                [Pours large glass, samples the bouquet, gulps down a large amount]

SCREEN   Portrait of Nostradamus
                [Caption: Michel de Notredame—"Nostradamus" (1503-

	1566)]
ORSON	The mysterious sixteenth-century prophet Nostradamus has fascinated generations with his predictions of the tragic death of the French king Henri II in 1559, the Great Fire of London in 1666, the conquests of Napoleon, the rise and fall of Adolph Hitler, the assassination of John F. Kennedy, and many other completely confirmed historical occurrences. However, more mysterious by far—and, until now, completely lost to history—was his half-brother Preposterodamus, shown in this hitherto unidentified portrait by Renaissance artist Linx of Bologna.
SCREEN	Portrait of Linx [Caption: "The Astrologer," Linx of Bologna (c.1560)]
ORSON	Who was this forgotten seer? Was he an even more gifted prognosticator than his famous sibling? Where did his occult path lead him? How did he unlock the magical forces of the cosmos to divine the hidden secrets of the dark future? What horrifying events did he foresee? When did he foretell the final cataclysm? Are we even now on the eve of the Apocalypse?
SCREEN	Orson, looking alarmed, takes another large swig. [Caption: Orson Welles, Actor/Director/Shiller o' Swill]
ORSON	Ahem. Scholars have identified Preposterodamus as the figure in the portrait and as the half-sibling of Nostradamus . . .
SCREEN	A parchment manuscript [Caption: "Anonymous Manuscript," Anonymous of Terra Incognita (c.1588?)]
ORSON	. . . thanks to the discovery of a hitherto unknown manuscript by the obscure scribe, Anonymous of Terra Incognita.
SCREEN	A map of France
ORSON	Preposterodamus was born in Provence in southern France in 1513. Anonymous of Terra Incognita reports that his nativity was marked by the apparition of a smiling winged pig in the constellation Capricorn. Preposterodamus was the illegitimate son of Nostradamus' father Pierre de

Notredame and a Provencal peasant prostitute named Ulala, who claimed—improbably—to be the descendant of
. . .

SCREEN	Portrait of Joan of Arc [Caption: St. Joan of Arc]
ORSON	. . . St. Joan of Arc, the Holy Maid of Orleans, and who worked . . .
SCREEN	Picture of an ark [Caption: Jean D'Arc's Dark John's Ark]
ORSON	. . . in Marseilles in a boat-shaped brothel that catered to Aragonese Moors and was known as Jean D'Arc's Dark John's Ark.
SCREEN	Orson [Caption: Orson Welles, Actor/Director/Hustler o' Hooch]
ORSON	Pierre de Notredame acknowledged his paternity of the boy and provided generously for his education. Young Preposterodamus attended a local grammar school in Marseilles under the dull headmaster Pedant of St. Denis.
SCREEN	Preposterodamus, with alphabet scrolling backward across screen with 6's
ORSON	Early on he showed signs of eccentricity, insisting on reciting the alphabet backwards and doing mathematical calculations in the ancient Babylonian sexagesimal system.
SCREEN	Preposterodamus with goat horns
ORSON	After being expelled for performing a lewd dance during the Guild of Goldsmiths' Corpus Christi procession, he studied theater under Crispin Cuspin the Caspian Thespian and traveled with a touring troupe of players as understudy for the part of Soter the Seldom-Sated Satyr in Francisco della Rovere's *Inflagrante Delicto, or The Goat's Tale*.
SCREEN	Preposterodamus studying [Caption: Student of Camelopard of Lyons and Carolus Tunapisces]
ORSON	Subsequently he mastered the *trivium* and the *quadrivium*

29

under the tutelage of Camelopard of Lyons and attempted to acquire a proper sense of good taste from the star-kissed aestheticist Carolus Tunapisces.

SCREEN   Preposterodamus, with vowels and dollar signs scrolling across screen
Caption: Buying a vowel

ORSON   About this time he developed an obsession with attempting to relate the place value normally assigned to numbers to the vowels in the Phoenician alphabet in order to determine their commercial potential and thus was led inexorably to a fascination with wheels of fortune. So began his career as a seer.

SCREEN   Horseman
[Caption: The "Gallop Pole"]

ORSON   With growing enthusiasm he studied prognostication with a retired cavalry officer from East Prussia known merely as the Gallop Pole . . .

SCREEN   A hallucinating person
[Caption: Lysergicus of Ergot]

ORSON   . . . learned about the interpretation of visions from Lysergicus of Ergot . . .

SCREEN   A scholar surrounded by effluvia
[Caption: Terminus of Flatulencia]

ORSON   . . . and read extensively about miasmas and curious vapors with Terminus of Flatulencia.

SCREEN   An apothecary
[Caption: Dermatitis the Apothecary of Padua]

ORSON   Inspired by his half-brother Nostradamus' growing reputation as a physician successful in treating the bubonic plague, Preposterodamus sought to carve out his own medical niche and spent six months learning to prepare soothing unguents with Dermatitis the Apothecary of Padua.

SCREEN	A monastery
	[Caption: Abbey of Psoriasis in the time of Abbot Quidnunc]
ORSON	Later he sold to the daughter of the count of Champagne an ointment guaranteed to restore virginity, but when it instead gave her an extremely irritating rash on the eve of her wedding, he had to flee into sanctuary at the Abbey of Psoriasis. There the Abbot Quidnunc sought to convert him to the monastic life but without success.
SCREEN	Henri II
	[Caption: Henry II]
ORSON	Preposterodamus followed Nostradamus to the court of King Henri II of France and Queen Catherine de Medici in 1557 and attempted like his brother to become a court astrologer.
SCREEN	Catherine de Medici
	[Caption: Catherine de Medici]
ORSON	Unimpressed, Henri and Catherine offered him instead a position as court jester.
SCREEN	John Dee
	[Caption: John Dee]
ORSON	Preposterodamus left the court in a high dudgeon and journeyed to Surrey, England, where he met the young John Dee.
SCREEN	Map showing the Black Sea
ORSON	On the return trip across the English Channel, he was captured by pirates and sold into slavery in the Ottoman Empire. Escaping months later near the Black Sea, he made his way to the north shore of the Danube, where—traveling in three-quarter time—he fell in with a band of gypsies, who introduced him to . . .
SCREEN	Wenus
	[Caption: Wenus of Wallachia, Pretender to the Principality]
ORSON	. . . Wenus of Wallachia, the disinherited descendant of Prince Vlad Tsepes the Impaler, the real Count Dracula. He

31

	now became the royal seer to this third-rate potentate and entered upon the most productive phase of his career.
MUSIC	He's Wenus of Wallachia Scourge of the frozen steppes Terror of Transylvania And the messenger of death
SCREEN	Preposterodamus writing [Caption: Writing *The Aspect of Uranus*]
ORSON	During his time he wrote an unconventional astrological treatise entitled *The Aspect of Uranus*, which is thought to have predicted, among other things, talk radio and reality television.
SCREEN	Preposterodamus and a goat [Caption: With Capricorndog]
ORSON	He also appears to have become the world's first known pet psychic, attempting to help Wenus's depressed pet goat Capricorndog to get in touch with his inner kid.
SCREEN	Preposterodamus and chemical apparatus [Caption: Seeking the philosopher's stone]
ORSON	Developing an interest in alchemy, he began efforts to discover the philosopher's stone, enlisting the aid of a hirsute pot maker to build the necessary alchemical apparatus, essentially a large still.
SCREEN	Orson with wine bottle [Caption: Orson Welles, Actor/Director/Bagger o' Burgundy]
ORSON	I'll drink to that!
SCREEN	Preposterodamus with foil cone [Caption: Experimenting with long distance communication]
ORSON	He sought to communicate over long distances using a pair of enchanted foil cones, trying repeatedly to contact his humble assistant Fantod.
PREP	Can you hear me now?

SCREEN	Fantod, looking stupid
	[Caption: Fantod, Humble Assistant]
ORSON	At first the experiments were fruitless.

SCREEN	Preposterodamus with foil cone
	[Caption: Still experimenting]
PREP	Can you hear me now?

SCREEN	Fantod, looking stupid
	[Caption: Fantod, Humble Assistant]
ORSON	But Preposterodamus and the faithful Fantod persevered.

SCREEN	Preposterodamus with foil cone
	[Caption: And still experimenting]
PREP	Can you hear me now?

SCREEN	Fantod
	[Caption: Fantod, Humble Assistant]
FANTOD	Yes!

SCREEN	Preposterodamus inches away from Fantod's ear
	[Caption: Eureka!]
PREP	Good!

SCREEN	Orson, still drinking
	[Caption: Orson Welles, Actor/Director/Chugger of Chardonnay]
ORSON	Perhaps most famously, he began composing four-line verses known as squatrains because they were recited while squatting on the steppes. These are believed to contain many accurate predictions about the future.

SCREEN	Preposterodamus, brandishing a wand
	[Caption: Attempting teleportation]
ORSON	On the final page of his manuscript, Anonymous of Terra Incognita tells us that late in his career Preposterodamus attempted experiments with teleportation, but here the manuscript suddenly breaks off.

| SCREEN | Preposterodamus walking away from camera in a ghostly |

	haze
ORSON	The date and circumstances of Preposterodamus' death are unknown, leading to speculation that he is in fact the mythical immortal St. Germaine and to numerous reports of him being sighted in the company of Elvis.
SCREEN	Orson [Caption: Orson Welles, Actor/Director/Baron o' Boone's Farm]
ORSON	Preposterodamus' claims to prescience were controversial during his lifetime and have remained so. One famous example is his boast that he successfully summoned the Devil, though this has not gone unchallenged.
SCREEN	The devil surrounded by flames Caption: Satan, Proprietor of Perdition.
SATAN	That is a complete lie! I would never respond to the pathetic incantations of a third-rate conjurer like this fool Preposterodamus. The idea is absurd!
SCREEN	Orson [Caption: Orson Welles, Actor/Director/Maven o' Mad Dog]
ORSON	For once, the Prince of Lies apparently is telling the truth. In fact, Preposterodamus actually appears to have called up another occult figure, a powerful wizard able to discern good and evil from afar, to enchant horned quadrupeds, to fly long distances, to disrupt the space-time continuum, to levitate inside chimneys, and to make himself very small. It now is clear that Preposterodamus was dyslexic and that in fact he summoned . . .
SCREEN	The word "Satan" appears, disappears, the word "Santa" appears
ORSON	. . . not Satan, but Santa.
SCREEN	Santa [Caption: St. Nicholas, a/k/a Kris Kringle, Right Jolly Old Elf]
SANTA	Ho! Ho! Ho! Oh, yes, I remember. It was a hoot. The silly bugger summoned me on the summer solstice. I thought to

myself, "Wrong time of year, but what have I got to do in June." So, what the heck, I responded. Well, of course I came down the chimney like I usually do. There was a big fire in the fireplace, but that never bothers me. You should have seen his face when I stepped out of the flames. Oh, it was priceless, just priceless. A real killer! Ho! Ho! Ho! And, by the way, don't think I don't know what time of year it is now. I'm watching you people out there!

SCREEN	Orson [Caption: Orson Welles, Actor/Director/Minister o' Merlot]
ORSON	Historians, scientists, and theologians dismiss Preposterodamus.
SCREEN	A scholar [Caption: Dr. William B. Robison, Historian]
ROBISON	There is little reason to regard Preposterodamus as anything other than a superstitious fraud.
SCREEN	Orson [Caption: Orson Welles, Actor/Director/Raconteur o' Rotgut]
ORSON	However, Preposterodamus still inspires widespread belief.
SCREEN	Humbert Fudad, an obvious idiot Caption: Humbert Fudad, Credulous Dupe
FUDAD	My name is Humbert Fudad. I am the founder and sole proprietor of Fudad's Quality Meats, where meat is our métier and our motto is "Hot dog, it's hog sausage!" I have been a UFO investigator for the United States Air Force's Project Blue Book, a clairvoyant cartographer specializing in maps of Atlantis, an expert on wild orchids in the Everglades, and a septic tank technician for Honeydippers, Inc. I am also a parapsychological prognosticator and the world's foremost authority on Preposterodamus the Forgotten Seer. I have seen, as he has, with the inner eye! The future is an open book to me. The price of meat will go up . . . and I'm not just jiving you with some cosmic debris. The heretics will perish in flames! The heretics will

perish in flames!

SCREEN	A fortune teller
	Caption: Sister Electra, Fortune Teller, 1-999-666-7137
ORSON	Preposterodamus also appeals to more prosaic fortunetellers.
ELECTRA	I am not a fortuneteller. I am a thaumaturgical engineer. I see all, I know all. Preposterodamus, he tell me. I see the future, I know the future! And I don't steal nobody money. People call me. They open their hearts to Sister Electra. And I share the great Preposterodamus' vision with them. If, in their gratitude, they send me a little present, what business is that of the IRS? I am not a crook! I am an honest woman making an honest living! I was framed! Framed! Bastards!

SCREEN	Jack
	[Caption: Jack O' Lantern, Neo-Pagan High Priest of the Fiery Druids]
ORSON	And there are other interpretations.
JACK	We believe that Preposterodamus was a victim of the narrow-minded, persecuting Church that burned over 50 million witches in the sixteenth century alone. In reality he was simply a pastoral peasant peacefully practicing our ancient nature religion and seeking to live in harmony with earth, water, and air and the sacred rhythms of the cosmos.

SCREEN	A scholar
	[Caption: Dr. William B. Robison, Historian]
ROBISON	There is not one shred of evidence to support that interpretation.

SCREEN	Jack and a woman who gazes adoringly at him
	[Caption: Jack O' Lantern and Wife, Jackie O]
JACK	That's just the sort of deceptive explanation you would expect from the academic establishment.

SCREEN	A postmodern literary scholar
	[Caption: Dr. Crystal Gazer, Postmodern Literary Critic]
POSTMOD	Close reading of the holograph of Anonymous of Terra

Incognita reveals a polymorphic hermeneutics of synchronic and diachronic inversion and metamorphosis that mingles intertextuality and intersexuality in a transgressive reification of patriarchally-imposed class tensions in a carnivalesque concretization of phobias concerning the body and the diabolical feminine that transmits, remits, submits, and emits oven mitts in a transgendered transmogrification of social mores in the intermittent oeuvre of the notionally real . . .

[Subtitles: I don't know what this means, but I need tenure and I owe money to my aromatherapist!]

SCREEN   Orson, reeling slightly
              [Caption: Orson Welles, Actor/Director/Wino]

ORSON   Is there no one who can provide an intelligent perspective?

SCREEN   Hermione with pictures of Harry and Ron in background
              [Caption: Hermione Granger, 5th Year, Hogwarts School for Witchcraft and Wizardry, Amicus de Henrico]

HERMIONE   Well, I have read every book in the Hogwarts Library about every astrologer who ever lived, and—unlike, say, Nicholas Flamel—I've never seen the first mention of Preposterodamus. At Hogwarts we believe that Preposterodamus is hogwash.

SCREEN   Moaning Myrtle, sitting near toilet
              [Caption: Moaning Myrtle, Spectral Drain Dweller]

MYRTLE   It's rubbish. And I know—I'm a ghost. It's all a lot of cobblers. Hmmph!

SCREEN   "Inquisitor" with photo of Preposterodamus and stupid prediction

ORSON   Still Preposterodamus remains fodder for the tabloids . . .

SCREEN   "Tripe" with photo of Preposterodamus and stupid prediction

ORSON   . . . week after week at your supermarket checkout line.

SCREEN	An obviously blitzed Orson, head on desk, wine bottle empty, mumbling [Caption: Orson Welles, Actor/Director/Blotto]
ORSON	Rosebud . . . Rosebud . . . Rosebud . . .
SCREEN	EEN Fundraiser with assorted ghouls talking on phones in the background Caption: EEN Fundraiser, 1-800-555-5555
MABLE	Hello, this is Mable Phipps. If you enjoy the kind of quality programming you are watching tonight, we hope that you will take a few minutes to pick up the phone and call the number on your screen and pledge a contribution to viewer-supported EEN. For a $50 contribution, we will send you a wonderful premium, this colorful lump of multi-dimensional protoplasm. For a $100 contribution tonight only, we will send you a framed copy of Preposterodamus' recipe for his Miracle Revirginating Ointment. Remember, this station belongs to you. We don't receive state funding like the big shots at university television stations; we depend on viewers like you. Won't you please pick up the phone and call while we return you to this fascinating program on Preposterostermus, Prepostarhinoceros, Preposterposthumous, Prepost . . . on the forgotten seer.
SCREEN	Orson looking slightly ill [Caption: Orson Welles, Actor/Director/Snockered]
ORSON	Rose . . . Ugh. Oh, boy. And so we come to the famous squatrains, some of which are actually believed to predict events occurring in our very own day. For example, a possible reference to contemporary politics . . .
SCREEN	In lands beyond the ocean sea In Anno Domini 2003 The throne given to a sturdy beggar The lederhosened Schwarzenegger
VOICE	In lands beyond the ocean sea In Anno Domini 2003 The throne given to a sturdy beggar The lederhosened Schwarzenegger
ORSON	Or to contemporary news media . . .

38

SCREEN   From the antipodes a lying fox
                    Appears upon the magic box
                    Then shall he cast a magic bone
                    And prate upon the no-spin zone

VOICE   From the antipodes a lying fox
                    Appears upon the magic box
                    Then shall he cast a magic bone
                    And prate upon the no-spin zone

ORSON   Or to contemporary political experts . . .

SCREEN   Ann anon no nun decline
                    Colt or ass or porcupine
                    Pseudo-pundit dominatrix
                    Blond and barbied bloviatrix

VOICE   Ann anon no nun decline
                    Colt or ass or porcupine
                    Pseudo-pundit dominatrix
                    Blond and barbied bloviatrix

ORSON   Or to the contemporary world of sports resurrection . . .

SCREEN   Helmeted lions eighteen years ere gone
                    To Strawberry Stadium home have come
                    But the nature of it knows no prophet
                    If the game shall profit Randy Moffett

VOICE   Helmeted lions eighteen years ere gone
                    To Strawberry Stadium home have come
                    But the nature of it knows no prophet
                    If the game shall profit Randy Moffett

ORSON   Or to a contemporary cinema legend . . .

SCREEN   In his dotage the Whoreson Ells
                    A jug of cheaper vintage sells
                    Cain disabled, Mercury marred,
                    Schlockmeister and tub of lard

VOICE   In his dotage the Whoreson Ells
                    A jug of cheaper vintage sells
                    Cain disabled, Mercury marred,
                    Schlockmeister and tub of lard

SCREEN	An infuriated Orson raging [Caption: Orson Welles, Actor/Director/Pissed]
ORSON	Hey, wait a minute! That's about me! Damn it, that does it! Hearst! I know you're behind this, William Randolph Hearst! I was a legend! A giant! Citizen Kane was the greatest movie ever made. But you, Hearst! You couldn't take the criticism! No honesty for you! Oh, no! So you destroyed my career, you rotten SOB! And now I'm reduced to peddling crap documentaries like some slightly more articulate Jerry Springer! Ruined! Ruined! Dead! And so great an actor!
SCREEN	Orson storms off
STAGE	Orson storms on to the stage, still raging, stalks off
SCREEN	Preposterodamus appears, toys with wand, suddenly disappears in puff of smoke
STAGE	Puff of smoke in front of podium, Preposterodamus appears behind it, sound effects go off, balloons, etc.

LECTURE ON NOSTRADAMUS

STAGE	Preposterodamus, Electra, Orson, et. al. throw candy to audience
SCREEN	Credits run as follows

NOSTRADAMUS: POET, PROPHET, PHARMACIST, PHRAUD

Written and Performed by	William B. Robison
Pottle Technical Director	Ellen Sovkopolas

PREPOSTERODAMUS THE FORGOTTEN SEER

Writer	William B. Robison
Director	Bibbet Robison
Filmed on Some Locations by	Buttered Buns Cinematography
Music	Tucker Robison
Sound	Robison Productions, Inc
Still Photography	Diosa Photography

Costuming	Togaman.com
Casting	Casting Caution to the Winds
Carpentry	Sweaty Pitts
Gaffer	Snookum Constable
Geezer	Wampus Cat Clark
Gooser	D. Duck
Key Grip	Snoop Beagle Dogg
Monkey Grip	Balto Golden
Hypermonkey Grip	Bob Golden, Jr
Public Relations	Boyd Hall
Masseuse	Autumn Felinius
Catering	Junk Foods

CAST (IN ORDER OF APPEARANCE)

Orson Welles	Wade Heaton
Preposterodamus	Bill Robison
Wenus of Wallachia	Chuck Dellert
Fantod	Tucker Robison
Satan	Wade Heaton
Santa	Bill Robison
Dr. William Robison	Himself
Humbert Fudad	Bill Robison
Sister Electra	Bibbet Robison
Jack O'Lantern	Matt Robison
Jackie O. Lantern	Natasha Sanchez
Dr. Crystal Gazer	Natasha Sanchez
Hermione Granger	Zoe Robison
Moaning Myrtle	Molly Robison
Mabel Phipps	Bibbet Robison

WITH SPECIAL THANKS TO
Southeastern Louisiana University
Fanfare
The College of Arts and Sciences
The Department of History and Political Science
The Center for Southeast Louisiana Studies
The Florida Parishes Social Science Research Center
The Southeastern Channel
Pottle Music Auditorium
Donna Gay Anderson

Keiron Couret
Kim Lewis-Gordon
Ellen Sovkoplas [Lipkos]
Joyce White
Everyone who has not sued us

SOUNDTRACK
Available on Happy Pigg Records
[Actually on *Show Tunes*]

2003 LECTURE
NOSTRADAMUS: POET, PROPHET, PHARMACIST, PHRAUD

Well, what was that about? [Referring to *Preposterodamus the Forgotten Seer.*] And how, my superiors are wondering, did we ever give this man tenure and make him a department head? It was magic!

Orson Welles, great actor and director, really did make *Citizen Kane*, which contains mysterious references to "Rosebud" and which many critics regard as the greatest film of all time; he really did have his career destroyed by the newspaper magnate William Randolph Hearst; thereafter he really did become the spokesman for Paul Masson wines; and in his dotage he really did make a "documentary" about Nostradamus, which was a far cry from the aesthetic brilliance of *Citizen Kane* and much closer—in its disregard for the facts, if not in its artistic value—to his famous Mercury Theater radio broadcast of *The War of the Worlds*, which panicked listeners into believing that Martians had invaded the Earth. Hence our little spoof.

Before I go any further, I do want to make one thing perfectly clear. Nostradamus did not have an illegitimate brother named Preposterodamus. I am here today to demystify Nostradamus, and I certainly do not want to create another false myth alongside him. However, much of what has been written, said, and believed about Nostradamus is as preposterous as what you have just witnessed onscreen here. Hence the title of our little spoof and the name of Nostradamus' fictional sibling.

I have one further caveat before proceeding. Much of Nostradamus' career occurred along the boundaries between magic and religion, between magic and science, and between religion and science. It will be clear in my discussion of Nostradamus that I prefer science to magic as an explanation for events in the natural world. However, that does not mean that I wish to denigrate religion or to appear contemptuous of anyone's faith.

Now, who was Nostradamus and what do we *really* know about him? And what do the answers to those questions have to do with the subtitle of today's lecture—*Poet, Prophet, Pharmacist, Phraud?* There are four categories of people when it comes to Nostradamus. First, there are those who have never heard of Nostradamus—obviously people who never shop at the supermarket and thus are never confronted with the weekly prophesies attributed to him in the tabloids at the checkout counter. Second, there are those who have heard of Nostradamus but do not know much more than his name and do not much care. Third, there are those who have read and heard a great deal about Nostradamus and who fervently believe that he was a prophet (e.g., like the nineteenth century writer Charles Ward or the contemporary John Hogue). Fourth, there are those who have read and heard a great deal about Nostradamus and who fervently believe that he was *not* a prophet. I am in the last group.

So why, you might ask, am I interested in Nostradamus if I do not believe that he was a prophet? The answer is that I have spent my whole career as a historian studying and writing about late medieval and early modern Europe, particularly the sixteenth century, and I believe that a careful examination of the real Nostradamus can provide us with valuable insights about the history of his era and about the modern understanding—or misunderstanding—of that history. I also think it is fun.

Nostradamus is widely remembered. There are almost 300 books currently on Amazon.com and many hundreds more in libraries, there are thousands of sites on the web (most of them of the greatest scholarly value), there have been movies, there has been music (including Al Stewart's album *Past, Present, and Future*), there are regular features in the tabloids, and astrology remains popular today.

Prophecy has a long history. The best we can tell, early man even in prehistoric times attempted to predict the future. We certainly know based on cave paintings that prehistoric man tried to do magic, that is, to influence the future, and if you believe you can influence it, presumably you believe that you can predict it as well. The Egyptians had their prophets, the Chaldeans their astronomers, the Persians their magi, the Greeks their oracles, the Romans their soothsayers, and the Middle Ages their apocalyptic millennialists, usually predicting the end of the world, the advent of the Antichrist, and the revelation that their enemies, whoever they might be, were in fact in a league with the Devil. These folks got especially exercised whenever numbers came up like the year 1000, the year 1500, and of course we have had an echo of that more recently with all of the hysteria about the year 2000.

Astrology was actually quite common in the sixteenth century, and that strikes some people as odd because that was the high point of the Renaissance. But, in fact, astrology was popular not in spite of the Renaissance but because of it. Much of the "knowledge" that went into the practice and study of astrology was recovered from the literature of the ancient world, along with other literature having to do with history, philosophy, poetry, drama, and so on. So you had scholars of the time like Girolamo Cardano, an astrologer who was very well known for having recovered a great deal of ancient knowledge. The thing about it is, though most of us regard astrology as bogus nonsense these days (and rightfully so), it was considered to be a legitimate field of knowledge in the sixteenth century, and you had to work very hard to be an informed astrologer. You had to learn languages, and you had to study difficult texts. It was as difficult to become an accomplished astrologer, as Cardano was, as it was to become a medical doctor, a lawyer, or any other sort of learned person. Astrology was held in high regard in the highest places. Queen Elizabeth— an extraordinarily enlightened woman in a lot of ways, very well educated, multilingual, talented in all sorts of areas—nonetheless believed very firmly in it and employed an astrologer, John Dee.

This was also a time in which the scientific view of the world was undergoing substantial change. The Middle Ages believed in a universe in which the Earth was literally at the center; a world in which the planets, the stars, the moon, and the sun were held in celestial crystalline spheres that rotated around the earth; a world in which it was believed that all life and, indeed, all non-life were organized into a Great Chain of Being in which everything had its exact place in relationship to everything else; a world in which the elements were considered to be only four (something you may have devoutly wished for in your chemistry classes), but all four of these elements were not really elements at all—earth, air, fire, and water are not elements; a world in which the body was believed to be controlled by the four humors—black bile, yellow bile, phlegm, and blood. It was also believed that celestial bodies—the planets and the stars, the sun and the moon—interacted with the elements, with the humors, with heat and cold, with wetness and dryness, with the time of year that you were born, with the year that you were born in, and all sorts of other factors that are really more occult than scientific in nature to affect your health, to affect your fate, and so on.

It is only in the sixteenth century that we get the first little steps away from this. Copernicus did publish his work denouncing the old earth-centered (geocentric) view of the universe and replacing it with a heliocentric view, but that idea did not really catch on until over a hundred years later. So the sixteenth century was still very much in the Middle Ages as far as cosmology was concerned. Change—even in the Renaissance, later on in the First Scientific Revolution, and still later in the Enlightenment— was always very incremental. There tended to be one foot in the future but one foot still firmly in the past. John Dee is a good example of this. Here is a man who was a very advanced scientist in a great many ways but who also attempted to practice magic, who attempted to contact angels through a medium, and who practiced astrology. These things went together. The distinction that we make between real science and something like astrology simply did not exist. Even Isaac Newton—the Einstein of the seventeenth century, the man who really represents the culmination of the First Scientific Revolution—still practiced alchemy. I do not know if he had as nice looking a still as Preposterodamus, but he did do it, and he did search for the philosopher's stone.

Nostradamus was born into this sixteenth century in France, a nation which had been having a growth spurt recently, having driven the English out in 1453 at the end of the Hundred Years War and having acquired considerable new territory in recent years, which will come back into our story in just a moment. He also grew up at a time when there was growing religious turmoil in Europe. This is, after all, the age of the Reformation. It was in 1517 that Martin Luther nailed his Ninety-Five Theses to the door of the church in Wittenberg, thereby beginning the Protestant Reformation, the Catholic Reformation as a backlash against that, and all that ensued therefrom. Where this impacted Nostradamus is that while there had been an Inquisition since 1231, the Spanish Inquisition—known to everyone from Monty Python if nothing else—only came into existence in 1478 at the behest of Ferdinand of Aragon and Isabella of Castile, the rulers of Spain and the same people responsible for sending Columbus to the New World and expelling the Jews from the kingdom in 1492. A lot of the Jews thus expelled went across the border into Provence in southern France, and one of those who did so was Nostradamus' grandfather, a Jewish doctor by the name of Guy Gassonet, who converted to Christianity and changed his name to Pierre de Notredame, his last name meaning "our Lady," a reference to the Virgin Mary. Pierre had a son named Jacques, who married Renee, daughter of Jean de St. Remy, also a converted Jew and also a doctor. Pierre and Renee were in turn the parents of Nostradamus, born on Christmas Eve in 1503 in St. Remy, Provence and christened Michel de Notredame [born 24 December according to the New Style dating of the Gregorian calendar adopted in 1582 or 14 December according to the Old Style Julian calendar in use at the time of his birth]. Like many doctors, the adult Michel Latinized his names as Nostradamus. It was later claimed that because he was the grandson of a Jew, he must have inherited the ancient Hebrew talent for prophecy.

At any rate, he was a bright little guy, went off to school at an early age, began his secondary education at Avignon in 1517, attended the University of Montpellier to study medicine beginning in 1522, took a baccalaureate degree and a license to practice medicine in 1525, by which time he already had begun to acquire a reputation for treating bubonic plague (supposedly in 1523, 1525, and 1528 in France and northern Italy). You might be impressed by that but for the fact that bubonic plague in about 99.9% of all cases was incurable, so acquiring a reputation for being able to cure it is a little bit suspect. He took a full medical degree at Montpellier 1529, taught there two years, moved to Agen to study with Jules-Cesar Scaliger in 1532, settled down, got married to a woman whose name we do not know, and had two children whose names we do not know. Shortly thereafter, plague struck in Agen, and his wife and children all died.

The next year matters got worse because Nostradamus discovered that the Inquisition in France was interested in him. There are a number of reasons why they might have been interested in Nostradamus. Here was a man who, after all, was the grandson of a converted Jew, which automatically made one suspect in Spain and France. He also may have begun to dabble in the occult by this time, although there is no evidence of it before the 1540s. Recent discoveries in some of his correspondence provide the even more intriguing possibility that he may have been closet Protestant. There are letters in which he shows very distinct sympathy with Protestantism, although for a man who as about to become the employee of the Catholic king and queen of France to actually own up to that would have been foolish in the extreme.

In any case Nostradamus left Agen, practiced medicine at Aix-en-Provence and Lyons, was at Marseilles by 1544 and Aix again by 1546. He remarried in 1547 to a wealthy widow named Anna Ponce Gemelle, settled in Salon, and proceeded to have six children and travel extensively, including visits to Venice, Geneva, and Savona. He spent much of the rest of his life writing, publishing his first astrological almanac in 1550. To his surprise, it made money, encouraging him to write some more. His most famous work is the 1553 *Excellent et Moult utile Opuscule* (combining the earlier *Traicte des Fardemens* and *Vray et Parfaict embellissement de la Face*), a collection of all sorts of quack medicines, love potions, recipes, skin restorers, hair dyes, and cosmetics (though nothing that allegedly restores virginity). Then in 1555 he published *Les Prophecies*, the first group of quatrains claiming to predict the future.

I want to make an important distinction here. Nostradamus claimed from the first that his quatrains were predictions of the future, but he did not claim that they predicted any of the events with which they have become associated. The quatrains all are written in extraordinarily vague, allusive language, and you can make almost anything out of them. Thus, in many cases it was individuals who lived long afterward, not Nostradamus himself, who associated his prophecies with particular events. During his own lifetime he did make a few specious claims to have predicted actual events that occurred before his death, and I will address the most famous of those shortly. He predicted things all the way to 3797, so we have a lot more of this stuff to put up with before we finally lay him to rest.

In 1556 Catherine de Medici summoned him to the court of her husband, the French King Henri II, because they both believed in astrology and wanted him to give them advice. He wrote more quatrains, which he published in 1557 and 1558. Subsequently he received several royal appointments, later on Catherine and her son, the future Charles IX, visited him at Salon, and in 1565 he was appointed physician-in-ordinary to the king, which was quite a high honor. To be made the king's physician is to be a given a position of enormous trust. However, he died shortly afterward in 1566, and that—so it might have been thought—was the end of that. But, in fact, his quatrains took on a life of their own.

I want to make clear that Nostradamus always cast himself primarily as a prophet, not as a magician, an astronomer, or even an astrologer but as someone who was informed in more mysterious ways. It has been suggested that he may have been influenced in some of his visions by his own medication, but that is strictly speculation. One thing we know is that his quatrains dealt with things that were going on writ large in his own day—war, violence, religious strife, concerns over civil liberty, scandal, court gossip, you name it—it all shows up, often very heavily veiled. The truth is that the man was talented—in a way. He knew the classics, and he was able to balance a good deal of sophisticated knowledge with a good deal of frippery in his writing. As to why he did it, we can only speculate. Perhaps it was in the hope of making money, perhaps it was to advance his court connections, perhaps he, too, was having fun. But in any case, it is worth noting that in his own day, Nostradamus was less well regarded than his contemporaries like John Dee and Girolamo Cardano. Others saw him as less accomplished, somewhat vulgar, or even dismissed him as a kooky stargazer.

The quatrains themselves, which have attracted so much attention as allegedly telling the future, are very vague, they often have multiple applications, their interpretations can be taken in all sorts of directions, and they are frequently misread. One thing that interpreters of the quatrains do is that they rely on anagrams, that is, taking words and rearranging the letters to make other words. If you sit down and do that with any sentence, you eventually can come up with some pretty wild stuff. Dave Berry, the humor columnist, does that all the time. Another thing interpreters do is tamper with punctuation, which can change the meaning of things considerably. They interpret symbols in all sorts of ways. They use parts of quatrains or parts of lines of quatrains, combine parts of different quatrains, or take words in one language and make them stand for something in another language. There is lot of circular reasoning.

James Randi, a former magician who has devoted his later life to debunking all sorts of nonsense like Uri Geller, for example, has come up with an interesting system of classification for Nostradamus' quatrains. He identifies six kinds. Quatrains of the First Kind are those that were made for the safely far future. Since they have all of recorded time in which to be fulfilled, they will very probably come true or already have within certain limits. Quatrains of the Second Kind are those that were apt to be fulfilled very soon after they were written, things that one could predict reasonably certainly without being much of a prophet. Quatrains of the Third Kind are those that were absolutely sure to be successful prophecies because they predict things that already have happened and were often written very soon after the event. Quatrains of the Fourth Kind are those that are such garbled, mystical nonsense, semantically and logically, that they cannot be examined with any kind of reason at all. Quatrains of the Fifth Kind are those that describe quite ordinary events in Nostradamus' time, with a little extra material thrown in. Finally, there are Quatrains of the Wrong Kind, those that already have been proved inaccurate.

Here is perhaps the most famous of all Nostradamus' quatrains, the one that is said to have made his reputation. In fact, it almost did just the opposite. This is the quatrain that is supposed to have predicted the death of Henri II of France, who died tragically young in 1559. There was a big celebration in Paris to mark the marriage of Henri's daughter Elizabeth to Philip II of Spain and his sister Marguerite to the Duke of Savoy in a big double wedding. Of course there was a tournament with jousting, and Henri II—being a young, vigorous man—participated. In the course of a joust he was struck in the helmet with a lance by Gabriel de Lorges, Comte de Montgomery. Henri did not have his visor all the way down, the lance went into the helmet and punctured his right eye, and he lingered near death for ten days and then expired. Now what does that have to do with the following quatrain?

> The young lion will overcome the old one
> On the field of battle in single combat
> He will burst his eyes in a cage of gold
> Two fleets one, then to die, a cruel death

Those who believe in Nostradamus argue that this refers to a younger man killing Henri on the field of battle and the king's eye being hurt; the cage of gold is supposed to be a reference to his helmet, which allegedly was golden; and what the fleets are about nobody has the remotest clue. The fact is that Montgomery was a little younger but not much, so this was not really a "young lion versus old" situation. Also, one would never refer to a king of France as a "lion." The lion was the symbol of an English king. To call a French king a lion would be an insult. Jousting is not a battle but a sport; in fact, participants were not supposed to shed blood. Additionally, there is not a shred of evidence that Henri had a gilded helmet. So the claim on behalf of this quatrain does not hold up. In fact, it has been suggested that it might apply retroactively to Sir Thomas More, a man who was killed by a king, Henry VIII of England, who could have been called a "young lion" to More's "old lion." More had been dead a quarter of a century when this quatrain was written. The real clincher, though, is that in 1557 edition of his quatrains, Nostradamus included a dedication to Henri II in which he predicted long successful reign! Now, you cannot have it both ways. Either the 1557 prediction is right, and he really did not die—and that opens up a whole can of worms—or we cannot claim that Nostradamus predicted his death.

Here is another quatrain, supposedly about Elizabeth I of England:

> She who was chased out shall return to the kingdom
> Her enemies found to be conspirators
> More than ever her time will triumph
> Three and seventy to death much assured

If your English teacher gave you this quatrain and asked what it is about, what would you say? This was seen to be about Elizabeth because she was in prison (though not exactly chased out of her kingdom), did have enemies who were conspirators, and she died when she was seventy though not "three and seventy." What this actually appears to have been is propaganda. Elizabeth's number one enemy early on in her reign was Henri II of France, the boss of Nostradamus. Why? Because Henri II's oldest son, the eventual Francis II, was married to Mary, Queen of Scots, the rival to Elizabeth. So Nostradamus apparently was writing something that people at the time would interpret as a prediction of Elizabeth's death in the near future. She reigned from 1558 to 1603—most of us should be so lucky.

Nostradamus also is supposed to have predicted the death of

Charles I of England, who was executed by the parliamentary party in the English Civil War in 1649. Here is what we get for that:

> Ghent and Brussels will march against Antwerp
> The senate of London will put to death their king
> The salt and wine will be against him
> To have them, the realm in disarray

Certainly we have a dead king here. Charles Ward, the nineteenth century Nostradamian, claimed that the first line applies to the Treaty of Westphalia, which ended the Thirty Years War in 1648 and thereby ended the Spanish threat to the Netherlands. In fact, there was no action in the Netherlands around Ghent, Brussels, or Antwerp, but there was in 1555, when the Holy Roman Emperor Charles V, who was also the king of Spain, was in the area threatening those cities, three months before Nostradamus published the quatrains. The death of a king in London may refer to Henry VI, who was indeed murdered there in 1471.

Nostradamus is also said to have predicted the Great Fire of London (1666):

> The blood of the just shall be wanting in London
> Burnt by thunderbolts of twenty three the Six(es)
> The ancient dame shall fall from [her] high place
> Of the same sect many shall be killed

This may actually apply to the persecutions under Bloody Mary, who began burning heretics in 1555, shortly before Nostradamus published the quatrains.

Then there is the famous one where he supposedly predicted Napoleon. This is an anagram quatrain.

> Pau, Nay, Oloron will be more in fire than in blood
> Swimming the Aude, the great fleeing to the mountains
> He refuses the magpies entrance
> Pamplona, the Durance River holds them enclosed

If you take the first three words of first line and move them around, you get "Nay Pau Oloron," which is kind of like "Napoleon" but not much.

Then there is the Hitler quatrain, shown here in French to reveal in the second line the word "Hister," which people have argued is an anagram for "Hitler":

> Bestes farouches de faim fleuues tranner
> Plus part du champ encontre Hister sera
> En caige de fer Ie grand fera treisner
> Quant rein enfant de Germain obseruera

Let us see what it actually says:

> Beasts mad with hunger will swim across rivers
> Most of the army will be against the Lower Danube
> The great one shall be dragged in an iron cage
> When the child brother will observe nothing

The second line could be about World War II, but it also could be about any other war in Germany from ancient times to the present. "Hister" does not seem to have anything to do with Hitler at all.

Nostradamus also purportedly predicted the careers of the Kennedy brothers—John, Bobby, and Ted. This was a big item back in the sixties because the argument then was that all three Kennedy brothers were going to be president. John was president, Bobby was assassinated while running for president, and Ted ran but never succeeded. The "prediction" comes from a quatrain that makes reference to three brothers who may one day hold power, but the three brothers in question were the sons of Henri II and Catherine de Medici—Francis II, Charles IX, and Henri III. During the Cold War it was popular to find in Nostradamus predictions of the nuclear arms race and nuclear holocaust. So far, so good—there was supposed to be such a holocaust in 1999, but we missed it. After the tragic events of 9/11 in 2001 there almost immediately were people claiming to have found lines written by Nostradamus predicting that. Interestingly, the first quatrain brought forward turned out not to be have been written by Nostradamus at all. But there is a quatrain that makes reference to terror from the sky. But how much can one really make of that? Where does an astrologer look for signs of the future? To the sky. If terror is going to come—as it frequently did, in the form of comets, meteor showers, eclipses—it is going to come from the sky. There is not much to suggest that Nostradamus foretold the atrocity of 9/11.

Before I close, I want to return briefly to three themes that I have addressed in my previous Fanfare lectures and, I hope, throughout my career. The first theme is truth. We are always better off knowing the truth about history even when it forces us to cast aside or alter old assumptions. Accurate knowledge and understanding of the past, informed by a judicious balance of faith and reason, is the only sound basis for making sense of the present and for making realistic preparations for, if not actual predictions about, the future. We ignore history at our peril.

The second theme is fun. Learning is, of course, serious business, and the consequence of ignorance is not bliss but misery. You have only to look at the state of our world to be reminded that ignorance is the handmaiden of evil. But the importance of learning does not require that education be conducted in stone-faced solemnity. Lessons learned with laughter linger, and they are good not only for the mind but also for the soul.

The third theme is gratitude. I am grateful to be an American and to live in a country and an age in which we are free to believe or disbelieve whatever we like without facing the wrath of an Inquisition and where we seek to change minds through evidence and persuasion and not by fear and torment. I am grateful to be a history professor at Southeastern Louisiana University. As far as I am concerned, there is not a better job in the world. I am grateful to my son Matt and my daughters Zoe and Molly for appearing as actors in *Preposterodamus the Forgotten Seer,* to my brother Tucker for acting and composing the original theme music, to my sister-in-law Natasha Sanchez for acting and doing still photography, to my graduate assistant Chuck Dellert for acting and providing technical assistance, to my good friend Wade Heaton for putting off the *dignitas* and *gravitas* of the toga and taking up the cigar and wine glass of Orson Welles, and to my wife Bibbet for directing and editing the entire production, thereby sacrificing what little reputation she had left after marrying me. Finally, I am grateful to all of you for being here today, and in the spirit of Halloween, I would like to offer you a little token of my gratitude. So please stay with me just a moment longer, and while you watch the credits up here on the screen, please yell—as loudly as possible—"Trick or Treat!"

Suggestions for Further Reading

Philip Ball, *The Devil's Doctor: Paracelsus and the World of Renaissance Magic and Science* (2006); Stephen Vanden Broecke, *The Limits of Influence: Pico, Louvain, and the Crisis of Renaissance Astrology* (2003); Nicholas Campion, *A History of Western Astrology,* (2009); William Eamon, *The Professor of Secrets: Mystery, Medicine, and Alchemy in Renaissance Italy* (2010); Anthony Grafton, *Cardano's Cosmos: The Worlds and Works of a Renaissance Astrologer* (2000); Mack Holt, *The French Wars of Religion 1562-1629* (2005); R.J. Knecht, *Catherine de Medici*

(1997); John Scott Lucas, *Astrology and Numerology in Medieval and Early Modern Catalonia: The Tractat De Prenostication De LA Vida Natural Dels Homens* (2003); Diarmaid MacCulloch, *The Reformation* (2005); Peter Marshall, *The Magical Circle of Rudolf II: Alchemy and Astrology in Renaissance Prague* (2006); William Newman and Anthony Grafton, eds., *Secrets of Nature: Astrology and Alchemy in Early Modern Europe* (2006); James Randi, *The Mask of Nostradamus: The Prophecies of the World's Most Famous Seer* (1993); Steven Shapin, *The Scientific Revolution* (1998); Nancy Siraisi, *Medieval and Early Renaissance Medicine: An Introduction to Knowledge and Practice* (1990); Keith Thomas, *Religion and the Decline of Magic: Studies of Popular Beliefs in Sixteenth and Seventeenth Century England* (1971); Gerhild Scholz Williams and Charles Gunnoe, *Paracelsian Moments: Science, Medicine, and Astrology in Early Modern Europe* (2003); Benjamin Woolley, *The Queen's Conjurer: The Science and Magic of Dr. John Dee, Adviser to Queen Elizabeth I* (2002).

2004 PREQUEL
MR. ROBISON'S SPOOKY NEIGHBORHOOD

This year witnessed a return to the live-action prequel with a parody of the opening of *Mr. Rogers' Neighborhood*. The bit opens with a bell chiming for midnight (despite the fact that it is daytime) followed by spooky organ music, maniacal laughter, and a voiceover welcoming the audience to *Mr Robison's Spooky Neighborhood*. Then, to the tune of Mr. Rogers' theme music played in a minor key on electric guitars, Mr. Robison comes onstage, takes off his coat and shoes, hangs them up, and puts on a sweater and slippers. Mr. Robison welcomes the audience, introduces Mr. McTogaman (a pitch for a later event), and begins the lecture.

Listen to audio at https://myspace.com/headongoolah/videos or on the CD *Show Tunes* by Headongoolah (which is me before Impaired Faculties).

2004 LECTURE
PAGANS, PIETY, AND PUMPKINS:
THE HORRIFYING, HOLY, AND HORTICULTURAL
HISTORIES OF HALLOWEEN

I am not really a children's television host, but I *did* stay a Holiday Inn Express last night. Now, let me begin by explaining the title of my lecture. It is designed mainly to attract attention, and I just happen to like alliteration. I am not a pagan, and I am not here to promote paganism or to condemn paganism. I am not a pumpkin, though I have consumed pumpkin in every form known to man (even soup). However, I am given to occasional outbursts of piety as well as of silliness. I used the term "histories" because Halloween has more than one history—sometimes horrifying, sometimes holy, and sometimes horticultural. It has been many things, depending on the time, the place, and the people involved. All of these aspects of Halloween are related but not always very closely.

Halloween has pagan origins, it was a Christian holiday for many centuries, and it now largely has been secularized. Many present-day observers attempt to link Halloween's long-ago pagan origins to its current observance. This includes both neo-pagans, who argue that the early Christian church usurped an ancient pagan holiday, and Christian fundamentalists, who in turn link paganism to Satan. Neither group is right. Of course neo-pagans are perfectly entitled to celebrate Halloween however they please, and fundamentalists are perfectly entitled to oppose Satan (in fact, that seems like a pretty good idea for all of us). However, the name "Halloween" is actually Christian in origin (more on that later), and so is the word "pagan," which urban Christians in the Roman Empire originally used as an insult to refer to rural, poorly educated peasants who persisted in practicing pre-Christian religions. Therefore, use of both terms is problematic. Ironically, as we will see, much present-day belief about the "pagan origins" of the modern Halloween may be the result of reading Christian practices back into the past.

There are several possible sources for the ancient pagan observation of what later became Halloween. One is the Roman festival of Pomona, the goddess of fruits and seeds. Another is Parentalia, a festival of the dead that the Romans actually observed in mid-February. However, scholars most frequently point to the Celtic observance of Samhain (pronounced sow-an, meaning "summer's end"). Samhain is one of the quarter days that fall between the equinoxes and the solstices. Samhain (October 31 or November 1) occurred near the midpoint between the autumnal equinox (September 22 or 23) and the winter solstice (December 21 or 22) and was paired with Beltane (May 1), which occurred six months later, near the midpoint between the vernal equinox (March 20 or 21) and the summer solstice (June 20-21). Beltane welcomes the sun, Samhain the winter.

Both Beltane and Samhain (like the equinoxes, solstices, and other quarter days) often are associated with the Druids, though these festivals likely are older than that mysterious group of Celts. I would like to show you a picture of a Druid, but no one really knows what the Druids looked like. Nor does anyone know much else about them. Almost all of modern "knowledge" about Druids is fantasy, invention, and/or speculation. Indeed, the most accurate assessment of what we know about them may come from the fictitious rock star Nigel Tufnel, who observes in the movie *This Is Spinal Tap* (1984): "No one knows who they were or what they were doing." Our only real sources of information about the Druids come from the Romans, who were extremely biased against them. Several Roman writers—Julius Caesar, Strabo, and Diodorus—claim that the Druids performed human sacrifice, which the Romans regarded as an especially abominable practice. Pliny the Elder describes them sacrificing white cattle. But none of these writers even mention Samhain, much less link it to Druids or human sacrifice. Caesar also mentions Celts conducting human sacrifice using an effigy called a wicker man, the inspiration for the 1973 horror movie, *The Wicker Man*, starring Christopher Lee [remade, badly, in 2006 with Nicholas Cage]. Some of the Irish sagas mention human sacrifice, so it is possible that Druids engaged in this practice. But the "evidence" for Druid sacrifice of humans—frequently at Stonehenge—comes mostly from modern fiction and thus is not evidence at all.

Another interpretation sees Samhain as a festival of dead. One of the earliest examples of this explanation is Sir James Frazer's *The Golden Bough* (1890), which claims that the ancient Celts thought that on Samhain the dead come back to visit the living and warm themselves by their fires. Strangely enough, this idea actually may come from reading the Christian All Souls Day back into the pagan era. There actually is no hard evidence that Samhain was a festival of the dead. However, it did mark the onset of winter and thus was a liminal festival, that is, it marked the boundary between the autumnal equinox and the winter solstice. The Celts associated this occasion with the supernatural and built bonfires for protection. However, little other Samhain ritual is known.

The assumption that Christians "took over" Halloween from pagans is also unfounded. The Christian Halloween is linked with All Saints

Day and All Souls Day, which the Roman Catholic Church has observed for centuries on November 1 and 2. "Halloween" is short for "All Hallows Eve," which occurs the day and night before All Saints Day, that is, on October 31. But the church did not originally observe any of these holidays on the current dates. Early on in the history of the church, Christians honored martyrs put to death by non-Christian emperors rather than saints. In the fourth century this happened on May 13. By about 800 there was a festival for saints, but there was no universal date—England and Germany observed it on November 1, Ireland on April 20. The first known observance of All Souls Day was in seventh-century Spain. The Cluniac order of monks popularized it at the end of the tenth century, but Abbot Odilo of Cluny celebrated it in February. Only later did the church move it to the day after All Saints.

In England near the end of the Middle Ages, All Saints and All Souls formed one of the six major feasts and holy days of obligation in the church. Christians marked it with masses and prayers and, as night fell on All Saints, rang bells for the dead in purgatory. Some people believed that this warded off demons, and many communities built bonfires to ward off malevolent spirits. They also consecrated graves with holy water and/or decorated them with flowers, lit cemeteries and churches with candles, and held torchlight processions. In many towns well-to-do citizens gave doles to the poor in return for their promise to pray for the dead relatives of the givers. This is the origin of "trick or treat." This was also the time of year when farmers slaughtered livestock, and they often used the bladders of the dead animals to make footballs, which they used in celebratory games. The liturgy referred to the wise virgins of Jesus' parable and to marriage. Choirs sang with their hoods up. Halloween began the season of masking that continued until Christmas. The festival included carnivalesque elements, including lords of misrule, mock mayors and sheriffs, mummers, and cross-dressing. Revelers paraded around collecting "donations" (treats) and abused those who refused to contribute (tricks), for example, by dunking them in bodies of water.

After the onset of the Reformation, the Tudors attacked some Hallowtide rituals. Archbishop Thomas Cranmer tried to abolish the ringing of bells for the dead, but Henry VIII refused to go along with that. Subsequently Edward VI's government did end the practice, but Mary I revived it, and Elizabeth found it difficult to stop unofficial observances. Fire rituals continued, including bonfires and torchlight processions around fields to protect crops. English Protestants also indulged in "souling," that is, baking "soul cakes" for all Christian souls, for which they went door-to-door collecting ingredients. Often they lit the way for these expeditions with lanterns made from a hollowed-out turnip with a candle inside (anyone who has ever struggled to make a Jack O' Lantern from a pumpkin will appreciate the skill required for carving one from a turnip). Treating also occurred on a number of other holidays in early modern England, including Guy Fawkes (5 November), St. Clement's (23 November), St. Catherine's (25 November), St. Andrew's (30 November), St. Nicholas's (6 December), and St. Thomas's (21 December).

On November 5, 1605 the government of James VI and I foiled the Gunpowder Plot, an attempt by a handful of radical Catholic conspirators to blow up the Houses of Parliament and kill the king, Lords, Commons, and bishops in one fell swoop. Thereafter, the annual celebration of that victory with bonfires, fireworks, and the burning of effigies (initially the pope, later Guy Fawkes) superseded Halloween as the principal fall holiday for Protestants in England. Scotland, on the other hand, celebrated both, which were often associated with high spirits and pranks. Understandably, Irish Catholics were less keen on Gunpowder Day, and in Ireland Halloween continued to have a vague connection to Samhain. By the eighteenth century the observation of Halloween in England became much concerned with courtship, in part because the English considered this a good time for diving omens that might predict love and/or marriage.

In America, Halloween—like Christmas—did not catch on until the nineteenth century. New England's Puritans did not approve of its festive revelry or its alleged pagan roots. For example, both Increase and Cotton Mather associated Halloween and Christmas with the Antichrist. What brought Halloween into the American mainstream was the arrival of Scots and Irish immigrants, though it never became an ethnic celebration like St. Patrick's Day. Again, like Christmas, Halloween enjoyed a sharp rise in popularity after the American Civil War, and by the 1870s it assumed a more secular character and became much more commercial with the deliberate marketing of masks and treats in the form of candy, fruits, and nuts.

With this also came a greater emphasis on tricks. Boys and young men in particular indulged in considerable rowdiness, blowing horns and making noise or sneaking around more quietly to attack unsuspecting passersby with pea shooters or bags full of soot, disfigure their neighbor's Jack-o-Lanterns (just how does one "disfigure" a Jack-o-Lantern?!), relocating booze ads to churches and churchyards, taking up boardwalks and taking down gates, tipping over outhouses (hopefully unoccupied), uprooting vegetable gardens, and so on. Some pranks involved considerable work. For instance, it was quite popular for a time to disassemble entire carriages and reassemble them on the roofs of buildings. My father distinctly recalled going to work in my grandfather's Lecompte, Louisiana hardware store on November 1 and finding their delivery wagon atop the two-story building housing the Hardy Brothers dry goods emporium next door.

Not surprisingly there was considerable misbehavior on college campuses. Nicholas Rogers cites instances in which Ann Arbor (Michigan) medical students stole cadavers and propped up a headless female corpse against the door of University Hall in 1900, Northwestern (Illinois) students were arrested for turning hoses on divinity students in 1907, Barnard College and Wellesley coeds held mock debates to ridicule presidential candidates in 1912, and students at various colleges harassed faculty (this last instance seems less appealing to me). As this suggests, Halloween enjoyed wide observance in America by 1900. That year a popular cartoon showed presidential candidate William Jennings Bryan attempting to divine his chances at the polls. Over time tricks evolved to suit the times. From the 1920s on pranks often included deflating automobile tires, soaping windows and screens, and stealing street signs and manhole covers. Alarmed by this youthful exuberance the U.S. Senate Judiciary Committee in 1950 recommended that President Harry Truman convert Halloween into "Youth Honor Day," an idea that was dead on arrival. Meanwhile, Halloween shared in the rampant consumerism also associated with Christmas and Easter. Attempts to direct it in a more philanthropic direction with "Trick-or-Treating for UNICEF" met with charges of abetting a United Nations conspiracy to promote communism.

Rogers also addresses the darker side of Halloween in his study of the holiday. He notes that the first rumors of candy apples containing razor blades and tainted candy appeared in the 1960s. However, though five-year-old Kevin Toston ate heroin-laced candy in 1970 and eight-year-old Timothy O'Bryan consumed Pixie Stix that his father laced with cyanide in 1974, most other reports turned out to be exaggeration, rumor, or urban myths. More seriously, burning and rioting on "Devil's Night" (October 30) has become a regular feature of the Halloween season in Detroit, gradually spreading to other cities as well. Meanwhile, less destructive enthusiasts can experience their violence vicariously with the ever-increasing body of Halloween horror movies. Certain groups also have politicized Halloween, notably the radical feminist group WITCH (Women's International Terrorist Conspiracy from Hell). In numerous cities gay Halloween celebrations combine a political agenda with old-fashioned revelry.

In recent decades Christian fundamentalist groups have criticized Halloween for allegedly promoting paganism or even Satan worship, notably by encouraging children to dress as witches, goblins, and so on. However, this seems overblown to me. One of my daughters was a witch one year and will be trick-or-treating as a pirate this Halloween, but she shows no sign of becoming either in real life. As a child I spent several Halloweens as Popeye, but I did not become a sailor. Indeed, all the fuss about what is really just a chance for children to have some harmless fun reinforces my belief that what we need in this country is a Mind Your Own Business Amendment to the Constitution. In any case, I plan to observe Halloween as usual. So, if you will say the magic words, it is candy time.

Suggestions for Further Reading

Diane Arkins, *Halloween Merrymaking: An Illustrated Celebration of Fun, Food, and Frolics from Halloween's Past* (2004) and *Halloween Romantic Art and Customs of Yesteryear* (2000); Lesley Prat Banatyne, *Halloween: An American Holiday, An American History* (1998); Stanley Brandes, *Skulls to the Living, Bread to the Dead: The Day of the Dead in Mexico and Beyond* (2007); Elizabeth Carmichael and Chloe Sayer, *The Skeleton at the Feast: The Day of the Dead in Mexico* (1991); Steven Heller, *Halloween: Vintage Holiday Graphics* (2005); Ronald Hutton, *The Pagan Religions of the Ancient British Isles: Their Nature and Legacy* (1993), *The Rise and Fall of Merry England: The Ritual Year 1400-1700* (1994), and *The Stations of the Sun: A History of the Ritual Year in Britain* (1996); Lisa Morton, *A Hallowe'en Anthology: Literary and Historical Writers Over the Centuries* (2008) and *The Halloween Encyclopedia* (2003); Nicholas Rogers, *Halloween: From Pagan Ritual to Party Night* (2002); David Skal, *Deaths Make a Holiday: A Cultural History of Halloween* (2002).

2005 PREQUEL
MONSTER MATINEE

Movie time again, but with onstage action as well. The 2005 lecture recombined the "More-or-Less Annual Halloween Lecture" with "History Goes to the Movies," this time showing how the changing nature of monster movies reflects the changing nature of American society in the twentieth and twenty-first centuries. Therefore, the 2005 prequel features a fictitious television show, *Monster Matinee*, hosted by Villiam the Video Vampire, a male character modeled on Vampira and Elvira, and two impish minions. He introduces *Godzilla, King of the Monsters*, the 1956 American adaptation of the 1954 Japanese film *Gojira*, which intercut scenes featuring Raymond Burr as American reporter Steve Martin in order to make it more audience-friendly in the United States. Excerpts from that movie conclude with buildings crashing down around Martin. The dust settles to reveal another reporter, Rupert Fox, who lampoons the American adulteration of the movie. Fox then disappears from the screen, and Villiam appears onstage, walks down a flight of stairs, puts his vampire teeth in a glass, and begins the lecture. At the end of the lecture Villiam leaves the stage, and another segment of film shows Villiam interacting with his minions again before reappearing onstage to throw candy to the audience.

Watch the video at https://myspace.com/headongoolah/videos.

SCREEN	EEN [large letters]
	Extrasensory Ectoplasm Network
VOICE	E . . . E . . . N
SCREEN	Empty Monster Matinee studio, with words "Monster Matinee" materializing
VOICE	Hello, movie mongrels, and welcome to "Monster Matinee."
SCREEN	The words "Monster Matinee" disappear, leaving studio empty
SCREEN	Villiam materializes in Dracula outfit with two minions
VILLIAM	Hello, I am William the Wideo Wampire . . . ahem . . . I mean Villiam the Video Vampire, your host for a special Halloween edition of Monster Matinee.

SCREEN   Villiam and minions

VILLIAM   Today we have a very special treat for you tricksters—the mother of all monster movies, *Godzilla, King of the Monsters!* Watch with me, if you dare, while this gigantic wizard tewwowizes Tokyo . . . ahem . . . while this gigantic lizard terrorizes Tokyo in a fit of radiation-inspired rage! Better leave on the lights, hold on to someone tight, and take that Walium . . . ahem . . . that Valium.

SCREEN   Villiam leaps up

VILLIAM   And now, on with the show!

SCREEN   Villiam and minions exit to the right of the video

SCREEN   Test pattern with words "Please stand by" and stupid music

SCREEN   Villiam and minions reappear from the left, puzzled

MINION 1   We seem to be going in circles . . .

SCREEN   Villiam and minions exit to the right of the video

SCREEN   Rainbow bars test pattern and stupid music

SCREEN   Villiam and minions reappear from the right, exasperated

MINION 2   How do we get out of here?

SCREEN   Villiam and minions exit to the left of the video

SCREEN   Snow and white noise

SCREEN   Villiam and minions reappear from the left, furious

VILLIAM   Oh, to hell with it!

SCREEN   Villiam snaps his fingers, and he and minions disappear

SCREEN   Excerpt of *Godzilla*

SCREEN   Cut to Rupert Fox in 1950s reporter garb, lying in the rubble

RUPERT   Yes, this is Tokyo. Hello, I am Rupert Fox, your fairly unbalanced reporter with the Irrational News Network. We interrupt this program to ask just what Raymond Burr is doing in the middle of a Japanese movie about a Japanese monster filmed in Japan by a Japanese director with an all-Japanese cast. Oh, sure, everybody loves Raymond . . . Burr. But he was Perry Mason. And then Ironside. And then Perry Mason again. So what is he doing in the middle of *Godzilla*?

SCREEN	Rupert Fox (Villiam—in the flesh—is offstage)
VILLIAM	[Evil laughter] Don't you know, you silly man?

SCREEN	Rupert Fox looks to his right (left of video)
RUPERT	What was that? What was that?

SCREEN	Rupert Fox (Villiam is offstage)
VILLIAM	Don't you know? Don't you know why Waymond . . . ahem . . . why Raymond Burr is in *Godzilla*, Mr. Reporter Rupert?

SCREEN	Rupert Fox, peers around, alarmed
RUPERT	Who said that? Who said that?

SCREEN	Rupert Fox
VILLIAM	I said it. It is I, Villiam. Now back with you to the Antipodes whence you came. Be gone! [Evil laughter]

SCREEN	Rupert Fox, outraged, disappears

THUNDER AND FLASHING LIGHTS

STAGE LIGHTS COME UP

STAGE	Villiam in the flesh walks on stage
VILLIAM	All right, then, let me explain . . .

STAGE	Villiam goes to podium, hangs cape on coat rack, puts teeth in glass of water, and begins lecture

LECTURE

STAGE   Villiam puts on cape, delivers the following line, then exits
VILLIAM And now it's time for candy! Uh oh, where is the candy?
      Please excuse me for just a moment. Stay right there! Don't
      go away! I'll be right back!

STAGE LIGHTS GO DOWN

SCREEN   Villiam materializes on screen, where the minions are sitting
      with a big bowl of candy; they jump and look startled.
MINION 1 I hate it when you do that!
VILLIAM I see you've gotten into the candy already.
MINION 2 Sorry . . .

SCREEN   Villiam takes the bowl, snaps fingers, and disappears

SCREEN   Minions deliver the following lines, then snap fingers and
      disappear
MINION 1 Guess we might as well leave . . .
MINION 2 Right, let's go find more candy!

STAGE LIGHTS COME UP

STAGE   Villiam and helpers throw candy to audience

2005 LECTURE
MONSTER MOVIES AND HISTORY

On Sunday mornings when I was a kid, I used to occupy myself between breakfast and church by watching old movies on television—Abbot and Costello, Westerns, Tarzan movies, and—of course—monster movies. Now, suddenly, monster movies are hot again. What do I mean by monster movies? Not all horror movies, not devil movies, not slasher movies, not suspense thrillers, not vampire, werewolf, or witch movies, not even *Frankenstein* [see 2006]. For me, monster movies must have larger-than-life, non-human monstrous monsters and monstrosities—in other words, giant creatures and creepy aliens, with (of course) lots of special effects. Monster movies like this are indeed hot, and none more so than *King Kong*, *War of the Worlds*, and *Godzilla* [remember, this was written in 2005].

On 15 November 2005 came the DVD release of the *King Kong* animated television series (1966); on 22 November 2005 the DVD releases of the original *King Kong* (1933), *Son of Kong* (1933), *Mighty Joe Young* (1949), Dino de Laurentiis' remake of *King Kong* (1976), and the animated *Kong, King of Atlantis*; on 29 November 2005 the DVD release of *King Kong vs Godzilla* (1963) and *King Kong Escapes* (1969); and on 14 December 2005 the opening in theaters of Peter Jackson's *King Kong*. Simultaneously, a number of new books have been published (see below under Suggestions for Further Reading).

In June 2005 came the direct-to-DVD release of *H.G. Wells' War of the Worlds* (Pendragon) directed by Timothy Hines and of *H.G. Wells' War of the Worlds* (Asylum) directed by David Michael Latt, as well as the theatre release of *War of the Worlds* (Paramount) directed by Steven Spielberg; in September 2005 the DVD release of *War of the Worlds* with Orson Welles' radio broadcast (1938), an interview with H.G. Wells and Orson Welles (1940), and *The Night America Trembled* (1957 with Edward R. Murrow as narrator); and in November 2005 the DVD release of *War of the Worlds* (1953), the first season of the *War of the Worlds* television series, (1988), and Spielberg's *War of the Worlds*.

In 1998 came the DVD release of *Godzilla, King of the Monsters* (1956), with Raymond Burr, to coincide with the theatre release of the *Godzilla* remake; in 2002 the DVD release of *Godzilla vs Mothra* (1964); in 2004 the limited U.S. theatre release of the original Japanese *Gojira* (1954); in 2004 the DVD release in Australia and New Zealand of *Godzilla 50th Anniversary Special Edition*, including both *Gojira* and *Godzilla, King of the Monsters*, as well as the release of *Son of Godzilla* (1967); and in 2005 DVD releases of additional titles (though there was no U.S. DVD release of the 50th anniversary special edition).

That said, why study history via monster movies? Because movies illuminate popular culture, popular culture illuminates history, and history illuminates who we are. At the same time, however, there are things that this lecture will not tell you. These movies do not provide insights into all aspects of modern popular culture. This lecture will not even examine all facets of these particular movies. This lecture will not offer a comprehensive explanation of modern history but will merely weave together a few strands of late nineteenth and twentieth-century history: the New Imperialism, the scramble for Africa, and discovery in the Pacific Ocean; the cult of science, good science (the Second Scientific Revolution), and bad science; exploration and invasion, emigration and immigration, ethnocentrism and xenophobia; the Second Industrial Revolution and "bigness"; and the atom.

The New Imperialism of the late nineteenth and early twentieth centuries saw European nations expanding their colonial and commercial empires into Africa, Asia, and the Pacific. Explorers like David Livingstone (1813-73), Henry Morton Stanley (1841-1904), and Sir Richard Francis Burton (1821-90) acquired celebrity status. The opening up of new lands brought with it a sense of opportunity and the thrill of discovery but also a profound fear of the unknown. While no one actually discovered an ape the size of King Kong, European and American adventurers found more than enough exotic fauna to fire the imaginations of those back at home. The anxiety this produced had more than a little entertainment value, for readers and moviegoers enjoy being frightened.

At the same time the growing cult of science created both the faith that scientists eventually will solve mankind's many problems and the fear of mistakes and deliberate wrongs that they may commit. Indeed, the Second Scientific Revolution undermined much of the certainty and comfort that the First Scientific Revolution (seventeenth century) and the Enlightenment (eighteenth century) had created. Where Isaac Newton and his contemporaries posited a mechanistic universe that those employing reason might fully understand, Albert Einstein's theory of relativity, Max Planck's quantum theory, and other exciting but disturbing new discoveries suggested a far more complex and less comprehensible cosmos. Where the Enlightenment regarded reason as the infallible guide to wisdom, Sigmund Freud suggested that mankind's thoughts and actions are more often the product of subconscious fears and urges that the conscious mind rationalizes rather than of rational thought. Where the philosophes expected rationalism to produce endless progress and embraced the idea of the perfectibility of man, Charles Darwin's theory of natural selection suggested a much grimmer evolutionary struggle, though he never described this as "survival of the fittest"—that phrase came from the "social Darwinist" Herbert Spencer, whom Darwin disavowed.

Nineteenth century science—which fueled both the contemporary cult of science and the monster movies of the next century—was a mixture of good and bad. Early dinosaur discoveries provide a case in point. Progress came early in England, where William Buckland provided the first scientific description of Megalosaurus in 1824 and Gideon Mantell the first of Iguanadon in 1825. Across the Atlantic William Parker Fouke discovered the first nearly complete skeleton of Hadrosaurus fouki in New Jersey in 1858. However, Sir Richard Owen, who coined the term "dinosaur" in 1842, was also a vehement opponent of Darwinian evolution. Nevertheless, at the popular level there emerged a fascination with these creatures that eventually would make Godzilla one of movie history's most famous monsters.

Along with the mysteries of unexplored jungles (in Africa, Asia, and the Pacific) and creatures of the ancient past, people of this era were also fascinated by outer space and most especially by the planet Mars. In 1876 the Italian priest Pietro Secchi first observed unexplained lines on the surface of mars. When Giovanni Schiaparelli published a map of the planet's surface in 1877, he called these straight-line features "canali," which English speakers mistranslated as "canals." Subsequently, in an 1895 book, the respected astronomer Percival Lowell (1855-1916) argued that an intelligent Martian race had built the so-called canals.

Thus, by the turn of the century there was plenty for Americans and western Europeans to fear and plenty of material for novelists and the nascent movie industry to exploit. Spencer's specious social theories gave an intellectual veneer to more vulgar racism, and the inevitable conflicts that exploration produced led to a rise in both ethnocentrism and xenophobia. And if non-western "aliens" stoked anxiety, the possibility that there might be extraterrestrial aliens on Mars did so even more. Meanwhile, the new physics uncovered a new set of forces that seemed almost occult in nature. The atom, atomic power, radiation, and the "ray gun" all became standard features of science fiction and horror, as did atomic and hydrogen bombs during the Cold War. Interestingly, all these strands were drawn together early in the twentieth century in the novels of Edgar Rice Burroughs, who wrote about apes and the uncharted jungle in his Tarzan series, dinosaurs and other giant creatures in his Pellucidar series, Mars in his Barsoom series, and other prominent celestial bodies in series on the moon and Venus.

The original *King Kong* (1933) was the brainchild of adventurer and filmmaker Merian C. Cooper (1893-1973). Born in Jacksonville, Florida, he had a privileged upbringing. Though he was kicked out of Naval Academy, he subsequently learned to fly and did so in World War I. When he was shot down in flames on 26 September 1918, he stayed with the plane to save the gunner. Later he joined the Kosciuszko Squadron to fight Bolsheviks, was captured, and made a spectacular escape. After the war he worked for newspapers, made documentary films, and traveled everywhere. In fact, Carl Denham in *King Kong* is basically Cooper. He was the first filmmaker to pair Fred Astaire and Ginger Rogers, gave Katherine Hepburn her first screen test, worked with John Ford on westerns, and invented Cinerama. When World War II broke out, he fought with General Claire Chenault's Flying Tigers.

Cooper directed *King Kong* with Ernest Schoedsack for Radio-Keith-Orpheum (RKO) a/k/a Radio Pictures, and the two shared production credit with David O. Selznick. In the film, Carl Denham (Robert Armstrong) charters the ship *Venture* to travel to the mysterious Skull Island, where he plans to make a film featuring his newly discovered "actress," Ann Darrow (Faye Wray). During the voyage Ann and the first mate Jack Driscoll (Bruce Cabot) fall in love. On the island a native tribe kidnaps Ann and offers her as a sacrifice to the giant ape Kong, who carries her away into the jungle, where—instead of harming her—he defends her against various dinosaurs, including a Tyrannosaurus Rex. Eventually Driscoll rescues Ann, and Denham uses a gas bomb to render Kong unconscious, after which he transports him to New York City and puts him on public display. However, Kong escapes, wreaks havoc in the city, and climbs the Empire State Building with Ann in his grasp. After reaching the top and releasing Ann, he fights against four military planes, which eventually kill him. Looking upon his gigantic corpse on the ground, Denham observes, "It was Beauty killed the Beast."

King Kong spawned a number of sequels, remakes, and imitations. (Sequels usually are not as good as the original, though that is not stopping Sylvester Stallone from making *Rocky VI*, which could be subtitled *He's Older Than George Foreman And Doesn't Have a Grill to Peddle*, and *Rambo IV*, which could be subtitled *Screw Medicaid, Send the Elderly to Iraq*). The first sequel, *Son of Kong*, came later in the same year as the original. The best—which involved Armstrong, Cooper, and Schoedsack—was *Mighty Joe Young* (1949), though it was not very successful. Next came a rather poor knock-off, *Konga* (1961), followed by two more sequels, the rather ludicrous *King Kong vs Godzilla* (1962) and *King Kong Escapes* (1967), and another imitator, *The Mighty Gorga* (1969). Then came the 1976 remake featuring Jeff Bridges and Charles Grodin, as well as introducing (and almost finishing off) Jessica Lange. Three ill-advised copycat films appeared in rapid succession: *Queen Kong* (1976), *A.P.E.* (1977, a/k/a *Attack of the Giant Horny Gorilla*), and *The Mighty Peking Man* (1977), after which there was a lengthy hiatus before *King Kong Lives* (1986) and an even longer one preceding the *Mighty Joe Young* remake (1998).

Finally, there came Peter Jackson's ambitious and largely successful remake in 2005. Jackson, in the forward to Mark Cotta Vaz, *Living Dangerously: The Adventures of Merian C. Cooper, Creator of King Kong* (2005), notes:

> I experienced my own moment of becoming at the age of nine: I saw a movie Merian Cooper made called *King Kong*. The film was made twenty-eight years before I was born, yet its power and magic had an instant and profound effect on my young imagination. From that day on I wanted to do nothing else with my life other than make movies—movies like *King Kong*. Watching that film propelled me into a love of making movies and learning how to do visual effects, the very stuff of movie magic.

Plans are afoot for yet another remake involving Tom Hiddleston and J. K. Simmons in 2017.] And now let's watch the final climactic scene from the original *King Kong* [readers, you are on your own for this].

The War of the Worlds is the mother of all space invasion stories, and the Stephen Spielberg/Tom Cruise version has revived it [reminder—this lecture was in 2005]. The tale of a Martian invasion of Earth began its life as a serialized novel by H. G. Wells in 1897, two years after Lowell's work speculating about intelligent life on Mars and in the midst of the German militarization that threatened British naval superiority, ruptured diplomatic relations between Kaiser Wilhelm II and his grandmother Victoria's realm, and was a contributing cause to World War I. Published in book form the following year, Wells' novel emphasized the growing mechanization of warfare and the dangers that entailed. It remains one of the all-time classics of science fiction. In it the heroes are two unnamed brothers, one in Surrey and the other in England. In subsequent versions they acquired names and relocated.

The story acquired rather spectacular notoriety with Orson Welles' extremely realistic CBS Radio *Mercury Theater* broadcast in 1938, one year after the Hindenburg disaster (the first ever broadcast live) and amid Adolf Hitler's rearming of Nazi Germany (the Munich Pact which allowed German annexation of the Sudetenland was signed on September 30, 1938, exactly one month before Welles' broadcast on October 30). The *Mercury Theatre* program competed with NBC's *Chase and Sanborn Hour* with Edgar Bergen and Charlie

McCarthy, then the top-rated radio show. But at commercial breaks many NBC listeners switched briefly to CBS, where they were hooked by the "news" from "reporter Carl Phillips" and "Princeton astronomer Professor Pierson" near Grover's Mill, New Jersey. The whole program was set up as a series news bulletins "interrupting" Ramon Raquello and his orchestra. The result was a national panic. Readers can get a unique view of Wells and Welles with *The War of the Worlds Deluxe Illustrated Edition* (2003), which includes the novel and a CD of the broadcast, Welles' apology, an interview with Wells and Welles at their first (and only) meeting, a foreword by Ray Bradbury, and an afterword by Ben Bova.

The first film version of *The War of the Worlds* appeared in 1953 as one of the plethora of space invasion movies that enjoyed such frightening popularity during the first years of the Cold War. Martians and other extraterrestrials made excellent stand-ins for Soviet Communists. Directed by Byron Haskin, the movie starts Gene Barry as Dr. Clayton Forrester, who also functions as the narrator, and Anne Robinson as Sylvia van Buren. It is set in California instead of England or New Jersey. The Martians, like many 1950s villains, are equipped with a death ray, which trumps the newest ultimate weapon—the United States Army's atomic bomb has no effect on the invaders or their ships. What finally destroys them after they have wreaked havoc on the Earth are microbes to which they lack immunity. Though dated in many respects, it remains quite watchable.

In 1957, Studio One—a live CBS show hosted by Edward R. Murrow—presented a teleplay "The Night America Trembled," dramatizing the events surrounding the Mercury Theatre broadcast of 1938. The cast included the then unknown actors Ed Asner, Warren Beatty, and James Coburn. Despite the subject matter, however, it did not mention Welles, then an expatriate, or writer Howard Koch, who had been blacklisted. In 1975 ABC got into the act with a television movie, *The Night That Panicked America* with Paul Shenar as Orson Welles, plus Meredith Baxter, Tom Bosley, Eileen Brennan, Cliff De Young, Will Geer, Casey Kasem, Vic Morrow, John Ritter, and Ron Rifkin. Nominated for several Emmys, it won for sound editing. A Fox television series that ran for two years in 1988-90 took the 1953 movie as its starting point and operated on the premise that the original Martian invaders were not dead but instead hibernating in sealed drums of nuclear waste, which made them immune to microbes. After being freed by terrorists thirty-five years later, they again plague the Earth.

In 2005 there were no less than three movie versions of *The War of the Worlds*. Timothy Hines's film for Pendragon was a period piece, unlike the other two. Originally slated for theatre release on 31 October 2002, it was postponed due to the attacks of 11 September 2001 and subsequently encountered legal problems that led to it being released direct to DVD in 2005. Michael Latt directed the second 2005 film for Asylum, which also was known as *Invasion* and *The Worlds in War*. Spielberg's film—with Cruise as Ray Farrier and Dakota Fanning as his daughter Rachel—was as good as might be expected, combining technically excellent special effects with non-stop suspense, though Tom Cruise's life offstage was scarier than on—I was afraid he might ditch Katie Holmes as a has-been and start dating Dakota Fanning [again, this lecture was delivered in 2005 before Holmes ditched him].

Between Orson Welles' *War of the Worlds* in 1938 and the first *Godzilla*—Gojira in Japan—came World War II, the atomic bomb, Hiroshima and Nagasaki, the hydrogen bomb, widespread fear of nuclear war and radiation, and the early years of the Cold War. Meanwhile, the original *King Kong* was reissued in 1952, and—as just noted—the first *War of the Worlds* movie appeared in 1953. Appropriately, then, *Godzilla* appeared in 1954 and featured a giant monster created by nuclear radiation. The question is, should we regard it as a "film" or a "movie," that is, is it art of just entertainment? In America the Godzilla franchise has a reputation for cheesiness, which has rubbed off on director Ishiro Honda. However, Honda often worked in partnership with Japan's most revered filmmaker. Akira Kurosawa. For example, the latter's *Kagemusha* (1980, which received financial support from Francis Ford Coppola and George Lucas) was filmed at Toho Studios—where Honda filmed *Gojira*, was produced by Tomoyuki Tanaka—who produced *Gojira*, and was co-written by Honda. Many Japanese actors appeared in films by both Honda and Kurosawa, including Minoru Chiaki, Akira Kubo, Takashi Shimura, and Yoshio Tsuchiya. Masaru Sato has done scores for both directors, and major classical composer Akira Ifukube has written them for Honda. It is important to remember that American studios often have altered *Godzilla* and other Japanese monster movies in ways that make them look ridiculous, e.g., adding or deleting footage and/or changing stories, actors, or music. Regarding the famously low-budget special effects in such films, realism is less important to the Japanese than beauty and fantasy. Most importantly, however, *Gojira* is a serious treatment of the consequences of nuclear war.

Back in 1915 Thomas Edison's Mannikin Films distributed *The Dinosaur and the Missing Link*, animated by Willis O'Brien, who later did Arthur Conan Doyle's *The Lost World* (a 1912 novel) for Watterson R. Rothaker in 1925, as well as *King Kong* and *Son of Kong* in 1933. O'Brien's protégé Ray Harryhausen worked on *The Beast from 20,000 Fathoms* in 1953. The following year Tanaka got the idea to combine a King Kong type story with fear of radiation, though not just as a gimmick as it was in many science fiction films of the 1950's. Japan, of course, was and remains the only nation to experience the effects of nuclear war. Tanaka hired science fiction writer Shigeru Kayama, who modeled his story on *The Beast from 20,000 Fathoms* (the working title translates as *The Big Monster from 20,000 Miles Beneath the Sea*, which left Harryhausen with a grudge). Originally, in fact, the monster was an octopus. Eiji Tsuburaya, who did the effects, previously had done propaganda films during World War II, loved *King Kong*, and wanted do a similar kind of film. "Gojira" came from the nickname given to a Toho technician combining the words gorilla and *kujira*, the Japanese word for whale. Tanaka liked it, and that was that.

Meanwhile, Honda fought in China during the war, was in Tokyo during the firebombing while on furlough, and heard about Hiroshima and Nagasaki while a prisoner-of-war in China. He returned to Japan in 1946 and assisted Kurasawa with early films. He visited Hiroshima in 1946, was fascinated by the horror thereof, and wanted to put it in a film. Thus, monsters become a symbol of the atomic bomb. If you think about the opening scene and imagine that you do not know that Godzilla is coming, everything said could describe nuclear war. This is also why Godzilla has a radioactive ray. Honda worked with screenwriter Takeo Mura to alter Kayama's story. They included more character development for the human characters, made Godzilla less animal and more monster, and dropped many of the "stolen scenes" from *Beast*. Honda and Tsuburaya wanted the film to have a documentary feel. In fact, once they were on the roof of a Matsuzakaya department store in the Ginza district of Tokyo discussing starting fire in Shinbashi district that would spread to Ginza and got stopped by security guards!

The cast includes Akira Takarada as Ogata (the romantic lead), Akihiko Hirata as Dr. Serizawa (a scientist), Takashi Shimura—whom the *New York Times* once called "the best actor in the world"—as Dr. Yamane, and Momoko Kochi as Emiko Yamane. Playing Godzilla were Haruo Nakajima, a veteran stuntman who continued the role and studied zoo animals in preparation, and Katsumi Tezuka. Honda shot at a fast speed, which he then slowed down to give the monster a "lumbering" effect. The costume was a rubber suit, which must have been a real joy under hot studio lights! And it was gray, not green. Akira Ifukube did the score and created Godzilla's roar by rubbing a leather glove across the strings of a double bass and adding echo. Honda had a 1/25-scale model of Tokyo built. The film is one of the most expensive ever made in Japan. It cost 60 million yen, which is equivalent to $900,000 1954 and $65 million now! Carefully marketed, it opened on 3

November 1954, eventually made 152 million yen, and won Japan's Film Technique Award for Tsuburaya. Japanese critics consider it one of the twenty best films ever. It is darker than *King Kong* and features a lot of emotional conflict

At the beginning of the film Yamane discovers Godzilla awakened after millions years by H-bomb testing and now radioactive. He wants to study the creature, but the Self Defense Force wants to kill it. Meanwhile, Emiko is engaged to Serizawa, who has invented an Oxygen Destroyer, but is in love with Ogata. When Godzilla destroys Tokyo, whose hospitals are overwhelmed, Emiko tells Ogata about the weapon, and he demands that Serizawa let them use it. Initially Serizawa refuses because of the possible consequences of the military obtaining it, but eventually Ogata persuades him, though he destroys the plans. The navy delivers the Oxygen Destroyer, and Ogata and Serizawa deploy it. Though it works, Serizawa cuts his own oxygen line. At the end Yamane notes: "I cannot believe Godzilla was the last survivor of his species. If we continue nuclear testing, others of Godzilla's kind will appear again somewhere in the world."

The message is strongly anti-nuclear. The United States had just tested the first H-bomb on 1 March 1954 near the Marshall Islands. A small Japanese fishing boat, the Daigo Fukuryo Maru (Lucky Dragon), was nearby, the crew became ill, and radioman Aikichi Kuboyama died on 23 September 1954. There were headlines for month, one of which proclaimed "The Second Atomic Bombing of Mankind." This led to a significant diplomatic issue. Japan demanded reparations for Kuboyama's family, President Eisenhower refused, and an Anti-Bomb Test Group formed in Japan

Nevertheless, there was a Hollywood bidding war for *Godzilla*. The winner was Joseph E. Levine of Trans-World Films, which released it through Embassy Pictures. Levine paid $25,000 (9 million yen), which was a lot then. All Toho releases were Americanized for Western audiences. They were not given subtitles like art films; rather, they were dubbed by individuals like Paul Frees (who did voiceovers for films and cartoons), Marvin Miller (Robby the Robot), and George Taeki (Sulu from *Star Trek*, the only Japanese-American used). *Gojira* was the only one not completely dubbed. Rather, Levine kept a lot of the original dialogue in Japanese by adding the character of American Steve Martin, played by Raymond Burr, with his translator as narrator. Some conversations among main characters are dubbed, however. Dubbing is bad by definition, so this led to a lot of criticism.

The American version is eleven minutes shorter, changes the chronology, and deletes some subplots, though it keeps the main idea. Terrell O. Morse directed the new scenes. Burr previously had played heavies, e.g., the wife murderer in Alfred Hitchcock's *Rear Window*. Martin is a friend of Serizawa. Another new character is the security official who escorts Martin. Morse recut scenes to create conversations between Martin and Japanese characters (who are never in the same frame). There are some glitches. Godzilla is mentioned several times in Japanese dialogue before he ever shows up. The changing scene order means a dead guy who washes ashore on Odo Island shows up alive later (perhaps the result of a racist assumption that all Japanese look alike). The American version eliminates numerous references to World War II and almost all those to the A and H-bomb. Nuclear testing is still blamed for bringing Godzilla to life, but there is no mention of the United States as the tester.

Toho planned no sequels, but the success of the first led to a rush job with a second six months later. It features a "new Godzilla"—Gigantis the fire monster, who continues to be the Godzilla of the series through 1975. It retreads the plot of the first but with a second monster Angilas added. It is called *Godzilla's Counterattack* in Japan (1955) and *Gigantis the Fire Monster* in the U.S (1959), where the leads were dubbed by George Takei (Sulu) and Daws Butler (Yogi Bear!). Honda subsequently was busy with *Half-Human* (1955), *The Mysterians* (1957), *The H-Man* (1958), *Varan the Unbelievable* (1958), *Battle in Outer Space* (1959), *The Three Treasures* (1959), *The Human Vapor* (1960), *Secret of the Telegian* (1960), and *Gorath* (1962). Toho also produced *Rodan* (1956) and *Mothra* (1961).

Then came the rather campy *King Kong vs. Godzilla* (Japan 1962, U.S. 1963), *Godzilla vs Mothra* (1964), *Ghidrah the Three-Headed Monster* (Japan 1964, U.S. 1965), *Godzilla vs Monster Zero* (Japan 1965, U.S. 1970), *Godzilla vs the Sea Monster* (Japan 1966, U.S. 1968), *Son of Godzilla* (Japan 1967, U.S. television 1969), *Destroy All Monsters* (Japan 1968, U.S. 1969), *Godzilla's Revenge* (1969 Japan, 1971 U.S.), *Godzilla vs Hedorah* (Japan 1970, U.S. 1972), *Godzilla vs Gigan* (Japan 1972, U.S. 1977), *Godzilla vs Megalon* (Japan 1973, U.S. 1976), *Godzilla vs Mechagodzilla* (Japan 1974, U.S. 1977), *Terror of Mechagodzilla* (Japan 1975, U.S. 1978), *Godzilla 1985* (Japan 1984, U.S. 1985), *Godzilla vs Biollante* (Japan 1989, U.S. home video 1992), *Godzilla vs King Ghidora* (Japan 1991), *Godzilla vs Mothra* (Japan 1992), *Godzilla vs Mechagodzilla II* (Japan 1993), *Godzilla vs Space Godzilla* (Japan 1994), *Godzilla vs Destoroyah* (Japan 1995), Roland Emmerick's remake of *Godzilla* (1998 from Tri-Star starring Matthew Broderick, hence *Godzilla vs Ferris Bueller*), *Godzilla 2000* (Japan 1999, U.S. 2000), *Godzilla vs Megaguirus* (2000 Japan, 2003 U.S.), *Godzilla, Mothra, and King Ghidorah* (2001 Japan, 2003 U.S.), and *Godzilla Tokyo S.O.S.* (2003 Japan, 2004 U.S.) [since this lecture was delivered *Godzilla: The Final Wars* appeared in 2014 with a Toho reboot of the original scheduled for 2016].

There was an unusual byproduct of the Godzilla series. I know I am going to get in trouble for this, but let's watch the classic cartoon *Bambi Meets Godzilla* [we did to the response of generalized groans]. You might say this was a smashing success. I guess Godzilla has no patience with fawning sycophants. Even those who are "deer" to us can be bothersome when they get underfoot. Sometimes you just have to put your foot down.

But seriously, folks, paranoia was widespread in the world after World War I and during the rise of fascism and communism, World War II, and the Cold War. Simultaneous fascination with the space race and fear of radiation, mutations, nuclear war, and invasion were rampant in the 1950s. If you care to see further evidence of this point, try doing a keyword search on Google for "Attack of," "Invasion of," "Space alien invasion," and/or "Space invaders," and look at what that produces.

In conclusion, it is clear that monster movies reflect the times in which they were made and thus reveal a good deal about history and popular culture. However, it is also worth noting that most of the fears that such films reveal have never come to fruition. While it sometimes may be true that "just because you are paranoid does not mean they are not out to get you," perhaps what we should do is simply relax, enjoy being frightened vicariously, and revel in the cheesiness and what Frank Zappa calls the "Cheepnis" of it all. And now it's time for candy! Uh oh, where is the candy? Please excuse me for just a moment. Stay right there! Don't go away! I'll be right back! [Back to *Monster Matinee*, Part 2]

Suggestions for Further Reading

Bruce Bahrenberg, *The Creation of Dino De Laurentiis' King Kong* (1976); David Brin, *King Kong Is Back! An Unauthorized Look at One Humongous Ape* (2005); Joe Devito and Brad Strickland, *Merian C. Cooper's King Kong: A Novel* (2005); John Gosling, *Waging the War of the Worlds: A History of the 1938 Radio Broadcast and Resulting Panic* (2009); Karen Haber, ed., *Kong Unbound: The Cultural Impact, Pop Mythos, and Scientific Plausibility of a Cinematic Legend* (2005); Paul Heyer, *The Medium and the Magician: Orson Welles, the Radio Years 1934-1952* (2005); Brian Holmsten and Alex Lubertozzi, eds., *The Complete War of the Worlds: Mars' Invasion of Earth from H.G. Wells to Orson Welles*, with foreword by Ray Bradbury, afterword by Ben Bova (2001); William Graves Hoyt, *Lowell and Mars* (1976); David Kalat, *A Critical History Filmography of Toho's Godzilla Series*, 2nd edition (2010); Richard Lupoff, *Master of Adventure: The Worlds of Edgar Rice Burroughs* (2005); Ray Morton, *King Kong: The History of a Movie Icon from Fay Wray to Peter Jackson* (2005); Steve Ryfle, *Japan's Favorite Mon-Star: The Unauthorized Biography of 'The Big G'* (1998); David Skal, *The Monster Show: A*

Cultural History of Horror, revised edition (2001) and *Screams of Reason: Mad Science and Modern Culture* (1998); David C. Smith, *H.G. Wells: Desperately Mortal: A Biography* (1986); William Tsutsui, *Godzilla on My Mind: Fifty Years of the King of the Monsters* (2004); Mark Cotta Vaz, *Living Dangerously: The Adventures of Merian C. Cooper, Creator of King Kong* (2005); Jenny Wake, *The Making of King Kong: The Official Guide to the Motion Picture* (2006); Bill Warren, *Keep Watching the Skies! American Science Fiction Movies of the Fifties, The 21st Century Edition* (2009); Weta Workshop, *The World of Kong: A Natural History of Skull Island* (2005).

2006 PREQUEL
IT'S A LIVE ONSTAGE REANIMATION

The 2006 prequel mimics the scene in the original 1931 *Frankenstein* and in Mel Brooks' 1974 *Young Frankenstein* in which Dr. Frankenstein reanimates the monster. And it features pyrotechnics by Ellen Sovkoplas!

Dr. Frankenstein is me, Igors 1 and 2 are Zoe and Molly Robison, the monster is George Sanchez, the disembodied hand that appears from behind the curtain belongs to Bibbet Robison, and the "little girl" is Donna Gay Anderson, former Director of Fanfare.

Watch the video and an edited-for-television version of the lecture at https://myspace.com/headongoolah/videos.

PRE-SHOW

SOUND   Play Music/Effects Tracks 1-8 starting at 10:30

SHOW

SOUND   Track 9 SFX Foreboding begins playing

STAGE   Curtain goes up with Dr. F is in a lab coat and goggles, Igor 1 and Igor 2, the monster's body on a gurney, and strobe lights flashing. To stage right of the gurney is a giant battery labeled "Diehard Reanimator," which is surmounted by a Van der Graaf generator and connected to the monster's electrodes by jumper cables. To stage left of the gurney is a control panel labeled "Acme Control Panel" with three switches labeled "Lo," "Med," and "Hi."

SOUND   Music fades.

DR F   Turn on the power!

STAGE   Igor 1 throws switch labeled "Lo"

SOUND   Tracks 10-15 SFX Electricity begin playing (same track 6 times—play as much as necessary for the scene)

STAGE   Dr. F listens to the monster's chest, shakes his head

DR F   I need MORE power!

STAGE   Igor 2 throws switch labeled "Med"

SOUND   Electrical hum (SFX Electricity) increases in volume

STAGE   Dr. F listens to the monster's chest, shakes his head again

DR F: I need MAXIMUM POWER!

STAGE   Igor 1 and Igor 2 look at each other in disbelief, then throw switch labeled "Hi" and run offstage in terror

SOUND   Electrical hum (SFX Electricity) increases in volume

STAGE   The monster begins to stir, raises his arm, groans loudly, and begins to sit up

MONSTER: [Groans]

DR F: It's alive! It's alive! It's alive! Now I know what it's like to be a god! A titan! An . . . an . . . academic department head!

STAGE   First explosion

MONSTER: [Screams]

STAGE   Second explosion

SOUND   Electrical hum (SFX Electricity) stops—silently advance CD to 28 seconds into Track 16 "Transylvanian Lullaby" for later

STAGE   Van der Graaf generator turned off

DR F: [Screams]

STAGE   Monster flees and exits stage right, and Dr. F flees and exits stage left. There is a long pause. Dr. F creeps back out with a fire extinguisher, sprays the lab, sets it down, and goes to podium.

DR F: Hello . . .

STAGE   Lecture begins and continues through the "We belong dead" clip

SOUND   Following the "We belong dead" clip from *The Bride of Frankenstein*, begin "Transylvania Lullaby" 28 seconds into the track through stage left speaker only.

STAGE   The monster enters from stage right, stumbles across stage, "picking berries" in the air (like Peter Boyle), and exits stage left. After the monster disappears, there is screaming from offstage.

SOUND   The music stops.

DR F: I told Dr. Evenson [then Head of the Department of Music] that he should soundproof those damn practice rooms! Oh, well . . .

STAGE   Lecture continues to end

STAGE   As Dr. F is concluding his lecture, a "little girl" comes out from stage right, sits on the edge of the stage, and begins examining the flowers in a basket she is carrying. The monster comes out from stage left and watches. Dr. F concludes and watches. The girl looks up at the monster.

GIRL: Would you like one of my flowers?

STAGE   The girl hands the monster a flower.

GIRL: We can throw them to our fans!

STAGE   The girl throws a flower to the audience. The monster throws his flower. They continue until the basket is empty.

GIRL: What shall we throw now?

STAGE   The monster leers at audience and reaches for the little girl. Dr. F intervenes, cauldron o' candy in hand.

DR F: No, don't throw her! Throw candy!

MONSTER: Candy good!

DR F: Right. But first, everyone in the audience has to say "Trick or Treat."

SOUND   Play Track 17 "Puttin' on the Ritz."

STAGE   Everyone throws candy to audience while "Puttin' on the Ritz" plays in the background

2006 LECTURE
IT'S ALIVE! THE HISTORY OF FRANKENSTEIN
FROM MARY SHELLEY TO BORIS KARLOFF TO MEL
BROOKS AND BEYOND

"It's alive! Now I know what it feels like to be God!" Those are the words with which Dr. Frankenstein greeted the first signs of life from the pieced-together corpse he reanimated in the 1931 movie classic *Frankenstein*. Though Universal Studios initially released the film with the line included, censors forced its removal, regarding it as blasphemy. Over a century earlier, Mary Shelley's novel, *Frankenstein, or The Modern Prometheus* (first published in 1818) also drew condemnation for its allegedly blasphemous content. From its inception and through all of its incarnations in literature and on stage and screen, the Frankenstein story has remained both popular and controversial.

Even now the name "Frankenstein" evokes powerful emotions, and it has become a catch phrase for dabbling with nature, whether the subject is *in vitro* fertilization, genetic engineering, stem cell research, cloning, or some other enterprise on the frontiers of science. At the same time the "monster" that Dr. Frankenstein created has become a ubiquitous presence in western culture. It has engendered imitations and spin-offs from Shelley's novel, most recently the novels of Dean Koontz. It has spawned cinema both sublime and ridiculous, and you will see examples of both today. It has inspired music from the many movie scores to Edgar Winter's *Frankenstein* to the punk rock of Electric Frankenstein. And it has led to a host of commercial items ranging from Halloween costumes to a breakfast cereal. Today I will examine the history of Frankenstein from the beginning to the present; show how the story has evolved, changed, and at times returned to its origins; explore what makes the story simultaneously so frightening and so entertaining; and try to derive some larger meaning about its place in our culture.

I will begin with a simple question—who is this on the screen? [The monster.] If you said "Frankenstein," you are wrong. That is the name of the man who created the "monster"—or "creature" if you prefer a more polite term—not the name of the monster itself, though the confusion of the two began almost as soon as the novel was published. If you said "Adam," you are still wrong. The popular notion that Mary Shelley named the creature "Adam" for the Biblical first man is a myth. If you said "Prometheus," nice try, but no cigar. The reference in Shelley's title is to the mythical entity whom the Greek gods punished for the sacrilege of giving fire to mankind. Actually, Shelley gave the creature no name at all, though the vast majority of people refer to it as "Frankenstein." If the creature has no name, its creator has had several, as we will see—Victor in the novel and numerous adaptations, Henry, Wolf, Ludwig, and Frederick.

Mary Shelley's last name changed when she married; otherwise, she remained Mary. That being said, who was Mary Shelley? Mary Shelley (1797-1851) was a writer. Mary Shelley's mother was Mary Wollstonecraft (1759-97), a proto-feminist activist and thinker in 18th-century Britain. Her numerous written works include *Thoughts on the Education of Daughters* (1787), in which she advocated education for girls, and *A Vindication of the Rights of Women* (1792), the subject of which is obvious. Wollstonecraft has been an extremely popular subject for scholars in recent years. Tragically for her daughter, she died when the younger Mary was born. Mary Shelley's father was William Godwin (1756-1836), a novelist and political philosopher. In 1793, during the bloodiest phase of the French Revolution, he wrote *Enquiry Concerning Political Justice and Its Influence on General Virtue and Happiness*, which occupied the middle ground between the reactionary views of Edmund Burke and the radicalism of Thomas Paine. He also wrote the novel *Things As They Are, or the Adventures of Caleb Williams* (1794). And he educated his daughter very well.

Mary became the lover and then the wife of Percy Bysshe Shelley (1792-1822), the famous poet whose works include *Ozymandias* (1817) and the unfinished *Prometheus Unbound*. The member of a well-to-do family, Percy Shelley was educated at Eton and attended Oxford University. However, he was kicked out for unacceptable behavior, which included writing a pamphlet called *The Necessity of Atheism* (1811). At the age of nineteen he married his first wife Harriet Westbrook, but subsequently friendship with William Godwin led to an affair with the latter's daughter Mary. They eloped when she was only sixteen. Their lives were full of tragedy. Mary's older sister Fanny Imlay and Shelley's first wife both committed suicide in 1816. Percy himself drowned in 1822, leaving Mary with a small child.

Percy and Mary Shelley were close friends with the notorious Lord Byron (1788-1824). George Gordon Noel Byron, 6th Baron Byron of Rochdale (1798), is equally famous for his outrageous lifestyle, the epic poem *Childe Harold*, and his death while fighting in the Greek Revolution against the Ottoman Empire. Another good friend with a part to play in the story of *Frankenstein* was John Polidori (1795-1821), a talented young doctor with literary interests.

The summer of 1816 found the Shelley's, Byron, and Polidori at the

Villa Diodati on the southern shore of Lake Geneva in Switzerland. On a dark and stormy night in August, Byron proposed that the four friends amuse themselves with a contest. There were three guys and a girl, just like in *Seinfeld*, though this was not the same kind of contest. Ironically, while Bryon and Percy were the famous poets, the two literary unknowns excelled them on this particular occasion. In fact, two of the greatest legends of the horror genre were born that night.

In the coming weeks Polidori produced *The Vampyre*, which was the basis for Bram Stoker's *Dracula*. Meanwhile, Mary Shelley emerged as the clear winner of the contest, with *Frankenstein*. The original manuscript is now at the university that expelled her husband, housed in Oxford's Bodleian Library, which put it on public display in 2005. Supposedly it came to her in a "waking dream" on the night of the contest. It incorporates elements of the Hebrew myth of the Golem, the myth of Prometheus as found in the Roman poet Ovid, John Milton's *Paradise Lost*, Samuel Taylor Coleridge's *Rime of the Ancient Mariner*, and Wollstonecraft's feminism.

The novel begins with a Captain Walton writing home from a voyage in the Arctic Circle, where he spots the monster and then rescues Victor Frankenstein, who takes over the narration. Victor relates that early on he studied alchemy and the late medieval/early modern practitioners of medicine, who were highly unscientific. After leaving his home and family in Geneva to study in Ingolstadt, he is introduced to the "modern" science of the Enlightenment and decides to create a living human. Shelly's novel does not explain how he does this, though there are vague references to chemical instruments. His creature, rather than being the perfect human being he intended, is a "monster," from whom Frankenstein flees.

The monster subsequently disappears and murders Victor's younger brother William. After a long illness, Victor returns home, where he finds that the authorities have blamed the murder of his family's maid, Justine, who is convicted and executed. Consumed with guilt, he goes into the mountains and encounters the creature, who tells him his own story. The creature reveals that he has lived in a hut next to the home of a peasant family and has learned to speak by observing them. Now he asks Victor to create a female companion. Initially Victor agrees but then changes his mind. The creature follows him to Britain, where he murders Victor's friend Clerval. Later he also kills Victor's new wife Elizabeth on their wedding night. Victor then pursues the creature into the frozen north. Walton reports that Victor has died and that he has encountered the monster, who announces that he plans to commit suicide and then disappears. The book was published anonymously in 1818 and then with Mary Shelley credited in 1823. It was very popular, though not well received by critics. It also evoked considerable criticism. Mary substantially revised it in 1831, changing the story to emphasize that Victor created the monster simply in the interest of science. In addition, Elizabeth—who was Victor's cousin in the original—now became an adopted child of his parents. Mary wrote a number of other novels, but none matched the popularity of *Frankenstein*. She died of brain cancer on 1 February 1851.

Dramatists almost immediately adapted Shelley's novel for the stage. The first production came in 1823 with Richard Brinksley Peake's *Presumption; Or, The Fate of Frankenstein*. This play introduced Dr. Frankenstein's sidekick Fritz, who became a standard character in later versions of the story. It also included several songs. During the nineteenth century there were several more melodramas, as well as a number of satires. Modern versions are still performed onstage today, and recently Mel Brooks produced a stage version of his movie, *Young Frankenstein*.

Many people assume that the first movie version of Frankenstein was the 1931 Universal Studios production starring Boris Karloff. However, Thomas Edison's (1847-1931) *Frankenstein* actually appeared in 1910. This fourteen-minute silent film was long thought lost but reappeared a few years ago. J. Searle Dawley wrote and directed the movie, which featured silent film star Charles Ogle as the monster, Augustus Phillips as Frankenstein, and Mary Fuller as Elizabeth. In this version Frankenstein is a young medical student who attempts to create a perfect human but instead creates a monster. He becomes ill, and his fiancé Elizabeth cares for him. The monster shows up on their wedding night, as he does in the novel. However, in the midst of a fight with Frankenstein, the monster sees himself in a mirror and flees in horror. He returns later, but in the midst of another struggle he suddenly vanishes, and his image fades away in mirror, overcome by Frankenstein's love for his wife. This is the only movie that ends this way, and it is the first movie to show the monster's creation. Dawley accomplished this by burning a figure and then running the film backward.

Of course the much more famous "first" film was Universal Studios' *Frankenstein* (1931). Carl Laemmle (1867-1939), a German native, founded Universal with three partners in 1914 and played a major role in turning *Frankenstein* into a feature-length film. Laemmle initially wanted the Bela Lugosi as the monster. Interestingly, Lugosi turned down the role, but later played it in *Frankenstein Meets the Wolf Man*. In 1931 the original director Robert Florey wanted Lugosi as Dr. Frankenstein. Universal also considered Leslie Howard (*Gone With the Wind*) as Dr. Frankenstein, Bette Davis as Elizabeth, and John Carradine as the monster, which indicates the importance it placed on this film. Carradine also turned down the role of the monster, but later played Dracula in *House of Frankenstein*.

A key development was Laemmle's replacement of Florey with British director James Whale (1889-1957). Whale was born in England and initially worked as a cobbler before serving in World War I. Afterward he became involved in the theatre, and his success in London's West End led him to Broadway and then Hollywood, where he achieved his greatest fame with horror films, including *The Invisible Man* (1933) and *The Man in the Iron Mask* (1939).

After Whale took over as director, he chose Boris Karloff to portray the monster and Colin Clive as Dr. Henry Frankenstein. How many of you can guess Boris Karloff's nationality? Actually Boris Karloff was born William Henry (Bill) Pratt (1887-1969) in London, the son of Edward Pratt and his third wife, Elizabeth Sarah Millard. His paternal grandmother Eliza Julia Pratt was part Indian, which explains his dark complexion. Her sister was Anna Leonowens, whose life is the subject of the musical *The King and I*. Educated at the University of London, William Pratt moved to Canada in 1909, began acting, and adopted the name Boris Karloff. He appeared in dozens of silent films and talking movies in bit parts before Frankenstein.

Frankenstein transformed Karloff from a supporting actor into a major star, often in partnership with Bela Lugosi. Karloff also adapted to the new medium of television. He hosted the series *Thriller* (1960-62), which competed with *Alfred Hitchcock Presents* in terrifying TV audiences. But perhaps his most memorable role other than the Frankenstein monster was as the narrator of the cartoon version of *How the Grinch Stole Christmas* (1966) and the voice of the Grinch himself. In *Frankenstein* Karloff's principle co-stars were Mae Clark as Elizabeth, John Boles as Victor Moritz, Edward Sloan as Dr. Waldman, Frederick Kerr as Baron Frankenstein, Henry's father, and Dwight Frye as Fritz, Dr. Frankenstein's assistant.

The plot of the 1931 movie is significantly different from novel. There are no references to the frozen north. The monster's creator is now *Dr.* Frankenstein. He also is named Henry, while his friend is Victor (Moritz). Whereas the novel does not explain how he creates the monster, Frankenstein here uses electricity, which was the transformative force *du jour* in horror and science fiction stories of the 1930s. He creates the monster from stolen body parts and accidentally puts in a diseased brain.

Seemingly mad, he brings it to life over the objections of his fiancé Elizabeth, his friend Victor, and his former professor, Dr. Waldman.

I already have alluded to controversy over the film's alleged blasphemous content. The state of Kansas banned the movie because it showed "cruelty and tended to debase morals." Perhaps even more controversial was the scene in which a little girl named Maria entices the monster to play with her, whereupon he throws first flowers and then the little girl into the lake. Censors originally removed this scene, though modern reissues have restored it. Following Maria's death, the monster turns up nearby on what proves to be Victor Frankenstein's wedding day and attacks the bride-to-be Elizabeth. A mob hunts down the monster, who apparently dies in a fire after being trapped in a windmill. But is he really dead? Well . . . with the exception of Albus Dumbledore, no one who dies in the movies is ever guaranteed to stay dead. And in horror movies it is almost guaranteed that the dead will not stay that way.

Fortunately, for movie lovers, the monster survives the fire, as we learn in *Bride of Frankenstein* (1935). For this film Whale, Karloff, and Clive return as director, monster, and Dr. Frankenstein, and Frye—who died as sidekick Fritz in the first movie—is resurrected as new sidekick Karl. Elsa Lanchester plays Mary Shelley briefly at the beginning and reappears as the monster's bride at the end. Karloff's other co-stars included a new Elizabeth in Valerie Hobson, a new villain in Dr. Pretorius as played by Ernest Thesiger, comic relief in the form of Una O'Connor's Minnie, and actor O. P. Heggie as a blind hermit who befriends the monster.

In this movie the evil Dr. Pretorius tries to persuade Dr. Frankenstein to become his partner and return to his experiments. Meanwhile, the monster—who has survived the windmill fire—meets a hermit, who treats him kindly and teaches him to speak (after a fashion). Subsequently Dr. Pretorius and the monster kidnap Elizabeth in order to force Dr. Frankenstein to create a female companion for the monster. However, the 'bride" rejects her groom, who destroys the laboratory and the castle that houses it.

The third installment in the Universal series is *Son of Frankenstein* (1939), with Rowland Lee as director. Basil Rathbone, better known for playing Sherlock Holmes, is Baron Wolf von Frankenstein, a role reportedly turned down by Claude Rains and Peter Lorre. In this movie, Ygor appears for the first time, played by Bela Lugosi. Wolf, the son of Henry Frankenstein, returns to his father's estate, discovers the laboratory, and meets Ygor, who persuades him to revive the monster from a coma. Mayhem ensues, with the monster murdering villagers and Wolf shooting

Ygor before ultimately destroying the monster.

But remember that death is not a certainty in these movies. In *The Ghost of Frankenstein* (1942), which Erle C. Kenton directed, Ygor (Bela Lugosi) revives the monster (Lon Chaney Jr) and tricks Dr. Ludwig Frankenstein (Henry's son, played by Cedric Hardwicke) into transplanting his (Ygor's) brain into the monster. All hell breaks loose.

In *Frankenstein Meets the Wolf Man* (1943), directed by Roy William Neill, the Wolf Man (Lon Chaney Jr)—already an established character in his own movie series—seeks Dr. Frankenstein, hoping the latter can kill him once and for all. Instead he finds the monster (Bela Lugosi), and there is more trouble.

In *House of Frankenstein* (1944), again directed by Erle C. Kenton, Boris Karloff returns as the insane Dr. Gustav Niemann, who—with a hunchback assistant named Daniel (J. Carrol Naish)—revives the monster (Glenn Strange), the Wolf Man (Lon Chaney Jr), and Dracula (John Carradine). This, of course, is bad . . . really bad.

The first great movie spoof of the story is *Abbott and Costello Meet Frankenstein* (1948), directed by Charles Burton. Bud Abbott (1897-1974) and Lou Costello (1906-59) are a pair of hapless freight handlers named Chick Young and Wilbur Grey, respectively. They unwittingly deliver two crates containing the Frankenstein monster (Strange) and the coffin of Count Dracula (Lugosi) to McDougal's House of Horrors, whose perpetually irate owner (Mr. McDougal) is played by Frank Ferguson. Dracula and the monster escape. Larry Talbot a/k/a the Wolf Man (Chaney) shows up to warn Chick and Wilbur that Dracula plans to revive the monster. Meanwhile, the dull-witted Wilbur is being courted by Dr. Sandra Mornay (Lenore Aubert), who is secretly in a league with Dracula. She plans to put Wilbur's brain in the monster so it will be stupid and easy to control. Eventually she lures Chick and Wilbur to the castle where Dracula and the monster are hiding. After much hilarity, Chick and Wilbur defeat the evildoers with the help of a female investigator Joan Raymond (Jane Randolph) and scientist Dr. Stevens (Charles Bradstreet). This movie finds Abbott and Costello in peak form.

After over a decade in which there were no serious Frankenstein movies, Hammer Films revived the creature in 1957 for what proved to be a series of six films. Terence Fisher (1940-80) directed all but one of these Hammer Horror classics, and all featured Peter Cushing (1913-94) as Baron Victor Frankenstein. In the Hammer films Frankenstein is unmitigatedly evil, and the monster is a much less sympathetic character. The initial and best installment, *Curse of Frankenstein* (1957) is the first

Frankenstein movie in color. Hammer wanted to film it in black and white with Karloff as the monster, but Universal threatened to sue, and Hammer changed the script and hired Christopher Lee as the monster, with Hazel Court as Elizabeth. Following this film, Lee went on to become Hammer's Dracula and arguably the best screen vampire ever. Younger moviegoers may be more familiar with Cushing and Lee from more recent films: Cushing in *Star Wars* as Grand Moff Tarkin, the only character other than the Emperor to have authority over Darth Vader, and Lee as *The Lord of the Rings'* good wizard gone bad, Saruman. In this film Wolf narrates the story to a priest who visits him in an insane asylum. He recounts how he and his teacher Paul Krempe experimented with the creation of life. However, their creation turns out to be less than cooperative.

Terence Fisher returned to direct *The Revenge of Frankenstein* (1958) before temporarily giving way to Freddie Francis, who directed the next sequel, *The Evil of Frankenstein* (1964). Fisher then returned again for *Frankenstein Created Woman* (1967), *Frankenstein Must Be Destroyed* (1969), and *Frankenstein and the Monster from Hell* (1974). Meanwhile, other studios got into the act, with varying degrees of success.

In *I Was a Teenage Frankenstein* (1957)—directed by Herbert L Storck, with Whit Bissell as Professor Frankenstein, and Gary Conway as Bob/Teenage Monster—Frankenstein builds a monster from body parts of athletes killed in a plane crash, after which the monster wreaks havoc on campus. *Frankenstein's Daughter* (1958) is set in modern Los Angeles, where Dr. Frankenstein's grandson attempts to create life. *Frankenstein 1970* (1958) begins the practice of giving the movies dates in the title well in advance of actual date. In this movie Boris Karloff plays Baron Frankenstein, a victim of Nazi atrocities, who creates monsters using an atomic reactor.

The Frankenstein monster also had its imitators on television. Copycat shows were common in the 1960s (e.g., *Thriller* and Hitchcock), and there were two competing shows with Frankenstein-like characters. In *The Munsters* (1962-64, 1981 *Revenge*), Herman Munster obviously was modeled on the Frankenstein monster. Fred Gwynne (1926-93) is perhaps best remembered for his portrayal of Herman, but he was already beloved for his role in *Car 54, Where Are You*, in which he as Francis Muldoon and Joe E. Ross as Gunther Toody formed a hapless police duo. *Times-Picayune* columnist Chris Rose recently has begun referring to New Orleans Mayor Ray Nagin as "Car 54," a reference to his frequent disappearance from the city. More recently, Gwynne appeared as Alabama Judge Chamberlain Haller in the 1992 comedy, *My Cousin Vinny*, where he actually gets the

Southern accent right.

In the *Addams Family* (1962-64, 1991, 1993), Lurch is only slightly less obvious as a "Frankenstein." Incidentally, the Addams Family in both of its incarnations is a good example of the principle of "six degrees of separation." John Astin (1930-present), television's Gomez Addams, is the father with wife Patty Duke of Sean Astin, who was Sam Gamgee in *The Lord of the Rings*. One of his co-stars was Ian McKellen, who played Gandalf in that film and director James Whale in the 1998 movie *Gods and Monsters*. Another co-star was Christopher Lee, erstwhile Frankenstein monster, Dracula, and Saruman. Raul Julia, the cinema's Gomez Addams, earlier played Dr. Victor Frankenstein in Roger Corman's 1990 *Frankenstein Unbound*. Television's Lurch was Ted Cassidy (1932-79), who was often annoyed at being confused with Richard Kiel, the actor who played Jaws in two James Bond movies. The cinema's Lurch was Carel Struycken (1948-present).

Besides pseudo-Frankenstein monsters like Herman Munster and Lurch, there also have been numerous television versions of the Frankenstein story: *Tales of Frankenstein (1958), Frankenstein Mark II (1966), Frankenstein (1968), Frankenstein (1973), Frankenstein: The True Story* (1973), *Frankenstein* (1981), *Frankenstein* (1984), *Frankenstein* (1987), *Frankenstein: The College Years* (1991), *Frankenstein* (1992), *It's Alive: The True Story of Frankenstein* (1994), *House of Frankenstein* (1997), *Frankenstein: Birth of a Monster* (2003), *Frankenstein* (2004), and the *Frankenstein* mini-series (2004).

The 1960s also witnessed further elaboration of the story in movie theaters, with *Frankenstein Conquers the World* (1965), the Japanese film *Frankenstein Meets the Space Monster* (1965), and *Jesse James Meets Frankenstein's Daughter* (1966), a companion piece to the equally improbable *Billy the Kid vs. Dracula* (1966). Curiously, prior to 1969 the Frankenstein monster never fought with Dracula, though they occasionally shared the screen. Suddenly, in just over three years there were three such movies—*Dracula vs. Frankenstein/Monster of Terror* (1969), *Dracula vs. Frankenstein* (1971), and *Dracula, Prisoner of Frankenstein* (1972). Alas, all are really bad.

In the wake of the sexual revolution, it was perhaps inevitable that possible latent erotic themes in the Frankenstein story would become more overt, sometimes ridiculously so. Audiences were advised about the namesake of *Lady Frankenstein* (1971) that "only the monster she made could satisfy her strange desires." The title of *The Erotic Rites of Frankenstein* (1972) is self-explanatory, though the title sometimes appears without the word "erotic" included. Andy Warhol's *Flesh for Frankenstein* (1973) provided him with his fifteen minutes of fame in the horror movie business.

Still more variations followed in the early 1970s, with Hammer's *Horror of Frankenstein* (1970), another anachronistically titled *Frankenstein 80* (1972), and an African-American monster in *Blackenstein* (1973) to match the African-American vampire in *Blacula*. The tagline for *Blackenstein*—"To stop this mutha takes one bad brotha"—readily identifies it as one of the 1970s' many so-called Blaxploitation movies. African-American comics Eddie Murphy on *Saturday Night Live* and Robert Townsend in the movie *Hollywood Shuffle* have lampooned this genre with devastating effectiveness.

Then in 1974 came a work of true genius. Many critics and movie fans alike see *Young Frankenstein* (1974 as the funniest movie ever made. Mel Brooks (1926-present) directed the film, with Gene Wilder (1933-present) in the title role as Dr. Frederick Frankenstein, grandson of the original Dr. Frankenstein. Brooks and Wilder had worked together before on *The Producers* (1968) and *Blazing Saddles* (1974). *Young Frankenstein* actually was Wilder's idea, which he developed while working with Brooks on *Blazing Saddles*. One thing that makes *Young Frankenstein* so successful is brilliant writing and directing. Another is the stellar cast. Wilder's male co-stars included Peter Boyle as the monster, Marty Feldman as an Igor whose hump keeps moving from side to side, and Kenneth Mars as the pompous Inspector Kemp. Female co-stars included the brilliant comedienne Madeline Kahn, dancer-turned actor Terri Garr (recently a regular on *The Sonny and Cher Show*) as Inga, and Cloris Leachman, a veteran of *The Mary Tyler More Show*, as the woman who frightened the horses, Frau Blücher.

In this movie Dr. Frankenstein's grandson Frederick inherits the family castle, discovers the laboratory thanks to the machinations of Frau Blücher, and repeats his grandfather's experiments with the help of Igor and the lovely Inga. This spoof is actually rather faithful to the original Universal movies and duplicates a number of scenes to hilarious effect, including the "It's alive" scene and the one with the monster and the little girl. One scene that definitely was not in any previous movies and that initially led to a huge argument between its creator Wilder and an atypically skeptical Brooks was the screamingly funny one in which Frankenstein and the monster dance to "Puttin' on the Ritz." Another involves a hilarious exchange about the "bags," a reference to suitcases that Igor misinterprets as applying to Elizabeth and Inga. A series of scenes with the monster and the hermit (Gene Hackman) duplicate familiar scenes from *Bride*, but things do not turn out so well with the soup, the wine, and the cigars. In the end, though, things go much better on the monster's wedding night

And then there is Peter Boyle's other "Frankenstein": in

91

"Halloween Candy," a 1998 episode of the popular television series, *Everybody Loves Raymond*, we get to see Frank Barone (Boyle) turn back into Frankenstein's monster, with Marie (Doris Roberts) as the Bride, and accidentally hand out Raymond's condoms to neighborhood children, mistaking them for foil-wrapped candy. The entire cast of the show also once posed as the Addams Family, with Raymond (Ray Romano) as Gomez, Deborah (Patricia Heaton) as Morticia, Robert (Brad Garrett) as Lurch, Frank as Uncle Fester, Marie as Granny, Ally (Madylin Sweeten) as Wednesday, and Geoffrey and Michael (Sawyer and Sullivan Sweeten) as twin Pugsleys. Meanwhile, in the cult classic, *Rocky Horror Picture* (1975), Dr. Frank-N-Furter (Tim Curry) is very loosely modeled on Dr. Frankenstein, which no one is likely to forget after seeing him in drag, singing, "I'm just a sweet transvestite from transsexual Transylvania."

And the horror continues with the *Terror of Frankenstein* (1977), *Frankenstein Island* (1981), *Frankenstein 90* (1984), *The Bride* (1985, featuring Sting), *Frankenstein General Hospital* (1988), Roger Corman's *Frankenstein Unbound* (1990), *Frankenstein 2000* (1991), *Frankenstein* (1992, television), and *Samurai Johnny Frankenstein* (1993, with Randy Quaid as the monster). Then, in 1994, Robert De Niro shows up as the monster in one of the most interesting—and grotesque—versions of the story in many years, *Mary Shelley's Frankenstein* (1994). Directed by Kenneth Branagh, who also played the role of Victor Frankenstein, the film also featured Helena Bonham Carter as Elizabeth, Ian Holm as Baron Frankenstein, and John Cleese as Professor Waldman. And that's not all, folks, for following soon thereafter were *Monster Mash* (1995), *Frankenstein Through the Eyes of the Monster* (1996, with Tim Curry again), and *Frankenstein and Me* (1997). The Frankenstein story also formed the backdrop for *Gods and Monsters* (1998), with Ian McKellen (is he Gandalf or Magneto?) as openly gay director James Whale and Brendan Fraser (is he George of the Jungle or Rick O'Connell?) as a younger straight friend.

At the turn of the century, things got weird—with Frankenstein embracing sex, drugs, and rock and roll in *Lust for Frankenstein* (1998), *Rock & Roll Frankenstein* (1999), and *LSD Frankenstein* (2002), as well as sex, rebirth, and chipmunks in *Alvin and the Chipmunks Meet Frankenstein* (1999), *Mistress Frankenstein* (2000), and *Frankenstein and the Wolf Man Reborn* (2002). The twenty-first century also brought more new films: *Frankenstein* (2004, with William Hurt and Donald Sutherland), Dean Koontz's *Frankenstein* (2004), *My Step Brother Frankenstein* (2004), *Van Helsing* (2004), *Frankenstein and the Creature from Blood Cove* (2005), and *Frankenstein Reborn* (2005). ·

Meanwhile, not to be forgotten are Tim Burton's *Frankenweenie*

(1984) [remade in 2012] and the recurring *Saturday Night Live Skit* (1987-early 1990s) featuring Tonto (Jon Lovitz), Tarzan (Kevin Nealon) and Frankenstein (Phil Hartman). Frankenstein's monster also has appeared in comics (Classic, Dell, Detective, Marvel, and so on), in children's television (*Saturday Morning with Frank*), in the form of stupid toys (Build Big Frankie) and bad cereal (Frankenberry), and in commercials for Bic, Doritos, Osteo-Biflex (especially funny), Shasta, and Twix. It even featured in a major exhibition at the National Library of Medicine in 1997-98, *Frankenstein Penetrating the Secrets of Nature*, which subsequently became a traveling exhibit.

Over the years Frankenstein has proven relatively easy to create, somewhat more difficult to kill, and impossible to keep dead. Why is that? In part, it is because the story is entertaining. It also taps into our anxieties. In Shelley's time modern science was still new and controversial, and body snatchers often stole corpses for use by anatomists. In the 1930s it played into the rise of totalitarianism, powerful, immoral or at least amoral, and the same was true in the 1950s with the Cold War. More recent efforts, sadly, seem to have more to do with movie fans' taste for gore. However, the better films also deal with man's hubris.

On the other hand, use of the term "Frankenstein" at times has created a problem with labeling, for example, in vitro fertilization, genetic engineering, stem cell research, and cloning. This introduces an emotional element that inhibits rational discussion of serious issues, often creating a straw man or presenting discussants with false choices. It is important to remember that the Frankenstein monster is a fictional creature made out of stolen body parts and a diseased brain—no serious scientist is proposing to do that. There are appropriate moral lessons to draw from the Frankenstein story, but it is important that we not let the Frankenstein metaphor run rampant in the same way that the monster has done.

Suggestions for Further Reading Kenneth Branagh, Steph Lady, Frank Darabont, *Mary Shelley's Frankenstein: A Classic Tale of Terror Reborn on Film* (1994); Stephen Cox and Butch Patrick, *The Munsters: A Trip Down Mockingbird Lane* (2006); James Curtis, *James Whale: A New World of Gods and Monsters* (2003); Deborah Del Vecchio and Tom Johnson, *Peter Cushing: The Gentle Man of Horror and His 91 Films* (2009); Marcus Hearn and Alan Barnes, *The Hammer Story* (2007); Bill Henkin, *The Rocky Horror Picture Show Book* (1979); Dorothy and Thomas Hoobler, *Monsters: Mary Shelley and the Curse of Frankenstein* (2006); Paul Leggett, *Terence Fisher: Horror, Myth and Religion* (2002); Michael Mallory, *Universal Studios Monsters: A Legacy of Horror*

(2009); Gregory Mank, *Bela Lugosi and Boris Karloff: The Expanded Story of a Haunting Collaboration, with a Complete Filmography of Their Films Together* (2009); Dennis Meikle, *A History of Horrors: The Rise and Fall of the House of Hammer* (2009); Mark Miller, *Christopher Lee and Peter Cushing and Horror Cinema: A Filmography of Their 22 Collaborations* (2010); Scott Nollen, *Boris Karloff: A Gentleman's Life* (2005); James Robert Parish, *It's Good to Be the King: The Seriously Funny Life of Mel Brooks* (2008); Caroline Picart, Frank Smoot, Jayne Blodgett, *The Frankenstein Film Sourcebook* (2001); Mary Shelley, *Frankenstein or the Modern Prometheus: The 1818 Text* (Oxford World's Classics) (2009) and *Frankenstein or the Modern Prometheus* (1831 Revision, Penguin, 2003); Tom Weaver, Michael Brunas, John Brunas, *Universal Horrors: The Studio's Classic Films 1931-1946* (2007); Gene Wilder, *Kiss Me Like a Stranger: My Search for Love and Art* (2005).

2007 PREQUEL
THERE'S A WAR . . . A WAR ON CHRISTMAS

A montage of movie and cartoon film clips shows various dysfunctional Christmases. Then comes the song, "The War on Christmas." Watch the video at https://myspace.com/headongoolah/videos and listen to the song on the CD *Show Tunes* by Headongoolah (which is me before Impaired Faculties).

SINGER: There's a war—WAR!—a war on Christmas
No Christmas trees at your local business
Nothing but a basket of wine and cheeses
No room at the inn for the baby Jesus

There's a war—WAR!—a war on Christmas
Santa is depressed and the elves are listless
It's the Dark Ages for Old St. Nicholas
And we can't even let Elmo tickle us

No mo' Santa
No hosanna

There's a war—WAR!—a war on Christmas
You can't put angels' pictures on the dishes
At the big carton store with the face that's smiley
I know it's true 'cause I heard it on O'Reilly

There's a war—WAR!—a war on Christmas
Happy Holidays is now what we wishes
Can't have a prayer at the school board meetings
And shop clerks got to say Seasons Greetings

No mo' holly
No mo' jolly

There's a war—WAR!—a war on Christmas
The Panama Canal is cut through an isthmus . . .

BILL   What? You try coming up with a bunch of words that rhyme with Christmas!

SINGER   There's a war—WAR!—a war on Christmas
           The Panama Canal is cut through an isthmus
           Down at the courthouse they don't have a manger
           And western civilization's in danger

           Let me hear you say ho
           Ho Ho
           Humbug
           Let me hear you say ho
           Ho Ho
           Humbug

E BUNNY   Santa and Christmas. Santa and Christmas. Everything is
           always all about Santa and Christmas. But there's a war on
           Easter, too, you know.

SINGER   There's a war—WAR!—a war on Easter
           It used to be the other big holy day feaster
           Tiny little children on happy little legs
           Hunting through the grass for colored Easter eggs

           There's a war—WAR!—a war on Easter
           Talk about the Passion, they'll knock you on your keaster
           Lotta bad things happenin' and it really ain't funny
           The pagans all want to kill the Easter Bunny

T FAIRY   Now wait a minute. That just doesn't make sense. Why
           would pagans want to kill the Easter Bunny? The Easter
           Bunny is a pagan symbol himself.

E BUNNY   Oh, and I suppose Santa Claus is in the Bible? You know
           the name "Santa" is an anagram for "Satan." Just rearrange
           the letters and see what you get. And if you want to talk
           about pagan holidays and Satan, what about Halloween?

SATAN   Oh, please. I hate Halloween. It's the eve of All-Saints Day,
           you know, and Satan doesn't do saints. Why do you think I
           cursed that wretched football team? Halloween gives me
           hives. Children are happy on Halloween. I don't like happy
           children. I like miserable children. That's why I created the

LEAP Test. You know who likes Halloween? Dentists, that's who! All that candy, all those bad teeth. I don't like bad teeth. You know how Hell is. Wailing and gnashing of teeth. You can't gnash bad teeth.

T FAIRY   Ew. I don't like that guy. But he's right about Halloween. You should see all the teeth I collect the morning after Trick or Treat.

SINGER   There's a war—WAR!—a war on Halloween
The dentists don't want you chewing' no Dentyne
Orthodontists moving in for the kill
Gonna charge you ten grand for fixing your grill

D GAY   Oh, dear. I would just like to apologize to all the dentists in the audience, especially Dr. Brown and Dr. Chandler. My greatest fear is that some day one of my performers is going to do something that gets me fired and shuts down Fanfare.

SINGER   There's a war—WAR!—a war on Fanfare
Bad behavior from performers that don't care
Next year the staff will be on welfare
And Donna Gay gonna be selling that Tupperware

D GAY   Oh, let's just get this over with. Please welcome our speaker.

2007 LECTURE
THE REAL NIGHTMARE BEFORE CHRISTMAS:
THE PURITAN WAR AGAINST CHURCH HOLIDAYS

Let me begin by saying that I love Christmas, Easter, and Halloween. I participate in and enjoy both the sacred and secular celebrations of each. In fact, I have celebrated more than fifty in a row [sixty now]. I have never been on the naughty list. No, really. I like my dentist, too. The slightly sarcastic video that you just saw is not directed against either the holidays themselves or people who enjoy them. Rather, I hope that it will serve as a humorous introduction to an issue that recently has been the subject of far too much ill-humored discussion. That question is this: Is there a war on Christmas? I do not think so, and I will you why not momentarily. However, once upon a time in the English-speaking world there *was* a real war on Christmas. By examining that conflict, I hope that we can better understand the so-called "culture wars" of our own day. Then perhaps we can move into the coming holiday season with less acrimony and more of the Christmas spirit.

Every fall for the last several years Fox News commentator Bill O'Reilly has taken to the air in his "No Spin Zone" to issue dire warnings against a war on Christmas that he regards as being part of a larger culture war gripping our nation. Others have echoed this notion. John Gibson has even written a book called *The War on Christmas: How the Liberal Plot to Ban the Sacred Christian Holiday is Worse Than You Think* (2005). In response, Comedy Central's Jon Stewart and Stephen Colbert and MSNBC's Keith Olbermann have devoted considerable airtime to ridiculing this notion. But what would a war on Christmas look like?

In seventeenth century England there was a very real war on Christmas. King Charles I favored absolutism in government and Arminianism in religion, which included belief in free will and elaborate ritual, which Archbishop Laud praised as "the beauty of holiness" but that Puritans found redolent of Catholicism. This provoked a Civil War between royalist Cavaliers and parliamentarian Roundheads during the years 1642-48 that culminated in the king's execution in 1649 and the establishment of a Puritan republic. During an eleven-year Interregnum (the period between Charles I's death and the Restoration of Charles II in 1660), Parliament legally banned Christmas and other holidays in the name of Christianity and on the grounds that they were pagan in origin and too "Catholic" in nature. This extended to the American colonies, where the impact lasted until after the American Revolution.

Before proceeding, let me offer two important points of context. First, the American Revolution is the third in a trio of "English" revolutions. Our Founding Fathers looked back to both the Glorious Revolution of 1688 and the earlier Puritan Revolution of 1649 for examples of how to do things and how not to do things. Second, there have been over 2000 years of Christian history during which there have been enormous changes in the observance of Christmas, Easter, and Halloween—all of which are explicitly Christian holidays, all of which are sometimes said to have pagan roots, all of which are part of the so-called "culture wars" in modern America, and all of which Puritans banned, after which those holidays only slowly recovered their popularity.

Why would Puritans oppose such holidays? They were devout, Bible-reading, Church-going, praying Christians, yet they objected that Christmas and other religious holidays like Easter and Halloween (the eve of All Saints Day) were non-Biblical, pagan, Catholic, and led to un-Christian frivolity. To get at the reason for this, let us look at the history, starting with Christmas, perhaps our most controversial religious holiday. This will show that there is no basis for the claim that Christmas and other Church holidays like Easter and Halloween are no more than the appropriation of pagan festivals, which some Christian fundamentalists consider Satanic and some neo-pagans regard as part of a medieval Christian conspiracy to suppress a still vital pre-Christian nature religion. In fact, there is nothing "Satanic" about any of these holidays, pre-Christian religions were extinct in Europe by the Middle Ages, and the only "pagan" elements of Christmas, for example, are the date and the adaptation of pre-Christian practices to Christian purposes. The religious observance of Christmas was the product of centuries of doctrinal development and liturgical evolution.

We begin with the nativity of Jesus Christ. At least in theory this should have occurred at the beginning of the year 1 A.D., that is, in the first year Anno Domini or in the first year of our Lord. In fact, historians and Biblical scholars now generally agree that Jesus probably was born about 4 BC, that is four years before the traditional beginning of the Christian era, the designation "BC" meaning "before Christ." So why are the years off? The Kingdom of Judaea, where Christianity began, used the ancient Hebrew calendar like other Jewish people of the time. In the wider world, the Roman Empire used the more accurate solar calendar that Julius Caesar, great uncle of the Emperor Augustus, had introduced in what we know as 46 BC. Though the Julian calendar remained in use throughout Western Christendom until 1582 and in Britain until 1782, it took no cognizance of Jesus' birth, for the Romans remained hostile to Christianity until the reign of Constantine (306-337). Rather, Dionysius Exiguus created the Christian system of dating in 525, long after the time of Jesus, and he made a mistake in estimating when Jesus was born. Actually, then, this year should be 2011 [the lecture was in 2007], but don't worry—we are not going to change it. It would foul up the Olympics, plus it would put us right in the middle of another presidential election year, and I doubt that any of us could stand that right now.

The gospels also seem to indicate that Jesus was born in the spring—hence the presence of shepherds abiding with their flocks by night. So why do we celebrate Christmas on December 25? The selection of that date has to do with the conversion of large numbers of pagans to Christianity. During its first 400 years, Christianity grew from a tiny persecuted sect in Judaea to become a much larger but still persecuted sect that spread throughout the Roman Empire by the end of the third century, then to one of many legally sanctioned religions under Constantine, and finally the official state religion of the Empire under Theodosius I (379-395). Thus, at any given time during that period a significant proportion of all Christians were recent converts. Therefore, the church adopted for Christmas an occasion already observed by rival religions.

There were numerous mid-winter festivals in the ancient world. The Jews—some of whom became the first Christians—celebrated Hannukah, the festival of lights, in November or December. Many Romans took part in the revelry of Saturnalia on December 17. The Winter Solstice, December 21 or 22, was significant to many ancient peoples. It was the original point in the year for celebrating the Yule in Scandinavia, a festival that lasted as long as the Yule log burned and that was associated with night flights by Odin. December 25 was the date for the Roman festival Sol Invictus, the victorious sun. It also was the birthday of Mithras, the central figure in Mithraism, Christianity's chief rival in the first 300 years of its existence, and one whom shepherds worshipped. As many followers of these other religions converted to Christianity, it was convenient to celebrate the birth of Christ at mid-winter (shifting, in effect, from "the rising sun" to "the risen son"). Rather than trying to outlaw pagan traditions associated with winter festival, the Church eventually adopted them—decorating evergreen trees with apples (from Eden), using holly to represent the crown of thorns, and so on.

In fact, though, the early Church paid very little attention to Christmas. Indeed, for the first couple of centuries there was no observance at all. Easter became the first major Christian holy day in the second century, and when some of the faithful also began celebrating Christmas, it provoked a backlash from some Church leaders. For example, St Origen—one of the renowned Early Church Fathers—denounced Christmas in 245 AD, over a millennium-and-a-half before Ebenezer Scrooge uttered his first "Humbug." Regular observance of Christmas arrived only in the fourth century AD and then it was partially in response to a major theological dispute. In 325 the Council of Nicaea gave official sanction to the doctrine of the Holy Trinity—Father, Son, and Holy Spirit—while also noting that Jesus Christ was both divine and human, "true God and true man." However, there were competing heresies that claimed he was purely God without any human nature or purely man without any divine nature. Therefore, the Church encouraged the observation of Christmas to stress the birth of the divine Savior to a human mother. In celebrating the Nativity, many Christians took over the old pagan practice of decorating homes (and churches) with festive greenery. Thus, Christmas was "on the calendar" by the beginning of the medieval era.

However, in the Early Middle Ages it was overshadowed by Epiphany (January 6), which marks the arrival in Bethlehem of the three 'kings," "magi," or "wise men." Still, it was important enough by 800 for Charlemagne to make a pilgrimage to Rome, where Pope Leo III crowned him as Emperor on Christmas Day. In the ninth century the Church developed an official liturgy for Christmas. Following the conversion of Scandinavia c.1000, the lighting of the Yule log was moved to December 25. By the twelfth century elements of revelry and misrule also became part of the holiday, creating the tension that led Puritans to ban it in the 1650s.

Meanwhile, the conversion of the Anglo-Saxons in the 6th and 7th centuries brought Christmas to what became the kingdom of England in the 10th century. In 1066, William the Conqueror, whose invasion of England had the blessing of Pope Alexander II, held his coronation on Christmas Day. In the High Middle Ages, the "Christ Mass" became one of the most important events of the year in England. It was the occasion for feasting with the Yule boar and Christmas ale. It was a time for caroling, an activity accompanied by the collection of ingredients for making Christmas cakes. However, the exchange of gifts took place not on December 25 but on January 1, one of two competing dates for New Year's Day (January 1 was the old Roman date, but many medieval Englishmen preferred March 25, which—nine months prior to Christmas—was an appropriate date for celebrating the conception of Jesus).

By the beginning of the Tudor period in 1485, the entire year was organized around the Christian liturgical calendar, which included over sixty holidays, Christmas and Easter being the most important. For example, most English Christians did not take the sacrament of Communion every Sunday but only on these two particularly holy days. However, the observation of Christmas was not limited to December 25. Celebration, both sacred and profane, lasted through Twelve Days of Christmas. December 25 marks the Nativity of Our Lord, a day on which the king attended no less than three solemn masses. December 26 is the Feast of St Stephen. Later, it became "Boxing Day," the day on which the well to do boxed up gifts for their servants until the late twentieth century and on which British television now features movies and special programs. December 27 is the Feast of St John the Apostle. December 28 is the Feast of the Holy Innocents, which commemorates Herod's massacre of young male children, regarded as the first Christian martyrs. December 29 is the Feast of St Thomas Becket, martyred under Henry II in 1170. December 30 is not a saint's day, though it is now known in the Robison household as the Nativity of St William [my birthday]. December 31 is the Feast of St Sylvester, who was the Bishop of Rome (pope) during the reign of Constantine.

January 1 is the Solemnity of Mary, Mother of God. January 2 does double duty. It is the Feast of St Basil the Great, a fourth-century Greek bishop who combated the Arian heresy, which denied the divinity of Christ. It is also the Feast of St Gregory of Nazianzus, a fourth-century Archbishop of Constantinople who in 381 with Emperor Theodosius convened the 2nd Ecumenical Council, which reaffirmed the Nicene Creed and thus Christ's dual nature. January 3 is the Feast of the Most Holy Name of Jesus. January 4 is not a saint's day. January 5 is the occasion for Twelfth Night, a time of merrymaking on the Eve of Epiphany. January 6 is the Feast of Epiphany, which not only commemorates the arrival of the Magi but also celebrates the revelation of God the Son as a human being in the person of Jesus Christ. In this part of the world it also begins the Carnival season. Though not part of the official Twelve Days, the first Monday after January 6 was Plough Monday, which witnessed the resumption of agricultural labor along with the procession of a plough through town and considerable revelry.

Now let us take a brief look at Easter and Halloween during the same centuries, as they are part of the story, too. Easter is perhaps the holiest of holy days in Christianity. The crucifixion of Jesus occurred around AD 27-33 at the time of Passover. The English name "Easter" for the passion of Christ is derived from the old Celtic Eostre, but—contrary to the claims of some neo-pagans—has nothing to do with the goddess Ishtar. Easter was the most popular holiday in the early Church, which apparently began observing it in the second century, from which comes our first reference. Subsequently, there was controversy over the proper date for observing Easter, both between East and West and later between Rome and the Celtic Church, and how to calculate the date remains a mystery to many (which is amplified in Louisiana and other places that observe Mardi Gras, since the dating of Easter also affects that holiday). Easter always falls between March 22 and April 25 on the first Sunday after the first full moon on or after March 21.

Many of the current observances associated with Easter developed in the Middle Ages. This includes Mardi Gras, which has roots in pre-Christian spring carnivals. Following "Fat Tuesday," Christians solemnly observed Ash Wednesday and then genuinely fasted throughout the Lenten season. During this period they contemplated the Stations of the Cross, held processions and the blessing of palms on Palm Sunday, and marked the Triduum of Maundy Thursday, Good Friday, and Holy Saturday prior to Easter itself. Easter Sunday was a feast day, like Christmas, that marked the end of a lengthy period of fasting. Bunnies and eggs are very likely relics of pre-Christian fertility symbolism.

While Halloween has roots in paganism, i.e., the Celtic Samhain and other fall festivals, the medieval Christian observance had nothing to do with pagans but was instead the eve of All Saints Day [see Chapter 4: "Pagans, Piety and Pumpkins," for more details]. Links to the Druids, about whom we know very little aside from what is found in biased Roman sources, are largely imaginary. James Frazer's suggestion that Samhain was a festival of the dead has no basis in the evidence, nor does the argument that Christians "took over" a pagan holiday. In fact, All Saints or All Hallows Day cannot be dated to earlier than the eighth century, and it was not always on November 1, so All Hallows Eve—Halloween—cannot be either. However, in medieval Britain, All Saints was one of six major holy days of obligation. Churches rang bells for the dead, relatives decorated graves with flowers, and there were torchlight processions, candles, and bonfires, which some people thought effective in warding off malevolent demons and the dead. Door-to-door processions collected donations or "treats" and abused or "tricked" those who refused them.

Witches and belief therein had little to do with Halloween. The Witch Hunt that erupted c.1460-1660 is often misunderstood. Some Christian fundamentalists believe that Halloween had Satanic associations and that those prosecuted as witches were Satan worshippers. Neo-pagans assume that they were practitioners of a pre-Christian nature religion. Evidence does not support either view. In fact, witch persecution and prosecution—about 50,000 cases in all—were based on the highly problematic notion that witches were guilty of diabolism, i.e., making a deal with the Devil in return for the ability to perform harmful acts called maleficia, or black magic [see Chapter 2].

After the beginning of the Protestant Reformation in the sixteenth century, Martin Luther and other Protestants condemned Christmas as popish and un-Biblical. Catholics responded by highlighting the holiday and emphasizing its religious nature. Many Protestants similarly rejected Easter, among them John Calvin, who was especially influential in England. There, of course, the Reformation began as the result of the "King's Great Matter," in which Henry VIII (1509-47) pursued a divorce from Catherine of Aragon so that he might marry Anne Boleyn and produce a son. Henry broke with Rome in 1533, but doctrine remained ambiguous for the remainder of his reign. Under Edward VI (1547-53) the Church of England became genuinely Protestant, but his older sister Mary (1553-1558) returned to Catholicism before Elizabeth I (1558-1603) restored Protestantism. Henry abolished some Hallowtide rituals, Edward's government did away with them all, Mary revived them, and Elizabeth tried without complete success to ban them.

The radical Catholic Gunpowder Plot of 5 November 1605 against James VI and I [see Chapter 10] led to annual celebrations of divine deliverance that virtually effaced Halloween until the late twentieth century. Treating occurred on both Halloween and Gunpowder (or Guy Fawkes) Day, as well as on numerous occasions between Halloween and Christmas.

During the Civil War and even more after the execution of Charles I, there was a real war on Christmas and other religious holidays. While the fighting continued, Puritans tried to ban Christmas and other holidays in the areas they controlled. In fact, they ordered churches to close and businesses to stay open unless Christmas fell on a Sunday. Of course this provoked considerable resistance from traditionalists [the following four paragraphs owe much to Chris Durston, "Lords of Misrule: The Puritan War on Christmas," and Ronald Hutton, The Rise and Fall of Merry England, cited in the Suggestions for More Reading].

An early harbinger of Puritan hostility to Church holidays was The Anatomie of Abuses, which Philip Stubbes wrote sometime in the 1580s, contending, "The more mischief is that time committed than in all the year besides, what masking and mumming, whereby robbery, whoredom, murder, and what not is committed? What dicing and carding, what eating and drinking, what banqueting and feasting is then used, more than in all the year besides, to the great dishonor of God and impoverishing of the realm." In 1642, at the beginning of the Civil War, Thomas Fuller commented in *A Holy Innocents Fast Day Sermon*, "On this day a feast and a fast do both jostle together, and the question is which should take place in our affections . . . [the young] be so addicted to their toys and Christmas sports that they will not be weaned from them [but elders should not be] transported with their follies, but mourn while they are in mirth."

On 19 December 1644, Parliament issued "An Ordinance for the better observation of the monethly Fast; and more especially the next Wednesday, commonly called The Feast of the Nativity of Christ, Thorowout the Kingdome of England and Dominion of Wales," which provided that "Whereas some doubts have been raised whether the next Fast shall be celebrated, because it falleth on the day which heretofore was usually called the feast of the Nativity of our Saviour. The Lords and Commons in Parliament assembled doe order and ordaine that publique notice be given that the Fast appointed to be kept on the last Wednesday in every moneth ought to be observed untill it be otherwise ordered by both Houses of Parliament: And that this day in particular is to be kept with the more solemne humiliation, because it may call to remembrance our sinnes, and the sinnes of our forefathers, who have turned this Feast, pretending the memory of Christ into an extreame forgetfulnesse of him, by giving liberty to carnall and sensuall delights, being contrary to the life which Christ himselfe led here upon earth, and to the spirituall life of Christ in our soules for the sanctifying and saving whereof Christ was pleased both to take a humane life, and to lay it down againe."

A 1645 Directory of Public Worship stipulated, "Festival days, vulgarly called Holy days, having no Warrant in the Word of God, are not to be continued." Referring to the Roundhead victory at the Battle of Naseby on 14 June 1645, where Charles I was defeated and capture, a Royalist Lament later dourly observed, "Christmas was killed at Naseby fight." Sure enough, in June 1647 Parliament abolished Christmas, Easter, and Whitsun (fifty days after Easter), in December 1647 numerous ministers were arrested for attempting to preach on Christmas, in 1650 the Council of State urged increased penalties for this offense, in 1652 a Christmas Eve proclamation ordered that shops be open on Christmas, in 1656 Parliament met on Christmas to discuss a bill to prevent celebrations in London, and in 1658 Richard Cromwell's Parliament repeated it.

If many pro-Parliament Englishmen were anti-Christmas, may pro-Royalists were also pro-Christmas, and illegal celebrations continued despite government efforts to stop them. In *The Feast of Feasts in* 1644, Edward Fisher exhorted his brethren, "Stand fast and hold the traditions which we have been taught, let us make them known to our children that the generations to come may know them." In 1647 the anonymous author of "A Ha! Christmas" commented, "At such time as Christmas, those who God Almighty hath given a good share of the wealth of this world may wear the best, eat and drink the best with moderation, so that they remember Christ's poor members with mercy and charity." But the same year Thomas Mockett, in "Christmas, The Christians Grand Feast," deplored "All the heathenish customs and pagan rites and ceremonies that the idolatrous heathens used, as riotous drinking, health drinking, gluttony, luxury, wantonness, dancing, dicing, stage-plays, interludes, masks, mummeries, with all other pagan sports and profane practices into the Church of God."

With the Restoration of Charles II, the monarchy, and the Church of England in 1660 came also the restoration of Christmas and other traditional holidays. Meanwhile, in colonial America, New England banned Christmas and other holidays from 1659 to 1681. On the other hand, Virginia celebrated it from the beginning, and it was there that eggnog made its first appearance, with rum of course. New York also enjoyed the Christmas season. After the American Revolution, citizens of the new nation rejected Christmas as "too British," and Congress met on Christmas Day most years from 1789 to 1856. Interestingly, class conflict in New York in the 1820s led to Christmas riots, which in turn prompted the creation of the New York City Police in 1828.

Christmas began to revive in America in the 1820s thanks to Washington Irving's stories and Clement Moore's *A Visit from St. Nicholas* (1822, now better known as *The Night Before Christmas*). Also, beginning in that decade, families began to focus more on children, and that entailed more emphasis on Christmas. In 1828 John Poinset, the American ambassador to Mexico, brought back the first poinsettia. In 1843, Charles Dickens published *A Christmas Carol*, and the first Christmas cards appeared in Britain, and in the same decade Prince Albert introduced the Christmas tree into Britain. All quickly caught on in the United Sates. The hanging of mistletoe became an excuse for ignoring the social proscription against kissing in public. In America, Christmas became "official" when it became a Federal holiday in 1870.

It was about the same time that Santa Claus became a major fixture in America. The jolly old elf is based very loosely on the fourth century Greek Christian, St. Nicholas of Myra, along with elements of the mythology of Odin and the Wild Hunt. The name derives from the Dutch Sinterklaas (who has a dark counterpart called Black Peter who deals with naughty children). In Britain he is known as Father Christmas, in France as Papa Noel, in Germany as Kris Kringle (with another evil analogue called Krampus), and so on. In America his rise to prominence in the nineteenth century owes much to Moore's *A Visit to St. Nicholas* and to Thomas Nast's cartoons in 1863 and thereafter. In 1890 Santa began appearing in American department stores in the weeks leading up to Christmas. By 1896 the Volunteers of America had Sidewalk Santas ringing bells and collecting money for charity. The following year eight-year-old Virginian O'Hanlon wrote a letter to *The New York Sun* seeking to verify the reality of Santa, to which Francis Pharcellus Church wrote the now famous reply, "Yes, Virginia, There is a Santa Claus."

In the 1920s Coca-Cola began using Santa Claus in its ads. In 1939 Robert May added significantly to Santa lore by writing *Rudolph the Red-Nosed Reindeer*, which his brother-in-law Johnny Marks adapted to music that Gene Autry turned into a major hit in 1949. Since then there have been cartoons (the first in 1944), comic books, and the Rankin-Bass stop-motion animated movie in 1964. Santa also has had a long and continuing career in film, his first major outing coming *Miracle on 34th Street* in 1947. In 1955 NORAD (the North American Aerospace Defense Command) began "tracking" Santa on its radar starting on Christmas Eve. During my own childhood in Central Louisiana, two of my slightly older friends—first Charles Neal and then the late Greg (Groundhog) Burns—appeared in Santa suits on local television station KALB, where they read letters from children and watched them through a magic spyglass.

In the late nineteenth and twentieth centuries immigrants added more elements to the ever richer and more varied traditions of Christmas in America. During the first year of World War I, the world watched in fascination as troops in Europe stopped fighting and came out of their trenches to celebrate the holiday before resuming the battle a few days later. The Macy's Thanksgiving Day Parade began in 1924 and, especially after the arrival of television, became for many the unofficial beginning of the Christmas season as it concluded with Santa's arrival. Simultaneously it became much more a family affair and a commercial opportunity. The combination is perhaps best exemplified by Sally's remark in the perennial favorite, *A Charlie Brown Christmas* (1965), "All I want is what I have coming to me. All I want is my fair share." Of course, there remain some Christian denominations that do not celebrate Christmas, while on the flip side there are non-Christians who do. In recent years the presence of

Christmas images (e.g., Nativity scenes) on the ground of public buildings and the observance of Christmas in public schools at times has produced controversy about the First Amendment separation of church and state.

Meanwhile, Easter and Halloween followed a similar trajectory to Christmas. Neither was popular in colonial America but both began to revive along with Christmas after the Civil War. Easter got a boost from Dolly Madison's practice of holding egg rolls at the White House in the early nineteenth century, and this became an annual event in 1880. Easter parades, which have a distant ancestor in medieval Paschal processions, became more and more widespread, as did Easter egg hunts and the Easter Bunny, who arrived in America with the Pennsylvania Dutch in the eighteenth century [and is part of the Guild of Nocturnal Gift-Bringers along with Santa, the Tooth Fairy, and the Great Pumpkin—see Chapter 10]. Puritans like Increase and Cotton Mather abhorred Halloween and Christmas, which they associated with the Antichrist. However, Irish and Scots immigrants brought Halloween traditions with them in the nineteenth century and began making Jack-o-Lanterns from pumpkins rather than turnips. Like Christmas and Easter, Halloween became increasingly commercial from the 1870s, with burgeoning sales of costumes, masks, candy, and other treats. It also became more secular

In conclusion, here are a few thoughts. Since the turn of the century we have been reminded in very painful ways that we have real enemies and that we are involved in a real war. So it is important to distinguish real enemies from imaginary ones. We are all Americans here, and our enemies are elsewhere. To keep things in perspective, we need to avoid falling victim to the politics of perpetual outrage, which warps perspective and prevents civil discourse. Hyperbole and capricious labeling, e.g., "the war on Christmas," also impede intelligent discussion. Americans still cherish Herbert Hoover's "rugged individualist," and we are all at least half libertarian, that is, what most what most Americans really want is to be left alone, though paradoxically many also have the desire to meddle. The so-called "culture wars" are really just cultural differences. In this new century our children have witnessed both 9/11 and Hurricane Katrina. What can the culture show them that is more horrifying than that? Yet at the same time both those events led Americans of all faiths and political persuasions to forget their differences and work together, which is the example we all should take to heart.

Meanwhile, Christmas is in no danger. In fact, it is probably more widely observed in America today than it ever has been. With that in mind, I would take a early opportunity to wish everyone a Merry Christmas, a

Happy Hanukah, a Happy Kwanzaa, a salubrious Solstice, a jolly Yule, and a satisfying Saturnalia. I also invite you to join us in observing an important civic holiday in two weeks with Veterans Day. Later in November we can all share Thanksgiving, a noncontroversial holiday, as we are surely the luckiest people who ever have lived. For today, Happy Halloween! Please enjoy Trick or Treat and remember to get regular dental check-ups. Because you are going to need them after you eat all this candy. Now what are the magic words?

Suggestions for Further Reading

Anthony Aveni, *The Book of the Year: A Brief History of Our Seasonal Holidays* (2004); Jim Baker, *Thanksgiving: The Biography of an American Holiday* (2009); Gerry Bowler, *Santa Claus: A Biography* (2005) and *The World Encyclopedia of Christmas* (2004); Paul Bradshaw and Lawrence Hoffman, *Passover and Easter: Origins and History to Modern Times* (2000); Chris Durston, "Lords of Misrule: The Puritan War on Christmas," *History Today* 35 (December 1985); Durston and Jacqueline Eales, *The Culture of English Puritanism 1560-1700* (1996); Jock Elliott, *Inventing Christmas: How Our Holiday Came to Be* (2002); Morris Fiorina, with Samuel Abrams and Jeremy Pope, *Culture War? The Myth of a Polarized America*, 3rd edition (2010); W.H.C. Frend, *The Rise of Christianity* (1984); John Grossman, *Christmas Curiosities: Odd, Dark, and Forgotten Christmas* (2008); Ronald Hutton, *The Rise and Fall of Merry England: The Ritual Year 1400-1700* (1994) and *The Stations of the Sun: A History of the Ritual Year in Britain* (1996); Cheslyn Jones, Edward Yarnold, Geoffrey Wainwright, and Paul Bradshaw, eds., *The Study of Liturgy* (1992); Joseph Kelly, *The Origins of Christmas* (2004); John McManners, *The Oxford Illustrated History of Christianity* (1990); Clement Miles, *Christmas in Ritual and Tradition, Christian and Pagan* (2008); Stephen Nissenbaum, *The Battle for Christmas* (1997); Penne Restad, *Christmas in America: A History* (1996); Geoffrey Wainwright and Karen Tucker, *The Oxford History of Christian Worship* (2005).

2008 PREQUEL
THE HEARTBREAK OF TUDORIASIS: A TEN-MINUTE ROCK OPERA

This film features clips from Tudor movies intercut with portraits of the monarchs and their spouses and set to music that I composed, played, and sang. At the end Henry VIII (me in costume) appears onstage and delivers the lecture. Yes, it's cheesy. Extremely so. Watch the video at https://myspace.com/headongoolah/videos and listen to the songs on the CD *Show Tunes* by Headongoolah (which is me before Impaired Faculties).

Introduction

Please turn off your cell phones, calm small children, silence barking dogs, and stay in your seats until the program is over—or we'll chop off your head! And now, please relax and enjoy today's presentation. We begin with the world premiere of *The Heartbreak of Tudoriasis*, history's first and worst ten-minute rock opera about the Tudor dynasty, featuring the St. Cretin's Corner Chapel Chorus and the Scataphagous Rictus Four-Piece Dinner Special Orchestra.

Just the Facts, Ma'am

What do Tudor films have to do with Halloween?

Fact!
When Henry VIII broke with Rome, he abolished all Catholic holidays, including All Hallows Day and—by implication—Halloween.

Fact!
During Henry's reign several plotters were executed for attempting to kill the king using necromancy.

Fact!
Anne Boleyn's detractors accused her of using witchcraft to lure Henry VIII away from his first wife Catherine of Aragon

Fact!
Elizabeth I employed a wizard named John Dee to foretell the future, and her enemies accused her of being a witch, the Antichrist, and the Devil.

110

Fact!
Many actors who have appeared in films about the Tudors also have appeared in films about Harry Potter.

Fact!
In 1540 Henry VIII married his fourth wife, Anne of Cleves. Before agreeing to this purely political marriage, Henry sent court painter Hans Holbein to paint a portrait of his potential paramour. Holbein made Anne look better on canvas than she was in reality. When Henry met her, he was dismayed, saying, "I like her not." He quickly divorced her. Researchers recently have discovered Holbein's original more accurate painting of Anne of Cleves. Here it is!

[At this point there appears the famous Holbein portrait of Anne of Cleves with a hideous Jack O' Lantern in place of her head. Then the singing begins—the terrible, terrible singing.]

Henry VII and Henry VIII' Song

Hen-er-y
Number Seven killed Richard III
Hen-er-y
Told the people I'm a man of my word

Hen-er-y
Kept his promise to Elizabeth of York
Hen-er-y
They got married and here came the stork

Arthur—Margaret—Henry—Mary

Hen-er-y
Number Eight was the son of Number Seven
Hen-er-y
His brother caught a cold and he went to heaven

Hen-er-y
After that his daddy died and then
Hen-er-y
Married Arthur's widow Catherine

Hen-er-y
As a youth was a handsome stud
Hen-er-y
But as a baby daddy he was a dud

Hen-er-y
Wanted half a dozen royal sons
Hen-er-y
But all he got was illegitimate ones

Bastards—bastards—bastards—bastards

Hen-er-y
Put down his scepter and got on his horse
Hen-er-y
Told Cardinal Wolsey man I need a divorce

Hen-er-y
Said to Catherine girl we're living in sin
Hen-er-y
So I've got to marry Anne Boleyn

Hen-er-y
People shouted she's a witch and a whore
Hen-er-y
So he dumped her for Jane Seymour

Hen-er-y
At last he had a wife who gave him son
Hen-er-y
But she died giving birth and the marriage was done

Hen-er-y
Anne of Cleves wasn't very hot
Hen-er-y
The king said I like her not

Hen-er-y
Catherine Howard was half his age
Hen-er-y

She cheated on him and suffered his rage

Hen-er-y
Catherine Parr was his final bride
Hen-er-y
She was with him till the day he died

Hen-er-y

Edward VI's Song

Hey Eddie, you're so fine
You're so fine you blow my mind
Hey Eddie, hey Eddie

Hey Eddie, you're so fine
You're so fine you blow my mind
Hey Eddie, hey Eddie

Eddie was a boy king and he wasn't ready yet
The council gave control to Protector Somerset

Somerset was ousted by the Duke of Northumberland
Who sent his enemy to sleep in dark slumber land

Eddie had a doppelganger who lived in a shanty
So is that the real king or is it Tom Canty

The young king was so smart, he seemed to learn just by osmosis
What a shame he died at sixteen from tuberculosis

Hey Eddie you're so dead
You're so dead it hurts my head
Hey Eddie, hey Eddie

Hey Eddie you're so dead
You're so dead it hurts my head
Hey Eddie, hey Eddie

Lady Jane Grey's Song

Lady Jane, Lady Jane Grey
Misbegotten, now forgotten, family was thoroughly rotten

Lady Jane, Lady Jane Grey's
Sad little reign only lasted nine days

Mary I's Song

Bloody Mary
You married the Spanish king
Bloody Mary
But your sister got your ring

Bloody Mary
Your pregnancy was fake
Bloody Mary
Can't you see what is at stake?

Elizabeth I's Song

Little Queen, Little Queen Bessie
You are a princess born and bred
Little Queen, Little Queen Bessie
And your hair is shiny red
Well, it's so sad, when you were three years old
Your daddy cut off your mama's head

The Privy Council came around to arrest her
For treasonably allowing Thomas Seymour to molest her
They chopped off his head, too—man, I ain't no jester
And this is what she said to the councilor who confessed her
I'll see less of Seymour 'cause there's less of Seymour to see
Anyway, I dig the Earl of Leicester

Leicester didn't want to be a farmer so he put on his armor to charm her
Leicester wanted to disarm her so he put on his armor to charm her
He didn't want to alarm her or harm her or let some killer bees swarm her
He just wanted to take her in from the cold, sit by the fire, and warm her

But damn, he said, my name is Earl of Leicester, I've got bad karma
She sent him off to the Netherlands to fight the Duke of Parma

Elizabeth was a virgin
To wed her councilors was urgin'
She said I can't stand Archduke Ferdinand
That sucker looks just like a sturgeon

Prince Eric's too blonde and Anjou's too fond
Of dresses and masculine mergin'
The Catholics are dirgin', the Jesuits are scourgin'
The Puritans are purgin', the planets convergin'
On my private business the parliament's vergin'

I'm the queen regnant, I'm not getting pregnant
I'm young and I'm happy, ain't changing no nappy
No breeding, no bleeding, no midnight breastfeeding
No marriage, no carriage, not even affair-age

I'm lord of this earth, I'm not giving birth
That way I won't need a surgeon
I'll hide away in my chamber
A long time I won't be emergin'

Except to go shopping with my new friend Sarah
For new clothes on which we'll be splurgin'

So, I told parliament thanks but no thanks
For that marriage to nowhere!
I'm a maverick.

Meanwhile . . .

Mary the Queen of Scots got married
To Francis the king of France
But he died really young and she went back home
In that sorry circumstance

In Scotland she and her cousin Lord Darnley
Had a new kind of romance

But she blew up his house and fled to England
Oh what a curious chance

Where Liz made a deadly decision
After decades of devious plots
To give a radical haircut
To the naughty Queen of Scots

Philip II's Interlude

Then in 1588 Philip II of Spain launched against England the greatest fleet
of warships ever assembled . . .

The Armada Song

My armada's invincible baby
And you know that it's coming for you
My armada's invincible baby
Ask the Turks if you don't think it's true

The Protestant Wind Song

But the Protestant wind came and blew them all away
Blew them all away, blew then all away
The Protestant wind came and blew them all away
And they're all at the bottom of the sea

Now the Spanish Armada is a bunch of sunken wrecks
A bunch of sunken wrecks, a bunch of sunken wrecks
And it's too late for all hands on decks,
And they're all at the bottom of the sea

And Liz was too old for marriage and sex,
Marriage and sex, marriage and sex
So she just played checkers with the Earl of Essex,
But she's not at the bottom of the sea

Essex raised rebels and she severed their necks
Severed their necks, severed their necks
And she finally died, Elizabeth Rex,

But she's not at the bottom of the sea

Of course the proper term is Elizabeth Regina,
Elizabeth Regina, Elizabeth Regina
But that word only rhymes with . . . angina
And she's not at the bottom of the sea

A Kingly Coda

Ladies and gentlemen, a kingly coda

Henry VIII was a big fat king
Killed his wives but it ain't no thing
Had half of dozen but everybody knows
All them women was witches and hos

The king is alright, he's alright
The king is alright, he's alright

Henry VIII was living large
Floating down the river on a party barge
He may not have been the very best spouse
But give it up, Hip Hop Henry's in the house

Put your hands together for the king
He got a funny hat and a whole lot of bling
Put your hands together for the king
Listen real good 'cause the choir gonna sing

I'm Henry the Eighth I Am

I'm Henry the Eighth I am
Henry the Eighth I am, I am
I've got servants so I never have to beg
When I get hungry for a turkey leg
And maybe a cup of sack or two or three
It makes me drunk, but I don't give a damn
I'm a gluttonous Lothario, I'm Henry
Henry the Eighth I am

2008 LECTURE
MISERS, LECHERS, ZEALOTS, AND VIRGINS:
THE TUDOR KINGS AND QUEENS ON FILM

I have a Tudor problem. In 1969, when kids only a little older than me were frolicking at Woodstock, my parents took me to see the movie, *Anne of the Thousand Days*, with Genevieve Bujold as Anne Boleyn and Richard Burton as Henry VIII. The effect was dramatic. First of all, I immediately fell head over heels in love with Genevieve Bujold. Secondly, I saw my first cinematic sex scene at the age of fourteen, sitting right next to my mother and father. This experience scarred me for life. I became a Tudor historian. I married a woman named Elizabeth. Our older daughter's middle name is Elizabeth, and our younger daughter's middle name is Anne. To this day I refuse to cut my hair because I want no one getting near my neck with sharp instruments. I have learned that the first stage of recovery is to admit you have a problem. For me, the second stage is to take that problem on stage. So here I am.

Today I want to examine the films made about the Tudor kings and queens with regard to three questions: whether they are good movies, what they tell us about the Tudor era, and what they tell us about the period in which they were made. Tudor movies have come in cycles: the first batch in the 1930s, a second in the 1960s and early 70s, and a third in the late 1990s and 2000s [this lecture does not examine the silent era, though *The Tudors on Film and Television* does so]. I will comment on this as we go along. However, I have chosen for today to focus in turn on the cinematic representation of each individual Tudor monarch, following chronological order and beginning with Henry VII.

Henry VII became king in 1485 after defeating Richard III at the Battle of Bosworth Field and ending the Wars of the Roses. He immediately married Elizabeth of York, thereby uniting the Lancastrian and Yorkist lines. Subsequently the couple had four surviving children: Arthur, Prince of Wales, who married Catherine of Aragon in 1501 but died the following year; Princess Margaret, who married James IV in 1503, the Earl of Angus in 1514, and Henry Stewart in 1528, and who was the grandmother of Mary, Queen of Scots; Prince Henry, who married six times; and Princess Mary, who married Louis XII of France in 1514 and Charles Brandon, Duke of Suffolk in 1515, and who was the grandmother of Lady Jane Grey.

Though an effective king, poor Henry VII is the Rodney Dangerfield of the Tudors. He gets no respect and very little screen time.

Most of his appearances come in film adaptations of William Shakespeare's play, *Richard III*, where he is merely Henry, Earl of Richmond, not yet king and definitely not the star. The first movie was made in 1912 and the most recent in 2008, but the most famous versions illustrate the point well. The 1955 film featured Laurence Olivier as Richard and Stanley Baker as Richmond, while in the bizarre 1995 version (set in a Britain that resembles 1930's Nazi Germany) Ian McKellen is Richard and Dominic West is Richmond.

In the British comedy *Black Adder*, Henry Tudor does not even get credit for defeating Richard III. In fact, he loses the Battle of Bosworth Field. When the idiotic Black Adder accidentally beheads King Richard, it is not Henry Tudor who takes the throne but the old king's nephew Richard, Duke of York, who apparently did not die in the Tower of London in 1483 after all. Though completely insane, he becomes King Richard IV, and his younger son—Edmund the Black Adder—spends the rest of the series trying and comically failing to usurp the throne.

The 2005 film *Princes in the Tower* also operates on the assumption that little Richard is alive. It assumes that little Richard, Duke of York did not die at the hands of Richard III, but this one is not intended to be a joke. Almost all historians believe that Richard III had York and his older brother Edward V murdered. However, this film takes seriously the claims of Perkin Warbeck, an imposter who claimed to be York and bedeviled Henry VII from 1491-97. Here Henry, played by Paul Hilton, is reduced to a supporting role and his legitimacy questioned. Otherwise, Henry VII's function in film is to die at the start, making way for his more colorful son, as he does on screen in the 2003 British television series, *Henry VIII*, which briefly featured Joss Ackland as the elder Tudor. Early on we see him giving some deathbed advice to his son, with the young Henry VIII played by Sid Mitchell. Of course we have no idea what Henry VII said on his deathbed, but we do know that this scene reflects a matter of major importance to both father and son. Henry VII had been very successful in producing heirs. Henry VIII would be less so, with enormous consequences for his realm.

Henry VIII became king just short of his eighteenth birthday—young, handsome, talented, and ambitious. His reign brought both an expected attempt to revive the Hundred Years War against France and the unexpected beginnings of the English Reformation. Henry's thirty-eight years on the throne were full of interesting characters who have made their way on to the screen, most of whom were named Thomas. Cardinal Thomas Wolsey, a brilliant but corrupt churchman and Lord Chancellor, was Henry's chief minister from about 1513 to 1529. Sir Thomas More was a close friend who shared the king's enthusiasm for Renaissance Humanism before they parted ways over religion. Thomas Howard, 3rd Duke of Norfolk, was the nation's highest-ranking nobleman and, above all else, a survivor. Thomas Boleyn was the father of both the king's mistress and his second wife. Thomas Cromwell, chief minister from 1531 to 1540, was the mastermind of Henry's break with the Roman Catholic Church. Thomas Cranmer, Archbishop of Canterbury from 1533, worked to make the Church of England genuinely Protestant. But most interesting of course are Henry's six wives.

Upon ascending the throne, he immediately married his brother's widow, Catherine of Aragon, who shared his enthusiasm for learning and who was a nearly perfect complement to his kingship for a decade-and-half, serving as regent in his absence and becoming a genuine soul mate. Her one "flaw" was her failure to produce a male heir. Her six pregnancies produced only one surviving child, a daughter Mary, born in 1516. The young king occasionally strayed. In 1519 his mistress Elizabeth Blount bore him an illegitimate son, Henry Fitzroy. And he had an affair in the early 1520s with Mary Boleyn.

However, near the middle of that decade he fell madly in love with Anne Boleyn at exactly the same time that he became convinced Catherine could not bear him a son and that their marriage was a violation of God's law as laid down in Leviticus. This led to a protracted courtship, a bitter divorce, Henry's break with Rome, marriage to Anne, and the birth of another daughter, Elizabeth, in 1533. Anne's sharp tongue, continued failure to bear a son, and the hostility she aroused at court led to her execution on trumped up charges of adultery in 1536. Henry then married Jane Seymour, who finally gave him a son, Edward, in 1537 but died as a result of injuries sustained in childbirth. His marriage to Anne of Cleves in 1540 was a failure, though she survived the experience, being pensioned off as the king's "sister." He then immediately married Catherine Howard, who was executed for very real adultery in 1542. The following year he married his final wife, Catherine Parr, who brought his family together and outlived him.

Henry VIII has had even more film roles than he had wives. The first sound movie to focus on his life was the 1933 production, *The Private Life of Henry VIII*, directed by Alexander Korda and featuring Charles Laughton as the king. The movie was nominated for Best Picture, and Laughton won the Academy Award for Best Actor, beating out Leslie Howard (later famous for *Gone With the Wind*) and Paul Muni. In retrospect this seems odd. Laughton plays Henry as a buffoon, and the film has the same feel about it as the "high society" comedies that were so popular in the 1930s. In fact, this movie deserves the blame for creating the popular image of Henry as a sort of jolly, gluttonous lecher. Though this film was meant to be serious, it is often hilarious to the modern viewer. The film begins with a caption stating: "Henry VIII had six wives. Catherine of Aragon was the first, but her story is of no particular interest—she was a respectable woman. So Henry divorced her. He then married Anne Boleyn. This marriage also was a failure—but not for the same reason." The action ensues with Anne already in the Tower, awaiting execution, and—among other things—features some very 1930-ish ladies in waiting, a bizarrely cheerful French executioner, and Henry himself discoursing on the decline of manners while devouring a roast capon.

This is very entertaining stuff but it is grossly inaccurate throughout. For example, Anne of Cleves—played by Elsa Lanchester (soon to be immortalized as the bride of Frankenstein)—makes herself ugly so Henry will divorce her and thus allow her to re-marry her nonexistent lover. While the movie contains some mild sexual innuendo, Henry's fifth wife Catherine Howard—who was between seventeen and twenty-one when they married—is played by an older woman. Interestingly, the year this movie appeared witnessed the foundation of the National Legion of Decency, an organization dedicated to "purifying" the cinema. Laughton reprised his role as Henry in *Young Bess*, about which more later. Four years after *Private Life*, Montague Love—a veteran of many historical dramas—appeared as Henry VIII in a 1937 movie adaptation of Mark Twain's novel, *The Prince and the Pauper*. This completely fictional tale, in which Prince Edward trades places with a look-alike pauper named Tom Canty, is one of the most enduringly popular tales about the Tudor era. In fact, the first Tudor movie of the 1960s was another version, this time with Paul Rogers as Henry. More would come later. Meanwhile *Thomas* More would come next.

The next major film to focus on Henry VIII was the star-studded *A Man for All Seasons*, which was released in 1966 and featured Robert Shaw as Henry VIII. This is an outstanding movie, and it won a host of awards, among them six Oscars, including Best Picture, Best Director for Fred Zinnemann, and Best Actor for Paul Scofield as Thomas More. Based on a 1954 BBC radio play by Robert Bolt, the movie focuses on More's moral dilemma when forced to choose between his conscience and faith in the Roman Catholic Church on one hand and his loyalty to his friend and king on the other. It would be a compelling story even if it were pure fiction. However, More really did choose to die rather than compromise his faith by accepting Henry VIII's break with Rome, his royal supremacy over the Church of England, and his divorce from Catherine of Aragon and marriage to Anne Boleyn.

While this movie does contain some inaccuracies, students and anyone else interested in the period can learn a great deal from it. Perhaps its greatest flaw is in overdrawing the distinction between More and his adversaries. The Catholic Church later canonized More on the basis of his martyrdom, and there is more than a little hagiography in this film. More appears throughout as the principled victim, while Cardinal Thomas Wolsey is an almost visceral symbol of corruption and Thomas Cromwell is a scheming manipulator with no apparent conscience. While Anne Boleyn appears briefly in the person of Vanessa Redgrave, she says almost nothing, and though Redgrave looks more like portraits of Anne than any other actress who has portrayed her, we are unable to see Anne below the surface. The reality was more complex.

More's passive resistance and principled sacrifice of himself made him the perfect hero in 1966 in the midst of the civil rights movement in America and elsewhere. However, what the movie ignores is that More himself was not just persecuted but also a persecutor. As Lord Chancellor between 1529 and 1532, he was responsible for burning as heretics several Protestants, individuals who also died rather than forsake their faith. He also engaged in a ferocious propaganda battle with Martin Luther. On the other hand, both Wolsey and Cromwell were reformers in some respects, and Cromwell's masterminding of the English Reformation arose at least in part from his commitment to Protestant ideals. Anne Boleyn, like Henry VIII, had much of the same Humanist learning that the film emphasizes in More and his family, and she also was committed to Protestant reform. This is not to suggest that either Catholics or Protestants were "right" in this situation or that More's death was less than heroic, but the actual history offers more gray than the sharp blacks and whites of the film. In a particularly memorable scene, More talks politics with Wolsey, played by Orson Welles, whose physical presence seems a perfect metaphor for the bloated corruption of the late medieval ecclesiastical hierarchy.

Next we come to *Anne of the Thousand Days*, directed by Charles Jarrot. As Henry VIII it featured Richard Burton, a man who was no stranger to multiple marriages. Though nominated in ten categories for the Academy Awards—including Best Picture, Burton for Best Actor, Bujold for Best Actress, and Anthony Quayle (a particularly unctuous Wolsey) as Best Supporting Actor—it won only for costume design. Burton, Bujold, and Quayle lost to John Wayne, Maggie Smith, and Gig Young. The film fared better at the Golden Globes, winning four, including Bujold as Best Actress. This film is very much a product of its time—by 1969 both the women's rights movement and the sexual revolution were in full swing. Bujold's Anne is an angry young woman, lashing out at Wolsey for interfering with her plans to marry Harry Percy and furiously resisting the king's sexual advances lest she become the mother of bastards (the real Anne did the same). But she also is a liberated female who speaks her mind about politics and religion and who has sex when she chooses—in France in her youth (by allusion), with Percy (almost), and with Henry once she decides that he really intends to marry her. And the movie deals frankly with sex, though it now seems extraordinarily tame—and tasteful— compared to Showtime's *The Tudors*. Like almost all historical movies, this one is guilty of a certain amount of time compression—one loses the sense that Henry and Anne's relationship lasted almost a decade. But like *A Man for All Seasons*, it gets most of the big issues right, and viewers will hardly come away from it with any gross misconceptions about Tudor history. One very important example is that the movie portrays Anne as innocent of the charges of adultery and treason brought against her in 1536. That is exactly what present-day historical scholarship says. The film even shows Anne resisting Henry's advances.

The Six Wives of Henry VIII, a 1970 BBC series (in six parts, naturally), is the first treatment of Henry to include all of his wives and the first to show the transition from the then little-known young, athletic Henry to the more familiar elderly, obese man he became. Keith Michell plays the king, supported by an excellent cast of wives and courtiers. Like the films of the preceding decade, this series sticks relatively close to the actual facts, though obviously there is some fictional invention. The main problem this series faces—one common to any that take on all of the wives—is that not all six lasted the same amount of time as royal spouse and not all are equally interesting. Catherine of Aragon had the longest and arguably the most tragic career and Anne Boleyn the most meteoric rise and dramatic fall; therefore, their lives make for a detailed and riveting story. Jane Seymour, Henry's favorite wife, was relatively unknown prior to her marriage to the king in 1536, and she died the following year from complications of giving birth to the future Edward VI, so her story— though highly melodramatic—is necessarily brief.

Anne of Cleves was married to Henry only a few months, though in some ways she was the luckiest of the six—when Henry divorced her, he set her up with a fine country home in Surrey and designated her "the king's loving sister." This allowed her to live very comfortably—by turns at court and in the country—until 1557, but once the marriage ends, her tale is rather prosaic. Catherine Howard offers the most salacious tale, though any sensible viewer has to be a little disgusted at the fifty-year-old king fawning over a girl who was aged somewhere between 17 and 21 when they wed. Unlike Anne Boleyn, Catherine really did commit adultery, right under the king's nose, and when caught, she suffered the identical fate. This offers momentary excitement, but again this relationship had little background, and it lasted less than two years. Finally, Catherine Parr, who was twice widowed before marrying Henry in 1543, gave the king comfort and brought all three of his children—Mary, Elizabeth, and Edward— under the same roof. While domestic happiness does not a thriller make, Catherine faced plots because of her sympathy for Protestantism and closeness to Prince Edward's Seymour uncles, but film accounts of her era suffer from the decline of Henry VIII—aging and sick, he no longer is very much fun. Watching Henry with each of his wives illustrates his on-screen aging.

Michell reprised his role as Henry VIII twice. The first was in the 1972 movie *Henry VIII and His Six Wives*, which otherwise features a different cast and in which a dying Henry looks back on his life. The second is the 1996 edition of *The Prince and the Pauper*, a mini-series for BBC television. After *Six Wives*, there was a long hiatus in Henry VIII movies, save for additional versions of *The Prince and the Pauper* in 1978, with Charlton Heston as Henry VIII, and 2000, with Alan Bates as the king. Heston also remade *A Man for All Seasons* as a filmed stage play in 1988 with Martin Chamberlain as Henry. Then suddenly in the twenty-first century Henry himself was in vogue again.

The first and best of the new films is a 2003 British television mini-series, *Henry VIII*, with Ray Winstone in the title role. It deals with all six wives, though it skips over most of Henry's marriage to Catherine of Aragon. The acting is good throughout, and while there are occasional inaccuracies, there are no glaring distortions. Several aspects of the series are noteworthy. One is Winstone's performance—he has a rather strong working class accent ("f" and "v" for "th" as in "I fink" and "muver" and "faver"), and he makes no apparent effort to avoid this. Thus we get a sort of twenty-first century proletarian king—*Everybody Loves Hank the Plumber, King of Queens*. He also plays both a harder and more vulnerable Henry, who rages with the best of them, is wantonly cruel at times, but who weeps over the stillbirths of children and the demise of marriages. As usual, Anne Boleyn is the most interesting wife, and she also seems a creature of the present day—she resists Henry's advances as determinedly as Bujold but she looks weary and beaten down by the process, and when she finally submits, you can see in her eyes—even if you do not know the end of the story—that tragedy lies ahead. Once again, Catherine Howard also offers an interesting contrast. More than any other movie about Henry, this one emphasizes her youth and the king's almost pathetic need to recover his own virility through her. The relationship is even more disturbing in this movie. Norfolk's exploitation of his niece for political ends is played well and accurately, and when Catherine briefly appears partially nude, there is nothing sexy about it.

Speaking of sex and exploitation brings us to the subject of the Showtime series, *The Tudors*, which began in 2007 and is now entering its third season. I do not have Showtime, so for months I had to defer comment when friends asked what I thought of the show. Having now watched it on DVD, I find that I can sum up my assessment in a scatological monosyllable. Oh, the show is entertaining after a fashion. The costumes are beautiful, and sometimes the actors and actresses actually keep them on for several minutes at a time. But in the end this show is an excuse to show an awful lot of nudity and on-screen sex. The cover of the DVD for Season One is revealing. We see young Henry VIII seated and looking, well, either seductively powerful or constipated—it is hard to tell. Behind him we see three women. Or rather we see three women's rather prominent cleavage but not their heads. Perhaps I am being overly analytical, but it seems to me that this suggests that what is in the women's heads is not very important. In any case, it is pretty obvious from the cover what Showtime is showing. With Season Two, of course, we get much more sensitive cover art.

What history there is here is mangled to the point where one wonders if it would not have been easier simply to tell it straight, with intermittent gratuitous sex scenes. Here is one example. In real life Henry's sister Margaret married James IV of Scotland well before her brother became king. In *The Tudors* she is one of a bevy of young and beautiful courtesans who marries the king of Portugal, whom she murders for some reason before returning to engage in a lust-laden marriage with Charles Brandon. In reality Margaret remarried twice after the death of her first husband but not to Brandon. Her younger sister did marry a continental king, but it was the aged Louis XII of France, whom she did not murder, although wags all over Europe joked when he died that it was sex with the young woman that killed him. It was this Tudor sister who married Brandon. The casting and acting also are problematic. Jonathan Rhys

Meyers may be a teen heartthrob, but he looks more like a cross between a punk rocker and a soccer player than a king, and the same is true of his courtiers. The portrayal of Holy Roman Emperor Charles V seems almost comical. When I see this, what it makes me think of is another scene from another movie. This is a great scene if you are making a comedy—on purpose. But if you are purportedly making a serious drama, you really do not want your audience thinking of Inigo Montoya. The characterization of Anne Boleyn is just ludicrous. Fine, she is beautiful and sexy. But it is impossible to imagine the real Anne—an intelligent and well-educated woman—flitting about the court like a wispy soap opera harlot and whispering "seduce me," as Natalie Dormer does early in *The Tudors*, in marked contrast to Bujold and Redgrave.

Taken together, the portrayal of the sex-crazed party-boy Henry and his bacchanalian court is as misleading—and likely to be as influential in molding popular opinion—as Laughton's pompous windbag among the society wives of the 1930s. All that being said, *The Tudors* is high art by comparison with the other recent installment in the Henry VIII canon. *The Other Boleyn Girl* is, in my estimation, the worst movie about the Tudors ever made. Looking for redeeming features in this abomination is like hunting for Easter eggs at Christmas. To start with, it is based on a novel that casts history to the winds for no apparent advantage in plot development. Anne Boleyn becomes the older sister, Mary the "ugly" younger sister—trying to pass off Scarlet Johansson as ugly is, in itself, misguided to the point of absurdity. Their scheming father (who looks like he is wearing a Tudor Halloween costume) and her evil uncle Norfolk (who looks like the generic husband on all those Family Channel and USA made-for-TV movies) pimp them both out to Henry for political influence. It is true that Norfolk did this with Catherine but not with the Boleyn sisters. Nobody, not even Henry, ever manipulated Anne. Unfortunately, not even Johansson and Natalie Portman, both fine actresses, can rescue this mess. The casting of Eric Bana as Henry is also problematic. Its only redeeming feature is that Henry was at this time still young, vigorous, and handsome. But Bana's attempt to act in a kingly manner consists mainly of striding around boldly, looking manly and determined. His costuming is meant to emphasize his broad shoulders, but it actually reminds me of the old Carol Burnett episode in which she is playing Scarlet O'Hara and makes a ball gown out of the drapes, forgetting to take out the curtain rod. What could make this any worse? Well, there are two versions of *The Other Boleyn Girl*. Back in 2003, the BBC did its own, which I will refer to here as *The Other Other Boleyn Girl*. Clearly it is time to move on to Edward VI.

Edward was only nine when he became king, and the Privy Council—ignoring Henry VIII's will—gave virtually complete power to his uncle, Edward Seymour, who became Lord Protector and Duke of Somerset. The Protector's jealous younger brother Thomas married the old king's widow, Catherine Parr, in whose household Princess Elizabeth resided, harbored the ambition of marrying her in turn, and may very well have molested her sexually—at the very least he behaved in an improper manner, which got him executed in 1549. Somerset faced unsuccessful wars with France and Scotland and revolts at home, and ultimately was ousted by John Dudley, who became Duke of Northumberland (but not Protector) and dominated the latter part of Edward's reign. Contrary to popular belief, Edward was not only smart and devout but also vigorous and healthy—much like his father—until he became ill in his sixteenth year. Like his grandfather, Henry VII, young king Edward gets short shrift in serious movies. Mostly he gets to be nearly kidnapped by his uncle Thomas Seymour and then die of tuberculosis, as in *Elizabeth R*. However, as the fictional Edward in *The Prince and the Pauper*, he is king of the movie palace. There are multiple versions, including the inevitable cartoon edition with Mickey Mouse. These include the 1937 version with Errol Flynn and Montagu Love, the 1962 version with Guy Williams, a 1969 version, the star-filled 1978 version, originally released as *Crossed Swords*, with Oliver Reed as Miles Hendon and Charlton Heston as Henry VIII, the 1996 version with Keith Michell, and the 2000 version with Aidan Quinn as Hendon and Alan Bates as Henry. These are good fun, and they do much better service to Mark Twain's novel than the abominable attempts to bring his other works, *Tom Sawyer* and *Huckleberry Finn*, to the screen. But they are not history. Once we get past that, they have featured some great actors. Incidentally, Edward and his doppelganger Tom Canty are usually played either by a single child actor or by sets of twins.

That brings us to the tragic tale of Lady Jane Grey. When it became clear that Edward was dying, Northumberland sought to maintain his hold on power and to keep the Catholic Princess Mary off the throne by marrying his son Guilford Dudley to Lady Jane, the great-granddaughter of Henry VII, and putting her on the throne. This lasted only nine days before popular support for Mary led to Jane's removal. Thus she entered into a marriage she did not want, took a throne that she did not want, and ultimately faced a death that, no doubt, she did not want. The story is told with considerable pathos and some sadism in the movie *Lady Jane*, with Helena Bonham Carter as Jane and Cary Elwes as Guilford. The movie takes some dramatic liberties, but it is well acted and adequately conveys the very real tragedy that befell poor Jane. Here are excerpts in which she becomes queen and in which faces execution under Mary.

Mary I—or "Bloody Mary," as she became known—was in many ways a tragic figure. Strangely, she has never been the subject of a serious movie that focused primarily upon her. She regularly figures as a child in movies about Henry VIII and as the bad old queen in those about Elizabeth. The only movie about her is essentially a horror flick, released early in 2008 by an independent British filmmaker, called *The Twisted Tale of Bloody Mary*, which features lots of scenes of the haunted little princess wandering about and lots of burnings. This is not one to show your history class. There are, however, some good portrayals of the adult Mary by Daphne Slater in the 1971 BBC mini-series *Elizabeth R* and Kathy Burke in the 1998 *Elizabeth*.

For sheer volume of screen time, Elizabeth takes the prize. And like her father, she brings along an interesting cast of characters: William Cecil, her secretary and chief advisor, who later became Lord Burghley and Lord Treasurer; Robert Dudley, son of Northumberland, who was her Master of the Horse and her on-again-off-again male favorite for much of her reign, and who later became Earl of Leicester; Francis Walsingham, another secretary and also her spymaster; the Earl of Sussex, like the preceding individuals a member of her Privy Council; Christopher Hatton, a councilor and alleged paramour; the adventurer Walter Raleigh, the only Elizabethan courtier to be named in a Beatles song; the Lord Admiral, Charles Howard, Earl of Nottingham, who commanded her fleet against the Spanish Armada; Sir Francis Drake the privateer; Sir John Hawkins the slave trader; her suitors, Emperor Ferdinand I; King Eric XIV of Sweden; the Duke of Anjou, later King Henri III of France; his younger brother the Duke of Alençon, whom she nicknamed her "Frog" and came very near to marrying in the early 1580s; the Earl of Essex, the favorite of her old age; and her longtime rival Mary, Queen of Scots.

Elizabeth's reign lasted 45 years, confronted her with extraordinarily complex problems, and is very difficult to sum up. However, most scholarly studies and most films focus on a handful of major issues, all of which were hashed out in her Privy Council and Parliament. These include her refusal to marry, conflict over religion with Catholics and Puritans, the threat to her throne posed by Mary Queen of Scots, the French Wars of Religion, the Dutch Revolt, and eventual war with Philip II of Spain. Elizabeth often had to remind her councilors that she would not defer to them simply because she was a woman. In turn, her indecisiveness (or calculation) drove Cecil and others to distraction.

She preferred to remain single, being unwilling to subject herself to a man or her country to a foreign prince She preferred a degree of religious toleration or, as she put it, not to make windows into men's souls. She preferred peace. And she stood on her dignity as a queen. She faced Puritan demands for further reform of the Church from day one, and members of her own privy council—including Leicester and Walsingham—favored Puritanism. The Catholic threat became much worse after 1570 when Pope Pius V issued the papal bull *Regnans in Excelsis* excommunicating her and freeing her Catholic subjects from their allegiance, though many remained loyal. Perhaps the greatest danger prior to 1587 came from a series of plots to overthrow Elizabeth and replace her with Mary Queen of Scots. Following her execution, England faced the attempted invasion of the Spanish Armada in 1588 and a continuing war with Spain until 1604. Yet Elizabeth died peacefully in her bed in 1603 and is now widely regarded as the greatest of English monarchs.

Given the problems Mary created, it is perhaps appropriate that the first sound film to deal with Elizabeth extensively was a biographical picture about the Scottish queen, *Mary Queen of Scots*, released in 1936 and starring Katherine Hepburn as Mary and Florence Eldridge as Elizabeth. It is not one of Hepburn's more distinguished efforts. It was followed a year later by Alexander Korda's *Fire Over England*, with Flora Robson as Elizabeth. Focusing on the Armada campaign, it is the first movie in which Laurence Olivier and Vivian Leigh appeared together, both in fictional roles. It is a good movie with a strong cast and plenty of action, but the main storyline is invented. And, frankly, Olivier's Michael Ingolby did give a damn about Leigh's Cynthia.

Most enduring of the 1930s Elizabeth's has been Bette Davis, who first played the queen in *The Private Lives of Elizabeth and Essex* in 1939 with Errol Flynn as Essex (though Davis initially wanted Olivier for the part). This is essentially a fictionalized romantic version of Elizabeth's relationship with Essex in the years between his victory over the Spanish at Cadiz in 1596 and his execution for treason in 1601. As background it also incorporates Essex's failure to suppress Tyrone's Rebellion in Ireland and his attempt to seize the throne for himself, but much of the detail is distinctly a-historical. Still, Davis is very believable as the domineering queen and Flynn as the feckless Essex. The following year, 1940, found Flynn in another fictional role in *The Sea Hawk* with a different but experienced Elizabeth, Flora Robson. This is another tale based on the Armada campaign, and it features a great deal of the swashbuckling action for which Flynn is famous. His character, Sir Geoffrey Thorpe, was inspired by real Sir Francis Drake. The cast also includes the ubiquitous Montagu Love as Philip II and Claude Rains as his ambassador to Elizabeth's court, where he—for a change—is one of the usual suspects. Thereafter, there is a lengthy gap before the 1953 *Young Bess*, which starred Jean Simmons as Elizabeth.

Young Bess concerns Princess Elizabeth's alleged love affair with Sir Thomas Seymour and includes the return of Charles Laughton as Henry VIII. Based on a novel by Margaret Irwin, it is not a great contribution to the history of the Tudors or of the cinema—at present it remains commercially unavailable except in the form of used VHS tapes. The other Elizabeth movie of the 1950s—a relative dry spell—is *The Virgin Queen*, which has an older Bette Davis playing a younger Elizabeth opposite Richard Todd as Sir Walter Raleigh. Her rival for his affections is a young Joan Collins, whose rather bitchy role here no doubt would shock those familiar with her later work.

By far the best film account of the Virgin Queen's reign is *Elizabeth R*, another six-part BBC series that in 1971 followed hard on the heels of the previous year's *Six Wives*. Glenda Jackson simply is Elizabeth for most people who saw that series in the 1970s, and her performance remains unsurpassed. Little inaccuracies here and there do not detract significantly from an overall faithful account of history. The superb cast members even look remarkably like the real individuals they portray. A series of scenes from early in Episode 3 remarkably encompasses the issues of the reign— Elizabeth's fury at the St Bartholomew's Day Massacre of French Protestants in 1572, the council's frustrated effort to persuade her to execute Mary Queen of Scots for her role in the Ridolfi Plot of 1571, Elizabeth's attempt to steer a middle path between Catholics and Puritans, her reluctance to take hostile action against foreign powers, her toying with marriage (this time with Alençon), her maddening indecision.

Less accurate and less successful was the movie, *Mary Queen of Scots*, made in the same year and also featuring Jackson as Elizabeth, Vanessa Redgrave as Mary, and a young Timothy Dalton (in a blond wig) as a very foppish Lord Darnley. The cast is different from that in *Elizabeth R* and— except for Redgrave, who is a better Mary than Vivian Pickles—inferior. Redgrave's Mary is also better than Hepburn's, but overall the film suffers by comparison with *Elizabeth R*.

Again there is along hiatus broken only by Princess Elizabeth's cameos in various versions of *The Prince and the Pauper* and by the appearance of "Queenie," as she is called in Black Adder II. Even here, poor Elizabeth is conflicted about marriage.

And then came 1998, with both *Shakespeare in Love* and *Elizabeth* (for which Cate Blanchett won an Oscar), films that gave movie-goers serious intellectual whiplash since both featured beautiful young, up-and-coming actresses (Gwyneth Paltrow and Blanchett), each had a different Elizabeth (Judi Dench as an elderly Elizabeth in *Shakespeare in Love*), and the films shared two actors in major roles—Joseph Fiennes as Shakespeare and as the Earl of Leceister, Geoffrey Rush as Philip Henslowe in *Shakespeare* and Francis Walsingham in *Elizabeth*. Both are gorgeous movies to watch, and neither has any regard for history whatsoever. *Shakespeare in Love* is probably the better film (with seven Academy Awards to prove it. But *Elizabeth* is more germane to our discussion today.

Like the later Cate Blanchett film, 2007's *Elizabeth: The Golden Age*, it starts well and ends well but is complete nonsense in between. *Elizabeth* begins with the Marian persecution, showing the burning of heretics, followed by Mary's increasingly irrational frustration at her inability to produce an heir, her death, and Elizabeth's reception of the news that she is queen at her residence, Hatfield House. Then, however, viewers are treated to a series of absurd fictions, including Walsingham as a bloodthirsty murderer, whose victims include Marie of Guise, regent of Scotland and mother of Mary, Queen of Scots; a lady-in-waiting who dies after trying on a poisoned dress intended for Elizabeth; improbable sexual escapades with Leicester; and so on—the list is long. The ending is bad history but appropriate as a metaphor. Elizabeth, after lots of haggling about marriage, cuts off her hair and covers her skin in white make-up, announcing that she is "becoming" the Virgin Queen. There is an obvious allusion to the Virgin Mary. Of course no such thing happened. However, there is a serious school of thought which argues that Elizabeth, in a Protestant England, benefited from the adoration formerly given to the mother of Christ in Catholic days.

Elizabeth: The Golden Age begins with a chilling scene in which Philip II is planning his invasion of England and ends with the spectacular defeat of the Armada, but in the middle it features a rather silly story focused upon Walter Raleigh, played by Nicholas Cage look-alike Clive Owen. From this movie one gets the impression that Raleigh almost singlehandedly defeated the Armada. There are plenty of other problems. Lord Burghley and the Earl of Leicester, still very much alive in reality, have vanished, their contracts apparently not kept up. Walsingham is still committing mayhem right and left. Here is the scene with Philip.

Sometimes in history movies the seemingly most ridiculous scenes are those most rooted in the facts. One example from *Elizabeth* involves the Duke of Anjou in drag. While this particular episode did not actually happen, Anjou's fondness for cross-dressing is well documented. The other example comes from *Elizabeth: The Golden Age* and is one about which my students expressed great skepticism at first. Elizabeth really did give the Tilbury Speech, though she was older than Cate Blanchett looks at the time and gave a rather different speech. The only other flaw in this scene is that Elizabeth subsequently goes to the edge of the cliffs of Dover and watches the battle off Calais, which in fact occurred several days earlier.

Between the two Blanchett films came two more English mini-series. The first is 2005's *Elizabeth I: The Virgin Queen*, with a rather frail Anne-Marie Duff as the queen and a cast of very young people around her—apparently part of the same "youth movement" that has given us *The Tudors*. The other, 2006's *Elizabeth I*, is much better and focuses on the older Elizabeth, played by Helen Mirren. This produced another case of mental whiplash since Mirren followed this role by playing Elizabeth II in the acclaimed film, *The Queen*. At any rate it is good film with a great cast, including Jeremy Irons as Leicester.

In the end many of these films are quite good artistically, while some are just the opposite. But they often tell us more about the period in which they were made and the attitudes and concerns of the filmmakers than they do about Tudor history. Still, Tudor movies are more popular than ever, and they have a profound influence on popular opinion about the history of sixteenth century England. Therefore, it ill behooves historians to simply dismiss or ignore them. It is far better that we engage them and "exploit" by using them to induce students and others to pursue their interest in the Tudors beyond the cinema and television. And speaking of inducements, I believe there was something in the advertisement for this lecture about candy. So Happy Halloween, and if you'll just say the magic words . . .

Suggestions for Further Reading

Stephen Alford, *Burghley: William Cecil at the Court of Elizabeth I* (2008); Susan Brigden, *New Worlds, Lost Worlds: The Rule of the Tudors 1485-1603* (2001); S.B. Chrimes, *Henry VII* (1992); Susan Doran and Thomas Freeman, eds, *Tudors and Stuarts on Film: Historical Perspectives* (2008); G.R. Elton, *Policy and Police: The Enforcement of the Reformation in the Age of Thomas Cromwell* (1972); Elizabeth Ford and Deborah Mitchell, *Royal Portraits in Hollywood: Filming the Lives of Queens* (2009); Sarah Gristwood, *Elizabeth & Leicester: Power, Passion, Politics* (2007); John Guy, *Queen of Scots: The True Life of Mary Stuart* (2004); Peter Gwyn, *The King's Cardinal: The Rise and Fall of Cardinal Wolsey* (1990);

Paul Hammer, *The Polarization of Elizabethan Politics: The Political Career of Robert Devereux, 2nd Earl of Essex* (1999); E.W. Ives, *Lady Jane Grey: A Tudor Mystery* (2009) and *The Life and Death of Anne Boleyn* (2004); David Loades, *Mary Tudor: A Life* (1990); Wallace MacCaffrey, *Elizabeth I* (1993); Diarmaid MacCulloch, *Thomas Cranmer: A Life* (1996); Sue Parrill and William B. Robison, *The Tudors on Film and Television* (2013); J.J. Scarisbrick, *Henry VIII* (1969); Chris Skidmore, *Edward VI: The Lost King of England* (2007); David Starkey, *Six Wives: The Queens of Henry VIII* (2004); Greg Walker, *The Private Life of Henry VIII: A British Film Guide* (2003).

2009 PREQUEL
REALITY TELEVISION: ALL HALLOWEEN! ALL HORROR!
ALL HISTORY!

The 2009 prequel is a spoof of various "reality television" programs, all of which seem to involve Henry VIII on this occasion. It uses footage from various Henry VIII movies and the television shows being subjected to spoofage. The guy racing on the bike is me in a Henry VIII costume on a small child's bicycle with two very flat tires. Watch the video on https://myspace.com/headongoolah/videos.

VINCE: You are watching The Reality Television Network. Welcome to an All Halloween, All Horror, All History, All Henry VIII weekend. We will be providing continuing coverage of a special Halloween edition of *The Amazing Race* featuring Eight Henry the Eighths. This is your host Vincent Vapid along with color commentator Betty Bloviatrix. Welcome, Betty.

BETTY: Thanks, Vince. This is a unique and very exciting competition, and what makes it so Halloween scary is that all of the competitors are dead!

VINCE: Dead, Betty?

BETTY: That's right, Vince. Today's *Amazing Race* features eight dead actors who have played Henry VIII showing off their equestrian skills. And here they are now!

Richard Burton . . .

Charles Laughton . . .

VINCE: Hey, he's not racing. He's eating!

BETTY: That's what he does, Vince. And here's . . .

Keith Michell . . .

Robert Shaw . . .

VINCE: Wait, he's in a boat. That's a little unorthodox, isn't it?

BETTY: Vince, we asked the officials about this, and apparently the rules allow alternate means of transport if you claim that you have had the swine flu. And now here's . . .

           Eric Bana . . .

VINCE: Wait, he's not dead.

BETTY: Did you see him in *The Other Boleyn Girl*?

VINCE: Oh, good point.

BETTY: Right. And here's . . .

           Jonathan Rhys-Myers . . .

VINCE: Hold it, he's not dead either.

BETTY: No, and *The Tudors* is not really about Henry VIII, but he is great for ratings. And here's . . .

           Ray Winstone . . .

VINCE: Oh, come on. This guy is not a dead actor.

BETTY: Yes, but apparently he stayed at a Holiday Inn Express last night. And now finally here's . . .

           Graham Chapman . . .

VINCE: Now, wait just a doggone minute, that's not Henry VIII!

BETTY: You're right, that's Arthur.

VINCE: You mean Henry's brother Arthur?

BETTY: No, the original Arthur. And he's not riding a horse either.

VINCE: No, there's a guy behind him with coconuts.

BETTY: Oh, this is big, Vince, we have just received word that Graham Chapman has been disqualified, and we are down to just Seven Henry Eighths.

VINCE: I hate fractions.

BETTY: Wait, we're getting word of a substitution. Apparently, there is a mystery Henry VIII joining the competition.

VINCE: Hey, that guy is on a bicycle.

BETTY: Well, that really is strange, Vince. We will try to find out more about the Mystery Cyclist after we pause for a commercial break.

VINCE: Wow, look at them go, Betty. Any word on the mystery cyclist?

BETTY: Nothing yet, Vince. But here he comes now.

VINCE: Tonight at 7:00 don't miss the most exciting episode ever of *Jon and Kate Plus Henry VIII*. Is the king coming between these happy parents?

KATE: You know, this is hard—Henry just shows up with his whole entourage expecting to be fed and entertained 24 hours a day.

JON: I think he's jealous of me. Yesterday I heard him tell one of his courtiers, "I got married six times, and all I have to show for it are two bastard daughters and one sickly son." This guy gets six babies at one pop. And his wife's kind of cute.

KATE: I think Henry is a bad influence on Jon. They've been going out clubbing together, and you know what kind of reputation Henry has.

JON: I think he's fooling around with Kate. He's had three wives named Katherine, you know. I think it's some kind of fixation.

VINCE: Is this marriage in jeopardy? Find out tonight.

VINCE: Then at 8:00 don't miss *The Bloody Bachelor*. In 1540 Henry VIII had been married three times, and all of his wives were dead. The question on everyone's mind was, "Who will be the lucky woman to be Wife Number Four?"

VINCE: Saturday morning a special Halloween edition of *American Bandstand* features "Horrifying Halloween Harmonies about Henry VIII" from Herman's Hermits.

VINCE: This weekend on *Jerry Springer* it's men who marry their dead brother's widows, cheat on them, have illegitimate sons, divorce their first wives, marry their girlfriend's sisters, chop off their heads, marry their maidservants, let them die in childbirth, marry half-wit German princesses, divorce them and call them their sisters, marry under-aged girls in a feeble attempt to restore their virility, chop off their heads, marry reluctant widows, and die. Also, men who decapitate and the women who love them.

VINCE: Later on *Oprah*, it's a special edition on the wrath of the king.

VINCE: Looks like Oprah has a candidate for anger management.

VINCE: Sunday night on *60 Minutes*, was Henry VIII a socialist? And how did the king who introduced the world's first law to help the poor influence that late twentieth century socialist, The Great Pumpkin, and his give-away programs to provide toys and candy to children all over the world?

VINCE: This week on *Survivor: The Tower of London*, it's the final showdown. We began with four teams: the wives, the ministers, the heretics, and the Surrey justices of the peace. All of the wives are dead except for Anne of Cleves, who has been disqualified for drinking excessively, and Catherine Parr. The ministers all have been beheaded. Last week the heretics died in a tragic accident when they got too close to the campfire. That leaves only three Surrey justices, who all have been arrested. They have become the focus of a worldwide effort to free the Surrey three. Will they be released? Will they escape? Will they continue to compete? Or will the winner of *Survivor: The Tower of London* be Catherine Parr? Don't miss the exciting conclusion!

LECTURE BEGINS

[The lecture is illustrated with actual portraits of the historical figures involved wherever they are available. However, where they do not, I created "portraits" by inserting the faces of various Southeastern Louisiana University personnel into period artworks.]

2009 LECTURE
THE WRATH OF THE KING: HENRY VIII, CARDINAL
WOLSEY AND THE SURREY JUSTICES IN STAR CHAMBER

Henry VIII was notorious for his wrath, especially when he failed to get his way or faced disloyalty, real or imagined. He was furious over Pope Clement VII's refusal to grant him a divorce from his first wife, Catherine of Aragon, and broke away from the Roman Catholic Church he earlier had defended against the Protestant Martin Luther. Famously, anger impelled him to execute two wives, Anne Boleyn and Catherine Howard; England's highest-ranking nobleman, Edward Stafford, 3rd Duke of Buckingham; his friend, Sir Thomas More; his political minister, Thomas Cromwell; and a host of rebels, traitors, heretics, and rival claimants to the throne.

Royal rage figures prominently in portrayals of Henry—whether scholarly studies, novels, or films—and rightly so. Today, however, I will discuss a case wherein the wrath of the king was fully justified, one in which Henry and Cardinal Thomas Wolsey brought three powerful local officials before the Court of Star Chamber in 1519 in the genuine interest of justice and reform. The case and related events are the subjects of a book that I hope to publish eventually.

As we proceed, it is important to remember that Henry and Wolsey were complex men. The young Henry was brilliant, well educated, and committed to the reforming impulse that Christian Humanism generated in Renaissance Europe. He shared this with his friend, the Biblical scholar Erasmus; with Thomas More; and in different ways with his first two wives, Catherine of Aragon and Anne Boleyn. Wolsey—Bishop, Cardinal, and Henry's Lord Chancellor—certainly deserved his reputation for concupiscence, but he also was a reformer with a particular interest in promoting justice.

Surrey, the focus of the king and cardinal's interest in 1519, is a county located just south of the Thames River from London. In Henry VIII's day it was the location of several royal residences, as the iconography of this map indicates. It also was home to Cardinal Wolsey's magnificent palace at Hampton Court. To the south lay the county of Sussex with which Surrey shared a sheriff responsible for law enforcement, collecting taxes, and conducting parliamentary elections. To the west lay the county of Hampshire with which Surrey formed the diocese of the Bishop of Winchester. To the east lay the county of Kent with which Surrey was joined for a variety of governmental functions and from the close proximity of which the Archbishop of Canterbury exercised his imposing authority.

However, the most important local officials in Surrey (or any county) were the men who sat on the commission of the peace, known as justices of the peace or JPs. Though lampooned by William Shakespeare in the person of Justice Shallow, JPs were responsible for maintaining law and order, holding courts called quarter sessions, and an ever-increasing list of administrative duties. A seat on the county bench as a JP was critical for any member of the gentry seeking local power and prestige. For the king, the JPs were essential to upholding royal authority in the counties—or shires, as they also were called. Thus, a JP who abused or neglected his authority was cause for grave concern. Yet precisely because the king was not all-powerful and was therefore dependent upon the JPs, the temptation and opportunity for official misbehavior in the counties was considerable.

At Henry VIII's accession several of Surrey's most influential JPs were grouped into two bitterly antagonistic factions headed by the Browne and Howard families. Sir George Browne, the first of his family to play an important role in Surrey politics, was active there by 1472. He was married to Elizabeth Paston, daughter of the judge Sir William Paston, an enemy of the Howards in Norfolk. His son, Sir Matthew Browne, was at the center of the trouble in Surrey along with his ally, John Scott. Sir George had a brother, Sir Anthony Browne I, whose son, Sir Anthony II, was a Surrey official and one of Henry VIII's oldest friends. Sir Anthony II had a half-brother, Sir William Fitzwilliam, who was equally close to the king.

No less well connected were the Howards. Though their power initially lay in Norfolk and Suffolk, John Howard, 1st Duke of Norfolk expanded his influence to Surrey. His son Thomas—1st Earl of Surrey, 2nd Duke of Norfolk, and the second highest-ranking nobleman in England—headed the family in the early years of Henry VIII's reign. He had three sons with influence in Surrey—Thomas Howard, 2nd Earl of Surrey and 3rd Duke of Norfolk; Lord Edmund Howard; and William Lord Howard of Effingham. Lord Edmund was heavily involved in the Surrey troubles along with his allies, the brothers John and Ralph Legh and their cousin Roger Legh.

The animosity between the Brownes and Howards dated to the Wars of the Roses, at least to Richard III's reign and probably to that of Edward IV. Richard III was controversial from the first because he usurped the throne from his nephew Edward V, who disappeared into the Tower of London with his younger brother Richard, Duke of York. The king's meddling with local politics in southern counties like Surrey made

140

matters worse. Richard purged several JPs, including Sir George Browne, from the Surrey commission of the peace. At the same time he granted substantial lands in Surrey to the 1st Duke of Norfolk, who became a JP along with several other outsiders.

Resentment led several Surrey JPs to participate in 1483 in the Duke of Buckingham's Rebellion, for which Sir George Browne was executed after being captured at Bodiam Castle. Soon afterward Richard appointed as a JP John Legh, a Howard ally. However, the 1st Duke of Norfolk died along with Richard III at the Battle of Bosworth Field in 1485, and the victorious Henry VII imprisoned his heir, Thomas Howard, 1st Earl of Surrey, in the Tower until 1489. The earl only gradually recovered his lands, became a JP only in 1501, and did not acquire the title of Duke of Norfolk until 1514.

Meanwhile, under Henry VII, the Brownes' fortunes improved. Sir Anthony I was briefly a Surrey JP in 1487. More important was the appointment in 1495 or 1496 of Sir George's son, Sir Matthew Browne of Betchworth. In 1497 Sir Matthew's ally, John Scott of Camberwell, also became a JP. Sir Matthew immediately took precedence on the commission of the peace over his rival, John Legh, and continued to do so even after the Earl of Surrey returned to the county bench and Legh was knighted in 1501.

By then, however, John Scott had become involved in a long and tortuous land dispute with Roger Legh. Scott and Legh had married sisters, and both claimed their father-in-law's inheritance. Sir John and Ralph Legh supported their cousin Roger. Whether Sir Matthew Browne was involved on Scott's side is uncertain. But about this time Sir John Legh sued Sir Matthew in the Court of Chancery in another land dispute. At any rate there was no settlement, and the case continued to cause trouble.

Meanwhile, Sir John and Ralph Legh, who became a JP in 1506, occupied land belong to one John Mills without paying rent, offered to buy it, cheated Mills out of half the price by fraudulent indentures, threatened him with violence, and sued him in the Court of Common Pleas before Henry VII and the royal council finally ordered them to desist on pain of imprisonment.

When Ralph Legh died, his widow Joyce married Lord Edmund Howard, who revived the suit against Mills at Sir John Legh's insistence. None of this augured well for justice, though Henry VII did not remove any of Surrey's contentious JPs from office. However, such local dissension may help to explain why the king appointed some of his own most trusted councilors to the Surrey bench during the last decade of his reign.

The beginning of Henry VIII's reign in 1509 brought significant changes in Surrey. The Howards rose in favor nationally. Sir John Legh was Henry VIII's first appointee as sheriff of Surrey and Sussex, while the king removed Sir Matthew Browne from the commission of the peace. Though he returned in 1511, he found himself ranked lower than his rival Legh. In 1511 Lord Edmund Howard became a JP, also ranked several places about Browne. In 1514 he was joined on the bench by Roger Legh, Sir John's cousin and John Scott's rival in the aforementioned land dispute. The same year the king created Thomas Howard as 2nd Duke of Norfolk and made his son Thomas 2nd Earl of Surrey. So there were more Howards.

By this time there were several other Surrey JPs with connections to the Howard group, including Sir Edmund Walsingham and John Westbroke. In 1513 they, along with Norfolk's servant John Shirley, attacked and wounded one Nicholas Eliot in Guildford. Sir William Fitzwilliam brought this to Norfolk's attention, but evidently he did nothing about it. The royal council later fined several JPs from the Guildford area for failing to conduct a proper inquiry.

Fitzwilliam's involvement in Surrey is important for another reason, however. A Yorkshire native, he acquired considerable land in Surrey and was a JP there by 1518, though probably earlier. His presence counterbalanced Howard influence and may have emboldened Sir Matthew Browne and John Scott. In any case, Browne and Scott were far from being intimidated into inaction by the Howards' recent successes. In fact, contention between the two groups increased dramatically between 1516 and 1519.

This came at a time when Wolsey was manifesting a determination to do something about "'the enormities in the realm,' which, he said, arose from failure to administer the law justly," and "to see the law enforced against the powerful." Perhaps Surrey's troubles were on his mind on 5 May 1516 when he held forth before the king and council on the need for conciliar oversight of law and order. In fact, Surrey's troubles were rare examples of "enormities" with which Wolsey's Court of Star Chamber actually dealt.

To appreciate how seriously Wolsey took this, note that while private litigation proliferated in Star Chamber under the Cardinal, there were only nine known official prosecutions there during his ascendancy, a handful of exemplary proceedings either related to the council's "periodic demonstration of law enforcement" or promoted by Wolsey for personal reasons. A third of these prosecutions concerned Surrey, for Wolsey brought separate suits against Sir Matthew Browne, Lord Edmund Howard, and Sir John Legh. Of the other six cases, two involved the offense of *praemunire* (appealing over the king's head to the pope) and were personal vendettas on Wolsey's part, two dealt with "offenses against public justice and public order" (a "heinous riot" and a case of perjury), and there were Sir William Bulmer's prosecution for illegally wearing the 3rd Duke of Buckingham's livery and a case arising from a murder investigation. Leaving aside *praemunire*, the Surrey cases comprehended all the evils of the other exemplary proceedings and more.

There certainly was ample reason to make an example of the Surrey offenders. It was a poor show for the rest of the nation that Surrey, right in the royal backyard as it were, should be so given up to lawlessness. Indeed Henry and Wolsey may have recalled that Surrey helped spawn the 1483 rebellion against Richard III. Amid the dynastic insecurity that characterized Henry VIII's early years, he was particularly sensitive to any disorder that might lead to rebellion.

One focus of heightened animosity between the Browne and Howard factions was the murder of Richard Rigsby alias Shepherd, a servant of Henry Knight of Knight's Hill in Surrey. Michael Cassinghurst, planned to marry Knight's maidservant, against her master's will, on Sunday 14 September 1516. On the Friday night before the wedding was scheduled to occur, Cassinghurst, Henry Henley, and several friends went to catch a couple of rabbits for the celebration. While they were hunting, Henry Knight and his servants attacked them. In the ensuing affray, Shepherd, one of Knight's followers, received wounds from which he eventually died—"smite in the back with an arrow" as the court records put it.

The next day Knight told Sir John Legh, who was again serving as sheriff, that he had mistaken the rabbit hunters for thieves and accused Cassinghurst and Henley of perpetrating the whole affair. Legh had Cassinghurst arrested when he came to church on Sunday to be married. He continued to hold him until Thursday despite efforts to bail him and carry on the wedding. Once Cassinghurst was finally free, he decided to marry on the following Sunday, but on Saturday night Knight and one of Legh's servants took the bride away to Legh's house. By this time Shepherd had died of his wounds.

Several quarter sessions inquired into the alleged "murder and riot" that Cassinghurst, Henley, and their fellows had committed against Knight, Shepherd, and their company. These quarter sessions became a forum for factional dispute. Sir John Legh and Lord Edmund Howard took Knight's part. Sir Matthew Browne and John Scott took that of Henley, who stood accused of murder. Henley was arrested and incarcerated, but—according to Roger Legh—Scott illegally released him on bail. At a gaol delivery session in Southwark, Henley appeared before Sir Thomas Neville, Sir John Legh, and John Scott and was "attainted" (i.e., indicted). At the next quarter sessions in Kingston-upon-Thames, Scott withheld the records of the Southwark proceedings "till the justices were up and then put them in," evidently ignoring proper procedure for Henley's benefit. Browne attempted to prevent Henley's indictment, first by trying to get the new sheriff, William Ashburnham of Sussex, to impanel a favorable jury. Then he attempted to intimidate and bribe the jury. He also spoke in Henley's favor at the quarter sessions itself, challenged the testimony of a Howard servant named Newdigate, and quarreled openly with Sir John Legh.

Ultimately Henley was convicted, a victory for the Howards and Leghs, if not necessarily for justice. But clearly the two Surrey factions were less interested in seeing justice done and proper procedure followed than in getting at each other. Lord Edmund Howard, Sir John Legh, and Henry Knight saw to it that Henley's company bore all responsibility for the affray, though it was clearly Knight's fault. Legh further abused his office by holding Cassinghurst without bail for several days and by kidnapping the bride-to-be. On the other hand Sir Matthew Browne and John Scott had no scruples whatsoever about subverting the law once Henley was on trial. This also involved several Surrey residents in the squabbles of their local rulers, who instead of maintaining royal authority were disrupting the peace of the shire.

The long-standing feud between Roger Legh and John Scott over their wives' inheritance erupted again about this time. Most recently it had been at issue in the Court of Common Pleas. Conflicting claims to timber now further complicated the matter. For some time Lord Edmund Howard had supported Legh against Scott, for which Legh gave him a "great quantity of wood that was growing upon the ground in variance." Browne and Scott claimed that the timber belonged to Scott. In any case Howard assembled eighty carts and 200 men armed with staves and carried away the wood. Perhaps he saw this as just recompense, but Browne claimed that was "for displeasure that be bore to . . . Scott." Either way, it set the stage for more trouble at quarter sessions.

Predictably Scott sought Browne's support. Browne advised Scott to report the matter to the council, but Scott demurred, saying, "I dare not do so for fear of displeasure of my lord of Norfolk." Though Browne later claimed that he acted for "zeal and intent of justice and equity," he "labored" the sheriff and jury in Scott's behalf, interfered with process serving, and appeared at quarter sessions at Scott's special request to speak for him. Roger Legh sought support from Lord Edmund Howard and Sir John Legh. Howard eventually admitted to illegally "bearing and maintaining" Roger Legh but denied that there had been a riot, while Sir John Legh insisted that he and Howard "have owed our lawful favor to . . . Roger because [he] is near kinsman."

Browne, Howard, and Legh's protestations of good intent did not impress Attorney General John Fitzjames, who later complained that because of the bearing and maintenance in this case "much vexation and trouble have grown amongst the king's subjects in . . . Surrey" and that the "matter hath caused much variance and debate in the said shire." Perhaps this is why Lord Edmund Howard was in the Fleet prison about this time "as convict[ed] of unlawful bearing by his own confession." The Howards were not immune from punishment—in May 1516 Edmund's brother, the 2nd Earl of Surrey, was "put out of the council chamber . . . indicted before the King's Bench, and also called before the Star Chamber for keeping retainers." But Lord Edmund was not in prison for long, for he found too much time to stir up trouble. His father the Duke of Norfolk's influence doubtless secured a quick release.

Another focus of factional strife was a 1516 debt dispute between John Russell, backed by Browne, and Thomas Powell, backed by Lord Edmund and Sir John. Russell obtained a writ to seize Powell's goods as payment. Sheriff William Ashburnham's officers and servants attempted to execute the writ at Ewell but met forcible resistance from thirty or forty armed men, possibly including six of Lord Edmund's servants. As Ashburnham's men approached, Powell's servant Ellis "bade them come upon their peril." Apparently finding themselves outnumbered, Ashburnham's men left without executing the writ.

Russell procured an indictment against Powell and the other rioters at quarter sessions in Southwark. Lord Edmund, who was sitting on the bench, claimed that the goods Russell sought were not Powell's but belonged to his servant Ellis. Henry Saunders, a JP from Ewell, disagreed and convinced Sir William Fitzwilliam that he was right. However, he provoked vocal disagreement from Sir John Legh. Later Saunders and another JP disgustedly told Fitzwilliam "they knew well enough [that the matter] would not be found as long as some were on the inquest that were, for they would say none otherwise than . . . Sir John Legh would have them." Apparently this was true—Powell went free, though clearly guilty.

Undaunted, Russell got the jury at the next quarter sessions in

Guildford to bring a similar indictment. Powell's servant Ellis in turn procured an indictment of trespass against Russell. Sir John Legh threatened Russell with a fine for "unfitting words," while Sir Matthew Browne spoke in Russell's favor. Browne further claimed that Lord Edmund's servants had assisted Powell at the riot. Howard then threatened Browne and Henry Saunders "that if any of them would so say, he would make it good upon their flesh that they both lied." Howard later admitted persuading the jury to find Powell not guilty but denied any wrongdoing. In fact, Howard, Legh, and Browne all were charged with maintenance, bearing, and/or embracery "in let of justice and in derogation of the king's laws."

This was not all. Sometime during the proceedings, perhaps following the Guildford quarter sessions, "a commission from the king" directed Lord Edmund, Legh, and one of their adherents, James Betts, to examine the matter between Russell and Powell. Thus the case was assigned, perhaps due to the Duke of Norfolk's influence, to JPs sure to favor Powell. The case provides one other example of improper official behavior. The council called the case up to Westminster and summoned a jury, but Browne "did labor the jury that they should not appear."

The continuing trouble probably accounts for changes that Wolsey made in the shire in 1517 and 1518. He took the unusual step of appointing two Surrey men in consecutive years as sheriff of Surrey and Sussex, Sir John Gaynesford in 1517 and Sir Nicholas Carew in 1518. He also made several new appointments to the commission of the peace designed to increase royal—and his own—influence. But matters got worse.

For Wolsey the last straw came in 1519. He had been plagued by disorder since his rise to power. In 1516 he intervened in Kent to stop violent feuding between the Guldefords and the Nevilles. In 1517 there was a major riot in Southampton and the notorious Evil May Day Riot in London. That year there was even a lunatic threat on Henry VIII and Wolsey's lives by a group of prisoners in the Marshalsea, several of whom were Southwark yeomen.

Judicial corruption and factional strife flared up in Surrey again in 1519. On 11 April Sir Matthew Browne and ten others, "for despite and displeasure that he bore to Thomas, Duke of Norfolk," destroyed the latter's rabbit warrens at Reigate. Recent scholarship on the history of crime has shown that this was a classic form of social protest against one's superiors in medieval and early modern England. Thus it was not only an act of wanton destruction but a calculated insult against Norfolk as well.

Presumably the rabbits were not happy about this.

Following this episode, Browne "for the bearing and maintaining of his . . . misdemeanor," appeared at the next quarter sessions at Reigate on 3 May with an unlawful assembly of servants, tenants, and friends, already having intimidated witnesses into staying away. There Sir Matthew "did multiply and spake many hasty words insomuch that Sir Henry Wyatt . . . desired him to keep silence and hold his peace or else he would rise from the bench and go his way." But Browne "would not order himself accordingly thereafter," boasting "that if such things that he had done concerning the said warren were to do he would do the same again and . . . he was sorry that he had done no more than he did."

Sometime between the Reigate quarter sessions and early July 1519 Wolsey began inquiries in Surrey concerning disruptive factionalism, obstruction of justice, failure to enforce various statutes, and illegal retaining. The council examined a number of Surrey JPs, including Sir Henry Wyatt, Sir John Gaynesford, Robert Wintershull, John Scott, Sir John Legh, Roger Legh, Henry Tingilden, and Lord Edmund Howard. Wolsey also obtained from Sir William Fitzwilliam a lengthy list of "misdemeanors contrary to the king's laws and statutes." And he ordered Sir Matthew Browne and Sir John Legh to produce certificates of the misdoings in Surrey. Neither went overboard to incriminate himself, but Legh's apparently was satisfactory, while Browne perjured himself. Wolsey also required Browne to certify "the names of all such persons as were warned by him or by his commandment to come to the said sessions at Reigate" that followed his destruction of Norfolk's rabbit warren. But Browne failed to give the council a complete list. The council caught on and examined others, who confessed that Browne had commanded them to attend the quarter sessions. Thus Sir Matthew added a second perjury to the charges against him.

Early in July Attorney General Fitzjames filed three bills of complaint in the Court of Star Chamber against Sir Matthew Browne, Sir John Legh, and Lord Edmund Howard. According to Edward Hall's *Chronicle*, the court also proceeded against John Scott, which seems reasonable, but there is no other evidence of this. On behalf of the king, Fitzjames showed "how that the good rule and execution of justice in the county of Surrey hath been of long time letted and misused by the great maintenance, embracery, and bearing . . . in many and diverse matters, as well between the king our sovereign lord and diverse of his subjects, as between party and party, to the great hurt and damage of the king's subjects and in contempt of our said sovereign lord and contrary to diverse statutes thereof made."

The three bills of complaint then went on to specific offenses. The Attorney General charged Browne with maintaining Henley and laboring to obtain his acquittal for murder; maintaining John Scott against Roger Legh; maintaining one Dandy, indicted of forcible entry, and preventing the restoration of his victim's property; maintaining John Russell against Thomas Powell; destroying the Duke of Norfolk's rabbit warrens in Reigate; and two counts of perjury. He charged Lord Edmund Howard and Sir John Legh with maintaining Roger Legh against Scott, Powell against Russell, one William White against Sir Matthew Browne, a Surrey priest against a Lady Rede, and one Codington against the queen, Catherine of Aragon. He also charged Howard with riotous assembly in taking wood claimed by Scott and Roger Legh. He further noted that Howard had confessed retaining twenty persons since 1515 or 1516 "for the execution of his office of provost marshal." The investigation turned up a great deal more evidence of official misconduct. Browne made numerous other allegations against Howard and Legh, though it is impossible to say whether these were real or contrived since the court did not proceed on them.

The council was concerned that Surrey JPs were failing to enforce statutes concerning laborers, vagabonds, apparel, and games. Wolsey was worried about retaining in Surrey, as well as in other shires. This involved noblemen giving their livery to retainers who essentially became private armies. Sir William Fitzwilliam's report revealed numerous instances, though only Lord Edmund was officially charged. Of course the Tudors tolerated retaining as a necessary evil, essential for military readiness, so it was not always prosecuted. But events recounted here show that several Surrey magnates had no qualms about using armed bands of followers to pursue personal aims. It simply turned out that most of these incidents were comprehended under charges of riot rather than retaining. Probably because Browne, Howard, and Legh all served the king in a military capacity, the government for the most part left the issue of retaining alone. As the actual charges show, Wolsey's main concern was with faction and maladministration of justice.

Next Browne and Legh filed written answers in which they denied or tried to explain away the charges against them. However, the Attorney General reasserted their guilt in his written replications. Howard, on the other hand, admitted his guilt, with some qualifications, to all of the charges except maintaining White and retaining men as provost marshal, which he explained away. For the rest he submitted himself to the king "as he hath done before" and "in most humble wise" besought Wolsey and the council "to be mediators to the king's highness for pardon," which he probably received.

On 10 and 11 July Attorney General Fitzjames re-examined Browne before the council on eleven interrogatories, but again Browne denied the charges against him. Fitzjames also re-examined Sir Henry Wyatt, Sir John Gaynesford, Robert Wintershull, John Scott, Sir John Legh, Roger Legh, Henry Tingilden, and Lord Edmund Howard. They added little to what was already known, though Howard did manage another charge of maintenance and bearing against Browne. About the same time the council administered further interrogatories to Browne, Sir John Legh, and Howard's servant Newdigate concerning Henry Henley's murder of Shepherd.

With the final hearing on 28 October the case reached a climax that, in terms of Star Chamber procedure, was quite spectacular. Just the day before Wolsey had delivered his second "notable oration" to the council on the administration of justice, in which he desired "the indifferent ministration of justice to all persons as well high as low." The oration embodied Wolsey's twin aims of making justice more equitable and humbling the mighty of the realm, as did the proceedings of the following day. The Cardinal was about to put the wrath of the king on display.

On 28 October, as John Guy notes, "Henry VIII was sitting in person with forty of the council, and timetable was arranged by Wolsey as a dramatic show of law enforcement." To begin with, Sir William Bulmer submitted himself for having worn the Duke of Buckingham's livery in the royal presence after having sworn loyalty to the king. Henry delivered a scathing denunciation to the unfortunate Bulmer, after which he pardoned him "at the intercession of the council on their knees." Then the king and council turned to Surrey matters. Sir Matthew Browne and Sir John Legh came into what must still have been a very heated atmosphere. First, the king and council fined Browne and Legh £100 apiece, an enormous sum in the sixteenth century. Then they ordered both men to be incarcerated in the Fleet Prison. Henry, Wolsey, and the council now had accomplished their purpose, however, so it was time for another round of good cop/bad cop. After Browne and Legh's "submission and intercession," Henry pardoned both. This was logical, for Browne and Legh—like Lord Edmund Howard—were prominent among Surrey's natural rulers and could be valuable servants to the Crown if only the king and cardinal could intimidate them into performing their duties in an upright manner. Having humbled them, Henry and Wolsey evidently assumed that they would do so—all three remained on the commission of the peace. Yet, as in all his efforts to improve the administration of justice, Wolsey was only partly successful. There were no more outbreaks of disorder in Surrey like those of 1515-19, but factional hostility continued.

Late in 1519 Sir John Legh got into a dispute with Thomas Hegger of East Betchworth over lands in West Cheam, control of which the previous owners had given to Sir Matthew Browne and his son Henry. Legh also encouraged several others to file a lawsuit against Browne. On the other hand Browne and John Scott persuaded Hegger in 1521 to enter a bill of complaint in Star Chamber against Legh, who replied that the bill "was feigned of malice by the means and excitation of John Scott of Camberwell . . . and other enemies," a standard response in such cases, but apparently true in this instance. On 14 November the council examined and then dismissed the plaintiffs against Browne, who deposed that, without any instigation from Legh, they had sought his "good help and furtherance." Hegger and Legh were dismissed after the former "openly desired to have his case determined at the common law." Most interesting of all is that Hegger "openly denied" a section of his own bill of complain which alleged that he had been imprisoned by Richard Hill, undersheriff of Surrey and Sussex and Legh's servant. Hegger stated that "he was not privy that it was so expressed in the said complaint." Obviously Scott and Browne had doctored the charges in Hegger's bill in order to create difficulties for Legh.

Faction thus lived on. The wrath of the king in Star Chamber had driven it underground. Furthermore, Wolsey followed this up by appointing a number of new JPs in the 1520s. But like Henry VII, Wolsey refused to risk a purge of local JPs like Browne, Scott, Howard, and Legh. He did not repeat Richard III's mistake of denying the natural rulers of the shire their place on the bench. In fact, the relative peace within Surrey during the remainder of Wolsey's ascendancy owed considerably to the changing relationships among local JPs and not just to steps the central government had taken. Sir Matthew Browne and John Scott benefitted enormously from Sir William Fitzwilliam's growing influence. Scott became sheriff in 1520, and by 1522 Browne had risen in precedence about Sir John Legh on the commission of the peace. Several new JPs appointed in the 1520s had connections to Fitzwilliam and Browne. At the same time the Howard-Legh alliance gradually disintegrated. Two allies, James Betts and Roger Legh, dropped off the commission in 1520 and 1522 respectively. Lord Edmund Howard and Sir John Legh had a falling out. By the time Legh died in 1524, he distrusted Howard enough to provide in his will that Lord Edmund and his wife Joyce (former wife of Sir John's brother Ralph) should have no inheritance from him if they meddled with the execution of his will. Neither did Legh's wife trust Howard.

The most likely reason was Howard's decline into abject poverty, which probably led him to ask for money. Certainly his impoverishment effectively removed him from participation in Surrey politics, for by 1527 he was so deeply indebted that he had to hide from his creditors and narrowly escaped being arrested. On top of that he suffered from kidney stones. What he clearly needed was some modern medicine. What he got— a remedy that he received from Lady Lisle—was a mixed blessing, to say the least. Here is what he wrote after trying it out.

Madam, so it is I have this night after midnight taken your medicine, for the which I heartily thank you, for it hath done me much good, and hath caused the stone to break so that now I void much gravel. But for all that, your said medicine hath done me little honesty, for it made me piss my bed this night, for the which my wife hath sore beaten, and saying it is children's parts to bepiss their bed. Ye have made me such a pisser that I dare not this day go abroad.

The days of the Howard-Legh alliance came to an end in 1524 with the deaths of Sir John Legh and Thomas Howard 2nd Duke of Norfolk. Legh's death ended his family's participation in country politics. Sir John had no sons and his heir, son of his brother Ralph, never obtained a place on the bench. The new 3rd Duke of Norfolk (formerly Earl of Surrey) was the implacable enemy of Wolsey, who gave him little opportunity to influence affairs in Surrey. Howard influence did not just vanish, but it was for the time being in eclipse. Thus, Browne, Scott, and their allies had less to fear from the Howards and were not so much inclined to harass their rivals, to flout the authority of the new Duke of Norfolk, and to violate the law for personal gain. True, the old enmity did not die. The Howards increased their power in Surrey in the years just after Wolsey's fall in 1529 and periodically thereafter, particularly in the person of William Lord Howard of Effingham. Sir Matthew Browne and his supporters continued to feud with them off and on until his death in 1557. And a new Protestant alliance emerged to oppose the Howards following the Reformation.

At no time, however, did factional strife in Tudor Surrey lead to the sort of disorder, maladministration of justice, and disrespect for authority among the JPs that had been characteristic of the first decade of Wolsey's ascendancy. The wrath of the king had the desired effect. On the other hand, this case demonstrates—as does the entire Tudor period—that there were limits to royal authority. Though changes in the Surrey commission of the peace were frequent, at no time in the Tudor period was there a thoroughgoing purge. All Tudor monarchs and their ministers found it necessary, in order to preserve royal authority, to give places on the bench to those local men regarded as the natural rulers of the shire. While Wolsey could modify the overall character of the Surrey commission of the peace by appointing powerful courtiers and councilors loyal to him and to the king, he could not afford to alienate the shire by denying those who were its natural rulers a place on the bench. Herein lay a fundamental dilemma for the Tudors and their ministers. Those men best able to enforce royal authority at the local level were also those most capable of undermining proper deference to the Crown and the laws in the shire through their failure to maintain order and administer justice and by their own disregard for legality. The Tudors struggled, usually with success, to make this faulty system of local government work. But the difficulties the Stuart dynasty faced in the seventeenth century—civil war, regicide, and revolution—clearly show that the problem of securing deference to royal authority in the shires did not go away.

Suggestions for Further Reading

John Bellamy, *The Tudor Law of Treason* (1979); Peter Clark, *English Provincial Society from the Reformation to the Revolution: Religion, Politics, and Society in Kent 1500-1640* (1977); G.R. Elton, *Star Chamber Stories* (1974); Stella Fletcher, *Cardinal Wolsey: A Life in Renaissance Europe* (2009); Louise Gill, *Richard III and Buckingham's Rebellion* (1999); S.J. Gunn and P.G. Lindley, *Cardinal Wolsey: Church, State, and Art* (1991); Gunn, *Charles Brandon, Duke of Suffolk, c.1484-1545* and *Early Tudor Government 1485-1558* (1995); John Guy, *The Cardinal's Court: The Impact of Thomas Wolsey in Star Chamber* (1977); Peter Gwyn, *The King's Cardinal: The Rise and Fall of Cardinal Wolsey* (1990); Barbara J. Harris, *Edward Stafford, Third Duke of Buckingham 1478-1521* (1986); David Head, *The Ebbs and Flows of Fortune: The Life of Thomas Howard, Third Duke of Norfolk* (1995); J.R. Lander, *English Justices of the Peace 1461-1509* (1989); Diarmaid MacCulloch, *Suffolk and the Tudors: Politics and Religion in an English County 1500-1600* (1986); H.C.G. Matthew and Brian Harrison, eds., *Oxford Dictionary of National Biography*, 60 vols. (2004); Helen Miller, *Henry VIII and the English Nobility* (1986); Carole Rawcliffe, *The Staffords, Earls of Stafford and Dukes of Buckingham 1394-1521* (1978); William B. Robison, "The Justices of the Peace of Surrey in National and Country Politics, 1483-1570," Ph.D. dissertation, Louisiana State University (1983); J.J. Scarisbrick, *Henry VIII* (1969); David Starkey, *Henry: Virtuous Prince* (2008) and *The Reign of Henry VIII: Personalities and Politics* (1985).

2010 PREQUEL
WHO KILLED THE GREAT PUMPKIN?

This film purports to explain why the Great Pumpkin never appeared to Linus van Pelt and features a couple of really moronic songs. Watch the video at https://myspace.com/headongoolah/videos and hear the songs on the CD *Show Tunes* by Headongoolah (which is me before Impaired Faculties).

SCREEN	The Peanuts kids trick-or-treating.
VOICE	Halloween is a happy occasion for most people if occasionally disappointing for a few.
SCREEN	Charlie Brown's "I got a rock."
SCREEN	Linus
VOICE	But for Linus van Pelt it has more sinister connotations. Every year he waits in vain for the Great Pumpkin in the most sincere pumpkin patch he can find. But Linus van Pelt has never seen anything except . . .
SCREEN	Snoopy.
VOICE	. . . a demented beagle.
SCREEN	Cartoon pumpkin patch
VOICE	Why hasn't the Great Pumpkin appeared? The chilling answer is murder. But why? And . . .
SCREEN	Who Killed the Great Pumpkin?
VOICE	. . . who killed the Great Pumpkin?
SCREEN	Map of southeastern Louisiana
VOICE	Our story begins in southeast Louisiana in . . .
SCREEN	Interstate sign for Pumpkin Center
VOICE	. . . the town of Pumpkin Center . . .
SCREEN	A pumpkin
VOICE	. . . where a little pumpkin named Peter grew up. At the first frost he became demoralized by thoughts of death at

the impending harvest, changed his name to Petey Rotten, and . . .

SCREEN	The Sex Pumpkins
VOICE	. . . joined a nihilistic punk rock band called the Sex Pumpkins . . .
SCREEN	The Sex Pumpkins
MUSIC	[Excerpt from "God Save the Queen"]
	No future, no future
SCREEN	Vomiting pumpkin
VOICE	. . . where he became famous for vomiting on audience members.
SCREEN	Pumpkin
VOICE	But remarkably, Peter survived and, in a reaction to his previous mood of doom, abandoned himself to the debauchery of disco, performing with the stage name . . .
SCREEN	Pump Daddy
	[Caption: Pump Daddy]
VOICE	. . . Pump Daddy.
SCREEN	Pump Daddy in suave outfit, under a disco ball, singing
	[Caption with lyrics]
MUSIC	I'm too sexy for my rind
	Too sexy for my vine
	Too sexy all the time
	So sexy
SCREEN	Disco record explosion
VOICE	Soon enough, though, Peter realized that disco sucks and turned to hip-hop, changing his name once again to . . .
SCREEN	Def Pumpkin in hip-hop outfit
	[Caption: Def Pumpkin]
NARR	Def Pumpkin
SCREEN	Def Pumpkin with subjects suggested by the lyrics

CAPTION   Lyrics [below]
MUSIC   Don't be a chump with the Def Pumpkin
Get off your hump with the Def Pumpkin
You can do the bump with the Def Pumpkin
Go to the dump with the Def Pumpkin

You can play trumpets with the Def Pumpkin
Pick up strumpets with the Def Pumpkin
Have tea and crumpets with the Def Pumpkin
Even use pumpets with the Def Pumpkin

A pumpet is a ball used to ink type

You can be a Flump
Pray like a frump
Act like a grump
Sit by a clump

Take a flying jump with the Def Pumpkin
Sing about a lump with the Def Pumpkin
You can have the mumps with the Def Pumpkin
Be a mugwump with the Def Pumpkin

Yell at a Bumpus with the Def Pumpkin
Raise a rumpus with the Def Pumpkin
Be callithumped with the Def Pumpkin
Get gazumped with the Def Pumpkin

To be gazumped is to be cheated in a real estate deal

You can work a pump
Even a sump pump
You can get plump
Show off your rump

Be in a slump with the Def Pumpkin
Get on a stump with the Def Pumpkin
Behave like a sumph with the Def Pumpkin
Go out and thump with the Def Pumpkin

Tump sumpin' over with the Def Pumpkin
Yell at the ump with the Def Pumpkin
You can be a wump with the Def Pumpkin
Buy yourself a zump with the Def Pumpkin

A "zump" is a sex toy. No, really.

You can galumph
You can harrumph
You can say humph
You can triumph

You can be a Schlump with the Def Pumpkin
Or Professor Klump with the Def Pumpkin
Be Helen Crump with the Def Pumpkin
Or Mr Schwump with the Def Pumpkin

You can be Jhumpa with the Def Pumpkin
Or an Umpa Lumpa with the Def Pumpkin
Be Donald Trump with the Def Pumpkin
Or Forrest Gump with the Def Pumpkin

Life is like a box of pumpkin seeds

SCREEN	Flying pumpkin
VOICE	Then one day Peter discovered that he could fly! Once again he changed his name, this time to the Great Pumpkin, and joined the Guild of Nocturnal Gift Bringers, along with . . .
SCREEN	Santa
VOICE	. . . Santa Claus . . .
SCREEN	The Easter Bunny
VOICE	. . . the Easter Bunny . . .
SCREEN	The Tooth Fairy
VOICE	. . . and the Tooth Fairy . . .
SCREEN	Forrest

[Caption: Barbara Forrest, author of *Creationism's Trojan Pumpkin*]

VOICE   Of course skeptics dismiss tales of flying pumpkins and nocturnal gift bringers, for example, Dr. Barbara Forrest, author of *Creationism's Trojan Pumpkin*, who blames the Intelligent Design movement for perpetuating such myths.

SCREEN   Pictures of Santa, et. al.

VOICE   In any case, the Great Pumpkin died before achieving recognition equal to his more famous colleagues.

SCREEN   Hitler, Stalin, Mao, Manson, Don Corleone, Saruman, Voldemort, Darth Vader

VOICE   In seeking the killer, the authorities have investigated the usual suspects.

SCREEN   Osama

VOICE   Many say the murder was part of Osama bin Laden's campaign against decadent Western vegetables.

SCREEN   Saddam

VOICE   Others blame Saddam Hussein's Weapons of Mass Depumkinization.

SCREEN   Linus

VOICE   Some even cast a suspicious eye on a vengeful and unbalanced Linus van Pelt.

SCREEN   Lucy

VOICE   His sister Lucille, known to have anger management issues, is not beyond suspicion either.

SCREEN   Charlie Brown

VOICE   Meanwhile, conspiracy theorists think frustrated place kicker Charles Brown tried to frame Ms. van Pelt to get even for her repeated practical jokes.

SCREEN   Sally

VOICE   Nor do investigators rule out Brown's sister Sally, who may blame her troubled romantic relationship with Linus van

Pelt on his fanatical devotion to the Great Pumpkin.

SCREEN   Gallagher

VOICE   Another suspect is Gallagher, a psychotic comic with a history of senseless violence against vegetables. Those who believe he acted alone accept the single mallet theory of . . .

SCREEN   Pigpen

VOICE   . . . the official Pigpen Commission, which claims a lone assassin launched his attack from the Garden Tool Depository.

SCREEN   Kurtz
[Caption: Michael Kurtz, author of *Slime of the Century*]

VOICE   But Michael Kurtz, in *Slime of the Century*, contends that the famed Zucchini Film reveals a patch of uncultivated ground known as the Grassy Row, which concealed a second attacker.

SCREEN   Sanders
[Caption: Randy Sanders, author of *Mighty Peculiar Punkins*]

VOICE   Randy Sanders, in *Mighty Peculiar Punkins*, blames Southern hostility to divergent species.

SCREEN   Hyde
[Caption: Samuel Hyde, author of *Pistols and Pumpkins*]

VOICE   Samuel Hyde, author of *Pistols and Pumpkins*, maintains that the Great Pumpkin wandered into a local feud in Bloody Tangipahoa Parish, where he was brutally bushwhacked by a pair of local toughs . . .

SCREEN   Old John
[Caption: Old John]
[Old John, played by George Sanchez, recently had featured in a play about the West Florida Rebellion at Southeastern Louisiana University]

VOICE   . . . the mysterious Old John and . . .

SCREEN   Elmer Fudd shooting a shotgun

VOICE	. . . his trigger-happy partner Elmer Fudd, here in this Southern heart of darkness.
SCREEN	Kurtz
VOICE	The horror! The horror!
SCREEN	Hollywood sign
VOICE	Depictions of this sordid murder are commonplace in popular culture. Charles Brown's cousin . . .
SCREEN	Dan Brown
	[Caption: Dan Brown, author of *The Da Vinci Gourd*]
VOICE	. . . Dan suggests in his novel, *The Da Vinci Gourd*, that the Roman Catholic Church suppressed the story that the Great Pumpkin is descended from the gourd used to fashion the Holy Grail . . .
SCREEN	The painting
VOICE	. . . basing this on a clue in Leonardo Da Vinci's *The Last Supper.*
SCREEN	Oliver Stone
	[Caption: Oliver Stone, Director of *Agent Orange and the Pumpkin Platoon Plot*]
VOICE	Meanwhile, Oliver Stone is working on a Vietnam-related film entitled *Agent Orange and the Pumpkin Platoon Plot*, while at the same time . . .
SCREEN	Mel Gibson
	[Caption: Mel Gibson, Director of *Lethal Pumpkin Passion and the Maya Papaya: The Juice Did It*]
VOICE	. . . Mel Gibson has a rival production, *Lethal Pumpkin Passion and the Mayan Papaya: The Juice Conspiracy* . . .
SCREEN	Michael Moore
	[Caption: Michael Moore, Director of Fahrenheit 350: Pumpkin Pie in the Corporate Sty]
VOICE	. . . Michael Moore blames capitalism in *Fahrenheit 350: Pumpkin Pie in the Corporate Sty* . . .

SCREEN   Picture of Glenn Beck
                 [Caption: Glenn Beck, Author of *Liberals Killed Gandhi and the Great Pumpkin*]

VOICE   . . . and Glenn Beck has responded with *Liberals Killed Gandhi and the Great Pumpkin.*

SCREEN   V for Vegetable Vigilante
                 [Caption: *V for Vegetable Vigilante*]

VOICE   Finally, V for Vegetable Vigilante sets the slaying in a futuristic Britain . . .

SCREEN   Fierce Great Pumpkin with Hitler moustache

VOICE   . . . where the Great Pumpkin is portrayed as a totalitarian dictator . . .

SCREEN   Eggplant in V mask

VOICE   . . . assassinated by a renegade eggplant obsessed with . . .

SCREEN   The gunpowder plot portrait

VOICE   . . . Guy Fawkes and the Gunpowder Plot of 1605.

SCREEN   Robison

VOICE   In the present day the murder remains unsolved . . .

SCREEN   Robison

MUSIC   Who, who killed the Great Pumpkin
                Who, who killed the Great Pumpkin

SCREEN   Robison
                 [Caption: Justice for the Great Pumpkin, Small Non-Sequential Bills, Fayard 335C]

MUSIC   Continues in background

VOICE   Still, you can help bring the killer to justice by leaving cash in small non-sequential bills in a paper bag outside the door of Fayard Hall 335C. Or you can bring money backstage later.

SCREEN   Igor from *Young Frankenstein*

IGOR   Act casual.

SCREEN   Snoopy rises from pumpkin patch.

STAGE   Lights come up.   Robison rises from behind podium. Presentation begins.

2010 LECTURE
GUY FAWKES, GUNPOWDER PLOT, AND
THE GREAT PUMPKIN: MID-AUTUMN
MAYHEM, MURDER, AND MYSTERY

Today we examine two cases of mid-autumn mayhem, murder and mystery, one involving Guy Fawkes and the Gunpowder Plot and the other the Great Pumpkin. You have just seen a documentary video that seeks to answer the question, who killed the Great Pumpkin? And now here is another question: have you seen the movie *V for Vendetta* (2006)? It depicts a futuristic Britain with a totalitarian government resembling the Nazi regime of the 1930s. The character V (Hugh Weaving) plots to blow up Parliament, and the movie ends rather spectacularly with the destruction of the Houses of Parliament.

Whence came this movie?

It is based on a ten-part graphic novel by writer Alan Moore and artist David Lloyd that Warrior Comics and DC published in 1982-85.

Whence came this comic?

It is based on the Gunpowder Plot of 1605, in which a group of thirteen radical Catholic conspirators plotted to blow up Parliament and along with it King James VI and I and all the bishops and nobles in the House of Lords and all the elected members of the House of Commons when Parliament convened on November 5. Among the thirteen was Guy Fawkes, whose image is the basis for the mask that V wears in *V for Vendetta*. So what is going on here? Before I answer that, let me offer a few disclaimers. This lecture deals with violence and religious intolerance. It is not intended to be anti-Catholic. It is not intended to be anti-Protestant. It does not advocate blowing up public buildings. Now on we go.

James Stuart, born in 1566, became King James VI of Scotland in 1567 and King James I of England in 1603. In 1605 he was the main target of the Gunpowder Plot. Why? To answer that, we must start with royal genealogy and religion. In 1485 Henry Tudor defeated Richard III at the Battle of Bosworth Field and established the Tudor dynasty as Henry VII (1485-1509). He married Elizabeth York, daughter of Edward IV (1461-83), and the couple had four surviving children. Henry VIII (1509-47) succeeded his father, famously had six wives, broke away from Roman Catholic Church and thereby began the English Reformation, and was followed on the throne by his three legitimate children, the Protestant Edward VI (1547-53), the Catholic Mary I (1553-58), and the Protestant

163

Elizabeth I (1558-1603), all of whom died childless to that the Tudor line came to an end in 1603.

Henry VIII's older sister Margaret had three husbands of her own, the first two of whom are relevant to our story today. She first married Scotland's James IV (1488-1513) and gave birth to his son and heir, James V (1513-42), who in turn married Marie of Guise, by whom he fathered Mary Queen of Scots (1542-67). Margaret then married Archibald Douglas, Earl of Angus and gave birth to his daughter Margaret, who in turn married Matthew Stuart, Earl of Lennox and gave birth to his son, Henry Stuart, Lord Darnley. Mary took her first cousin Darnley as her second husband in 1565 and gave birth in 1566 to the future James VI and I, who thus was descended from Henry VII through both his mother and father. When Darnley was murdered in 1567 and the Catholic Mary married the man most likely responsible, the Earl of Bothwell, the Protestant Scots nobility forced her to abdicate. Facing an armed revolt, she fled to England, where she expected to received aid from her cousin Elizabeth. Instead the English queen kept her imprisoned for nineteen years before finally allowing her execution in 1587.

Meanwhile, Mary's son James became king and grew up in extraordinarily challenging circumstances. Civil war wracked his kingdom from 1568 to 1573, and his first three regents—the Earls of Moray (1568-70), Lennox (1570-71), and Mar (1571-72)—all were assassinated. The fourth, the Earl of Morton (1572-78) survived his ouster by Esmé Stuart (1578-83), only to be executed in 1581. The following year James was kidnapped in the so-called Ruthven Raid. After his escape he began his personal rule in 1583 but continued to face adversity. In 1587 his mother's execution made him the direct heir to the English throne, but in 1589-92 he had to deal with treason by the Earls of Angus, Errol, and Huntly, who were in a league with Philip II of Spain, in 1591-95 he faced threats from a new Earl of Bothwell, and in 1600 he confronted the Earl of Gowrie's conspiracy.

Earlier, in 1589, James married Anne of Denmark, who gave him three surviving children—Henry (1594-1612), the heir until his untimely death; Elizabeth (1596-1662) the future bride of Frederick V, Elector of the Palatinate of the Rhine; and Charles I (1600-49), the actual heir. The king developed quite a reputation as an intellectual, though critics later derided him as "the wisest fool in Christendom." He was a prolific author, publishing—among other things—*Daemonologie* (1597), a study prompted by his concerns about witchcraft, as well as *The Trew Law of Free Monarchies* (1598) and *Basilikon Doron* (1599), which argued in favor of divine right absolutism, a position that later put him at odds with the English Parliament.

When James became king of England in 1603, he inherited the seventy-year legacy of fluctuations in official religious policy that began with the English Reformation. Exactly seven decades earlier in 1533, Henry VIII had broken away from the Roman Catholic Church and established himself as Supreme Head of the Church of England; however, the doctrinal position of that institution relative to Catholicism and Protestantism remained ambiguous and in flux for the remainder of his reign. Under his son and heir, Edward VI, the Church became genuinely Protestant. However, after Edward's premature death at sixteen in 1553, his Catholic sister Mary I restored England's allegiance to Rome and married one of the leading Catholics in Europe, Philip of Spain, son of Holy Roman Emperor Charles V, whom he succeeded on the Spanish throne in 1556. When Mary died childless in 1558, her younger sister Elizabeth I—as Supreme Governor of the Church—reestablished Protestantism. However, the Elizabethan Settlement of religion did not really settle things, Elizabeth's own views remained unclear, and the moderate Calvinist Church of England that enjoyed her official approval encountered opposition from both Catholics and Puritans bent on further reform. James thus faced both the hope from each group that he would favor their position and the suspicion that he would not.

Elizabeth was a hard act for James to follow in England for several reasons. Despite the difficulties of her last decade, she remained popular, she had enjoyed a long and successful reign, and she was unequivocally English, just as James was indisputably a Scot, a strike against him from the outset. Not the least of James' problems was that he was uncertain until the very last whether he would succeed Elizabeth at all. The Treaty of Ayton, which in 1502 set the terms for Margaret Tudor's marriage to James IV, prohibited a Stuart succession; the Act of Succession of 1544 named no heir beyond Elizabeth; Henry VIII attempted via his will to bar the Stuarts from the English throne; and Elizabeth, though unmarried and childless, refused to name a successor. The main factors in his favor were that he was male, married, and had produced multiple heirs.

Complicating matters, though, was that Elizabethan England had faced a long series of Catholic threats, most of which were associated with James' mother, Mary Queen of Scots, until her death. Her unexpected arrival in England in 1568 came in the midst of the French Wars of Religion (1562-98) and the Dutch Revolt against Spain (1568-1648). It led to her imprisonment far from London and the royal court and a series of attempts to liberate her and place her on the throne. The first was the Northern Rebellion of 1569, followed by Pius V's bull *Regnans in Excelsis* excommunicating Elizabeth in 1570, the Ridolfi Plot of 1571, the infiltration of seminary priests beginning in 1574 and Jesuits in 1580, the Throckmorton Plot of 1583, the eruption of war with Spain in 1585, the Babington Plot of 1586, Mary's execution in 1587, the Spanish Armada in 1588, the Lopez Plot and the outbreak of Tyrone's Rebellion in Ireland in 1594, a second Armada in 1596, a third in 1597, the Poison Pommel Plot of 1598 (which involved Edward Squire and future Gunpowder Plotters Robert Catesby, Francis Tresham, Christopher Wright, and John Wright), and—though not purely a Catholic plot—the rebellion of Robert Devereux, 2nd Earl of Essex, in 1601 (which included Catesby, Tresham, and the Wrights, plus future plotters John Grant and Thomas Winter).

When Essex fell, one of those who benefited most was his rival, Robert Cecil, Elizabeth's secretary and the son of her longtime and most trusted minister, William Cecil, Lord Burghley, who died in 1598. This was very fortunate for James, as Cecil was a strong advocate for his candidacy as heir to the throne. The two of them engaged in a secret correspondence that helped to smooth the transition at Elizabeth's death. Cecil's aid was crucial as James, while the most obvious successor, had numerous rivals. One of the most prominent was his first cousin, Arbella Stuart, daughter of Darnley's brother Matthew Stuart, Earl of Lennox, and—like James—a great-great-grandchild of Henry VII through his elder daughter Margaret. Other great-great-grandchildren of Henry VII through his younger daughter Mary were Edward Seymour, Lord Beauchamp, grandson of Mary's elder daughter Frances, and Ferdinando Stanley, 5th Earl of Derby, grandson of Mary's younger daughter Eleanor. There were numerous other potential rivals among the English and foreign descendants of Edward III.

However, when Elizabeth died on 24 March 1603, Cecil had a horse and rider ready to deliver the news to James, who knew before most people in London. He was quickly proclaimed king, left Edinburgh on 5 April, and entered London on 7 May, receiving an enthusiastic welcome along the way. His coronation took place on 25 July. Such smooth sailing did not long continue. Though experienced and successful as king of Scotland, James could be arrogant and authoritarian, he was a profligate spender and his large family and Scottish entourage were expensive, he squandered both financial and political capital through the inflation of honors (his liberal distribution of titles), and his innate clumsiness and obsessive fear of assassination made him the object of ridicule. He inherited a government short of funds due to the recent economic depression and the expenses of war, feuded with Parliament over the extent of its role, and immediately faced difficulty over religion.

James was a devout Calvinist but vehemently disliked Presbyterians, who had been frequent antagonists in Scotland. He favored episcopacy, which put him at odds at with many Puritans, and though he disliked Catholicism, it was rumored that his wife Anne was a closet papist. However, prior to taking the English throne, he had been deliberately vague about his religious opinions, in order to discourage sectarian opposition from any quarter. The Anglo-Spanish War persisted for the moment. The French Religious Wars were temporarily in abeyance, but the tensions that would reignite them in 1624-29 remained alive. The Dutch Revolt continued until 1609, halted temporarily during the Twelve Years Truce, and resumed 1621-48. And in the Holy Roman Empire, the uneasy Peace of Augsburg that had kept peace between Catholics and Protestants there was beginning to crumble, with the outbreak of the Thirty Year War (1618-48) just fifteen years away.

Among James' fellow rulers, Henri IV of France was Catholic but a friend, Maurice of the Netherlands a Calvinist and a friend, Philip III of Spain a Catholic and at least initially a foe, and Emperor Rufolf II a Catholic but also highly eccentric, if not downright mad. In England he faced a host of expectations. Anglicans (Church of England moderates) wanted him to maintain the status quo, a position he favored. However, Catholics wanted at very least toleration, though some dared to hope for restoration of their faith. Puritans naturally appealed to him for further reform, and Presbyterians urged him to abolish episcopacy, to which he supposedly responded, "No bishop, no king." All but the Anglicans were to be disappointed.

Trouble was not long in coming. In June 1603 Cecil uncovered the Bye Plot, in which George Brooke and the Appellant priests William Clark and William Watson planned to kidnap the king and force him to repeal fines for recusancy (the refusal of Catholics to receive communion in an Anglican Church). All three plotters were executed. In fact, they were betrayed by a Jesuit rival Henry Garnet, who was later involved in the Gunpowder Plot. The investigation of the Bye Plot led Cecil to the Main Plot, in which Lord Cobham and Sir Walter Raleigh sought—with Spanish assistance—to replace James with Arbella Stuart, who reported them instead of cooperating in the plot.

When James arrived in England in 1603, Puritans presented him with what was known as the Millenary Petition because it supposedly had over 1,000 signatures. It called for further reform of the church. In January

1604 James convened the Hampton Court Conference to address English religion, but its actions disappointed both Puritans and Catholics. The Canons of 1604 reaffirmed existing belief and practice, which displeased both groups. The only positive development for Puritans was the plan for a new English translation of the Bible, completed in 1611 and subsequently known as the King James Bible. For Catholics there was nothing. Later, in May and June, English and Spanish diplomats met in the Somerset House Conference and agreed to the Treaty of London, which ended the Anglo-Spanish War. This further angered the Puritans, who regarded Catholic Spain as an irreconcilable enemy, and gave false hope to Catholics, who thought it signified a thaw in relations with the Crown.

Meanwhile, James summoned his first Parliament (1604-10), the first session of which (March-July 1604) witnessed disputes with the king over sovereignty, revenue, religion, and James' proposal for a Union of England and Scotland. Disappointed and angry, the king prorogued Parliament on 7 July. It was at this point that the Gunpowder Plot began to take shape. Its ringleader was not the more famous Guy Fawkes, but Robert Catesby, who in 1603 sent Fawkes, Thomas Winter, and Christopher Wright to Spain in an attempt to persuade Philip III to invade England. However, the Spanish king was eager for peace, and Pope Clement VIII opposed the plan as being too reckless. Therefore, Catesby began to plot without them.

The plot involved only a handful of especially fanatical Catholics. Their plan was to blow up Parliament on the day that it reconvened for a second session by renting an adjacent building, breaking into the cellar beneath the Houses of Parliament, and filling it with gunpowder. After the explosion killed the king, members of Parliament, the bishops, and the judges, there was to be an uprising in the Midlands that would place James' daughter, Princess Elizabeth, on the throne, where they might influence her to give more favorable treatment to Catholics. The plotters sought the involvement and protection of Henry Percy, 9th Earl of Northumberland, but although he was imprisoned afterward, it is unclear whether he was involved. It is also uncertain if their intended victims included Prince Henry and Prince Charles.

In February 1604, Catesby, an Oxford-educated Warwickshire Catholic, recruited two previous associates: John Wright, a Yorkshire Catholic, and Thomas Winter, a Worcestershire Catholic and veteran of the continental wars. Catesby sent Winter to Flanders to seek aid, and though he returned without it in April, he brought with him Fawkes, a Yorkshire Catholic who had fought with Spain against the Dutch and was an explosives expert. A fifth conspirator, Thomas Percy—second cousin of the Earl—joined the group at a meeting on 20 May at the Duck and Drake in London, and on 24 May he rented a house in London. Fawkes, posing as Percy's servant and using the name John Johnson, took up residence there. In October Robert Keyes joined the plot, to which Catesby's retainer Thomas Bates was privy by this time. But the plan was delayed by the outbreak of plague on Christmas Eve, which led the postponement of the opening of Parliament from February to October 1605.

On 25 March the plotters reconvened, with John Grant, a Warwickshire Catholic, plus Robert Winter and Christopher Wright joining them. In June the plotters rented the cellar next to that of Parliament, but between then and August they encountered several difficulties. Catesby revealed the plan to Father Henry Garnet, who opposed it. Still the plot went ahead, and by 20 July the plotters had thirty-six barrels of gunpowder in the cellar. But thanks to another round of plague, on 28 July the government postponed the opening of Parliament to 5 November. In August Fawkes discovered that the powder had decayed, and they had to acquire a new batch, which they hid in—of all places—a stack of firewood. Three new recruits—Suffolk Catholic Ambrose Rokewood on 29 September, Northamptonshire convert Sir Francis Tresham on 14 October, and Leicestershire convert Sir Everard Digby on 21 October—brought the number involved to an unlucky thirteen.

In October the plotters finalized the plan. Fawkes was to light the fuse and then flee to the continent, where he would explain their intentions to Catholics there, while the Midlands revolt installed Elizabeth as a puppet ruler. However, a new complication arose when the plotters, Percy especially, became concerned about the fate of Catholic members of the House of Lords, i.e., the Earls of Arundel and Northumberland and Lords Monteagle, Montague, Stourton, and Vaux. On October 26 Monteagle received an anonymous letter warning him to stay away from Parliament. He immediately showed it to Secretary of State Cecil, whom the king recently had created Earl of Salisbury. He in turn revealed its contents to two members of the Lords suspected of being papists, the Earls of Northampton and Worcester. Salisbury already had suspicions that the letter confirmed, but for the moment he bided his time so that he might learn more about the plot. Later that month Monteagle's servant Thomas Ward, a relative of the Wrights, warned Catesby, who accused Tresham of writing the letter, which he denied. The writer's identity remains uncertain, though the suspects include Monteagle and even Salisbury.

On Friday, 1 November, Salisbury showed the letter to James, who suspected "some stratagem of fire and powder." On Saturday, 2 November, the king discussed with the Privy Council and ordered that a search of Parliament be conducted on Monday, 4 November. Meanwhile, on 3 November, Catesby, Percy, and Thomas Winter had their final meeting. The next day Digby and a "hunting party" were at Dunchurch, ready to take Elizabeth, and Catesby, Bates, and John Wright arrived in the Midlands. Back in London, Percy gave Keyes a watch for Fawkes, and Rokewood collected swords. The king entrusted the search to the Earl of Suffolk, joined by Monteagle and the landlord John Whynniard. The first search revealed the firewood, but Fawkes told them it belonged to Percy. Unsatisfied, James order a second search led by Thomas Knyvet in the wee hours of the morning. This time they found Fawkes wearing a cloak, hats, boots, and spurs, carrying a lantern, matches, and the watch, and claiming to be John Johnson. Then the searchers found the gunpowder.

Thereupon, they arrested Fawkes and took him before the king. Percy and Christopher Wright fled, followed by Rokewood, and eventually they caught up with Catesby, Bates, Keyes, and John Wright. All went to Ashby St. Ledgers, where they met Robert Winter, except for Keyes, who headed for Huddington Court, where Thomas Winter met him. The other six plotters went on to Dunchurch. Catesby wanted to put up a fight and lied to Digby that James and Salisbury were dead. They then headed west, robbed Warwick Castle for supplies and Norbrook for weapons. Catesby sent Bates to deliver a letter to Garnet while they made their way to the home of Stephen Littleton in Staffordshire. There an accident with gunpowder burned Catesby, Grant, and Rokewood. On 8 November the Worcestershire sheriff Richard Walsh and 200 men killed Catesby, Percy, and the Wrights, wounded and captured Rokewood and Thomas Winter along with Grant, and then apprehended Bates, Digby and Keyes. On 12 November Tresham was captured and on 9 January 1606 Littleton and Robert Winter. Northumberland found himself under house arrest.

Meanwhile, on 6 November Chief Justice John Popham interrogated Rokewood's servants and got the names of several plotters. Fawkes was moved to the Tower, where he was tortured and confessed on 7-9 November. Between November and January Attorney General Sir Edward Coke conducted an investigation that culminated in a trial on 26 January in Star Chamber, where the plotters were convicted of treason and sentenced to be hanged, drawn, and quartered. Bates, Digby, Grant, and Robert Winter died on 30 January and Fawkes, Keys, Rokewood, and Thomas Winter the following day. The Jesuits with links to the plot were arrested at Hindlip Hall, and in April and May Garnet, Humphrey Littleton,

Edward Oldcorne, John Winter, and layman Ralph Ashley were executed. Northumberland was in the Tower until 1621, and Lords Mordaunt and Stourton until 1608, when they moved to the Fleet Prison.

The legacy of the Gunpowder Plot includes the punitive Popish Recusants Act of 1606; a persistent fear of Popish Plots for the remainder of the century; a bevy of conspiracy theories, including one blaming Salisbury for instigating the whole thing; possibly William Shakespeare's *Macbeth*, according to some critics; a humorous political poster exhorting the electorate, "Vote for Guy Fawkes, the only man ever to enter Parliament with honest intentions"; and a bad television movie, *Gunpowder Treason and Plot* (2004), starring Clémence Poésy (better known as Fleur Delacour) as Mary Queen of Scots, Robert Carlyle (better known as Hitler) as James, and Michael Fassbender (better known as Lieutenant Archie Hicox) as Fawkes.

The most notable legacy is Bonfire Night, the perfect replacement for Halloween, the eve of All Saints Day, a pre-Reformation Catholic holiday that Puritans sought to eliminate. In January 1606 Edward Montagu introduced into Parliament "An Act for a public Thanksgiving to Almighty God every year on the fifth day of November." It applied to every church in England and remained in the Anglican Book of Common Prayer until 1859. It acquired additional weight with the Glorious Revolution, when the Protestant William of Orange landed in England on 5 November 1688 to oust the Catholic James II. He became William III (1688-1702) and his wife—James' daughter—Mary II (1688-94), preserving the Protestant succession and leading in 1689 to adoption of the Act of Toleration and the Bill of Rights. Under Queen Anne (1702-14), the Henry Sacheverell Affair linked 1605, 1649 and 1688 in the minds of many Protestant Englishmen. Protestant hatred of the Catholic Stuarts increased with the Jacobite Rebellions of 1715 (led by James II's son, James Edward the 'Old Pretender') and 1745 (led by James Edward's son, Bonnie Prince Charlie).

The Act of Succession of 1701 further guaranteed that the throne would pass to the Protestant Hanoverians, which eventually included George I (1714-27), George II (1727-60), George III (1760-1820), George IV (1820-30), William IV (1830-37), and Victoria (1837-1901, technically part of the House of Saxe-Coburg from her husband, Prince Albert). Perhaps because the Protestant succession was now secure, English anti-Catholicism gradually declined from the mid-eighteenth century. After about 1760 there were no further prosecutions for recusancy. Though the Catholic Relief Act of 1778—loosening restrictions on Catholic ownership of land and service in the army—provoked the foundation of the Protestant Association in 1779 and the Gordon Riots in 1780, the act stood, there were no further major anti-Catholic disturbances, and a 1791 Catholic Relief Act broadened the legislation to include the law, schools, and religion. Though William Pitt the Younger failed in his attempt to give greater rights to Irish Catholics in conjunction with the Act of Union (1800), Parliament repealed the Test Act (requiring a religious test for officeholders) in 1828 and approved Catholic emancipation in the Catholic Relief Act of 1829. The Oxford Movement of Catholic converts led by John Henry Newman in the 1830s and 40s led to reestablishment of a Catholic ecclesiastical hierarchy in 1850, and in 1859 the Anglican Prayer Book dropped observance of the Fifth of November.

As James Sharpe notes, the Fifth has been subject to frequent reinvention. Sermons on the Fifth in the seventeenth century rarely mentioned Fawkes, usually focusing on Catesby and Garnet. Generally that century burned effigies of the pope on Bonfire Night, though revelers adopted Guy as the new effigy of choice in the eighteenth and the holiday came to involve more festivity and less hatred. It became a focus of patriotism during the French Revolution and Napoleonic Wars, and in the nineteenth century references to religion declined. Strangely, there were plays in the nineteenth century that made Fawkes a hero against the tyrannical Stuarts! Emphasis on the anti-Catholic aspect of the Fifth also dropped off in scholarly histories. Numerous variations in observance emerged, including "Pope Day'" in colonial New England, rolling burning barrels of tar in Lewes in Sussex, vandalism by the Guildford Guys in Surrey in the 1850s and 60s, and street fighting in Exeter that peaked in 1867. No one is safe from being burned in effigy. In the last two centuries this has included Napoleon, Horatio Nelson, Benjamin Butler, most modern British prime ministers and American presidents, and a host of celebrities.

The reign of Edward VII (1901-10) marked the true end of the nineteenth century in Britain, and the twentieth and twenty-first centuries brought new enemies. Under George V (1910-36) came World War I, under George VI (1936-52)—after the abdication of Edward VIII (1936)— came World War II, and under Elizabeth II (1952-present) the Cold War and the war on terrorism. This made it fairly obvious that there are worse things than Catholics or Protestants, Jews, Muslims, Buddhists, Hindus, or any other faith whose members value human life. Today Bonfire Night is a festive, family affair with Bonfire Societies holding processions, rolling tar barrels, burning comic effigies, and setting off fireworks. Catholics participate along with everyone else.

In 2005, on the four hundredth anniversary of the Gunpowder Plot, Richard Hammond hosted a British television show on the ITV network in which demolition experts blew up an exact replica of Parliament in 1605. The results, which still can be found in video form online, were quite spectacular. It is well that the plot was foiled.

One other legacy of the Gunpowder Plot is a phoenix named Fawkes who shares rooms with Albus Dumbledore, the Master of Hogwarts School of Witchcraft and Wizardry in the Harry Potter novels and films. Together Fawkes and Dumbledore remind us that there are better ways to deal with illicit authority than blowing things up, warn us against substituting the mere appearance of education for real substance, and repeat the lesson that those in the right should never go quietly. Given that Fawkes and Dumbledore have left the building, it must be candy time. But first, Happy Halloween, please do not forget to vote on November 2, and Happy Guy Fawkes Day. Now say the magic words . . .

Suggestions for Further Reading

Fiona Bengsten, *Sir William Waad, Lieutenant of the Tower, and the Gunpowder Plot* (2006); David Cressy, *Bonfires and bells: national memory and the Protestant calendar in Elizabethan and Stuart England* (1989); Pauline Croft, *King James* (2003); Susan Doran and Thomas Freeman, eds, *Tudors and Stuarts on Film: Historical Perspectives* (2008); Richard Dutton, *Ben Jonson, 'Volpone' and the Gunpowder Plot* (2008); Antonia Fraser, *Faith and Treason: The Story of the Gunpowder Plot* (1996); Alan Haynes, *The Gunpowder Plot: Faith in Rebellion* (1994) and *Robert Cecil, Earl of Salisbury 1563-1612: Servant of Two Sovereigns* (1989); Alice Hogge, *God's Secret Agents: Queen Elizabeth's Forbidden Priests and the Hatching of the Gunpowder Plot* (2005); Ralph Houlbrooke, ed., *James VI and I: Ideas, Authority, and Government* (2006); Leanna de Lisle, *After Elizabeth: The Rise of James of Scotland and the Struggle for the Throne of England* (2006); H.C.G. Matthew and Brian Harrison, eds., *Oxford Dictionary of National Biography*, 60 vols. (2004); Alan Moore, *V for Vendetta* [graphic novel, basis for movie of the same name] (2005); Diane Newton, *The Making of the Jacobean Regime: James VI and I and the Government of England 1603-1605* (2005); Mark Nicholls, *Investigating Gunpowder Plot* (1991); Northcote Parkinson, *Gunpowder, Treason and Plot* (1976); James Sharpe, *Remember, Remember: A Cultural History of Guy Fawkes Day* (2005); Alan Stewart, *The Cradle King: The Life of James VI and I, the First Monarch of a United Great Britain* (2003); James Travers, *Gunpowder: The Players Behind the Plot* (2005); Hugh Ross Williamson, *The Gunpowder Plot* (1996).

2011 PREQUEL
IT'S POISON!

This video features a montage of clips from films, television, music videos, and safety messages concerning poisons, potions, and preparations. Watch the video at https://myspace.com/headongoolah/videos.

[Onstage, next to the lectern, is a large, black, bucket-like container full of candy and labeled "Poison."

2011 LECTURE
THE EVIL DRAUGHT:
POISONS, POTIONS, AND PREPARATIONS IN HISTORY

Hello, and welcome to today's cheerful installment of the More-or-Less Annual Halloween Lecture, "The Evil Draught: Poisons, Potions, and Preparations in History." Let us begin with some terminology. "Poison" is any substance designed to kill or severely impair victims who ingest it, breathe it in, absorb it through the skin, or have it injected into them. It can be good if it is being used to eradicate pest like rats or roaches. It can be bad if humans or pets get it into their system. Or it can be really bad if deliberately used to harm an individual or a crowd of people. "Potions" are concoctions that may or may not have a magical element and that are used to achieve some desired effect, good or bad, like causing someone to fall in love or to go mad (if there is, in fact, a difference). A "preparation" (like the one with the suffix "H"), in the context of today's discussion has, or is intended to have, pharmaceutical benefits. Of course, there is considerable overlap. Potions can be deadly, and preparations may contain low, medicinal doses of substances that are poisonous. There is also a problem with tackling this subject in a public lecture. There are so many poisons, so many potions, so many preparations, and so little time. So we had better get started.

The use of poisons, particularly in warfare and for bringing down wild game, began in prehistory during the Paleolithic (Old Stone) Age, while humans still followed a peripatetic hunter-gatherer lifestyle. Already in that period man knew how to use aconitum, acokonthera, curare, strychnos, the bark of the sandbox tree, exudations of the aptly named Poison Dart frog, and preparations made from the Diamphibia Beetle. The semi-mythical Menes (or Narmer, c. 3100 BC), the proto-dynastic pharaoh who unified Egypt, purportedly did research on poisons. In ancient India, Sushruta (fl. 800 BC), the "Father of Surgery," developed 300 surgical procedures, 120 instruments, and antidotes to a variety of poisons.

History is full of famous poisoners and victims of poison. The Athenian philosopher Socrates (469-399 BC), a victim, was a notorious critic of government who found himself condemned for corrupting the youth (as if youth are not perfectly capable of that themselves) and introducing new gods, accepted his death sentence, and calmly drank a cup of hemlock. This event has been commemorated many times, for example, on canvas by Jacques-Louis David in "The Death of Socrates" (1787) and on television by Steve Martin in a *Saturday Night Live* sketch. The Persian eunuch Bagoas was both a poisoner and a victim, who poisoned Artaxerxers III in 338 BC and Artaxerxes IV in 336 BC before Darius III poisoned him later that year. Alexander the Great, King of Macedon (born 356, reigned 336-323), who created the world's largest empire up to his time in a little over a decade, died at the age of thirty-three (as depicted, for example, in Karl von Ploty's painting, "The Death of Alexander," 1886). He may have died of natural causes (perhaps acute pancreatitis, malaria, typhoid, or West Nile Fever), but there is also suspicion that the cause was poisoning (perhaps accidentally by alcohol or deliberately with strychnine), as suggested by Oliver Stone's most problematic film, *Alexander the Great* (2004). However, scientists recently have suggested that his final illness may have resulted from drinking water from the River Styx (Marvoneri) containing highly toxic bacteria that produces a deadly compound, calicheamicin.

A few years later, Alexander's famous enemy Demosthenes of Athens took poison while being pursued by Antipapter, one of Alexander's former generals. Meanwhile in India, Chanakya (c.350-283 BC)—often called the "Indian Machiavelli," author of *Arthrashastra*, and teacher of Chandragupta—recommended that rulers use poison, advised them to have food tasters as a precaution against being poisoned, and suggested taking low doses to build up immunity (much like the fictional Westley in *The Princess Bride*). Back in Greece, according to both Plutarch and Polybius, Aratus of Sicyon, leader of the Achaean League that resisted Philip V of Macedon, was poisoned.

One of the most notorious poisoners in the ancient world was "the Poison King," Mithridates VI Eupator of Pontus (born 134 BC, reigned 120-63 BC), the bitter enemy of the Romans and recently the subject of a full-length study by Adrienne Mayor. Mithridates has a number of things in common with the modern fictional wizard, Harry Potter. His name means "sent by [the god] Mithra," that is, he was a "chosen one." Tradition has it that at the time of his birth, comets "like scimitars" appeared in the sky and that he was struck by lightning and had a crown-shaped scar on his forehead. His father Mithridates V died from poison in 120 BC, and for a time he shared rule with his mother Laodice and his younger brother Mithridates Chrestus, whom his mother favored. From 120 to 113 Mithridates was in hiding. On his return he imprisoned his mother and brother and married his younger sister Laodice to maintain a pure royal bloodline. In 88 BC he was responsible for the massacre of 80,000 Romans, which led to the Mithridatic Wars (First 88-83 BC, Second 83-81

BC, Third 73-63 BC). Captured by Pompey the Great, he tried to commit suicide by taking poison, but he had built up immunity during his many years of research. He also purportedly developed a universal antidote called Mithridatium.

Anti-Roman Jews poisoned Antipater the Idumean (died 43 BC), founder of the Herodian Dynasty in Judea, father of Herod the Great, and a pro-Roman who supported Julius Caesar against Pompey and Cassius against Mark Antony. Another poison victim, in a manner of speaking, was Cleopatra, Queen of Egypt (born 69 BC, reigned 51-30 BC), who famously had affairs with both Caesar and Antony. But after she and the latter got into a war with Octavius (Augustus) and lost the Battle of Actium in 31 BC, both committed suicide, she by allowing herself to be bitten an asp, as famously depicted in the epic film *Cleopatra* (1963), starring Elizabeth Taylor and Richard Burton. Still another was Drusus Minor (13 BC–AD 23)—born during Augustus' reign (27 BC–AD 14), son of Tiberius (14-37, cousin of Caligula (37-41) and Nero adoptive brother of Germanicus, and married to Claudius' sister Livilla, who poisoned him at the behest of her lover Sejanus. Among this nest of poisoners and victims was Caligula's sister Agrippina the Younger (AD 15–59), who hired the poisoner Locusta to give her husband Claudius (41-54) poison mushrooms so that her son Nero (54-68) might take the imperial throne.

Nero later employed Locusta to poison Britannicus in 55 BC. He also rewarded his mother's support by committing matricide. Accounts differ about how he did this, but one version involves poison. According to Cassius Dio, Nero had a ship with a collapsible hull built as a "gift" for Agrippina, who swam ashore when it sank, only to be stabbed by an assassin. Tacitus dismisses poison as too obvious and offers a variant story of the boat with a collapsible ceiling, though in his version Agrippina is killed by three assassins after escaping the shipwreck. However, Suetonius claims Nero attempted to have her poisoned three times and also tried to kill her with a collapsible ceiling over her bed before the episodes with the boat and the assassin(s), which Nero claimed was suicide. John William Waterhouse's painting "The Remorse of Nero" (1884) suggests that the emperor regretted this, but there are strong grounds for skepticism. Appropriately, during the Early Roman Empire, Pliny the Elder (23-79) wrote a *Natural History* in which he described over 7,000 poisons and offered policy advice on their use.

Poisons, potions, and preparations were commonplace in the Middle Ages, during which the worlds of the apothecary, the alchemist, the magician, the cunning man/woman, and the witch overlapped considerably. Some modern researchers have suggested that ergot, a bread mold with a chemical composition similar to LSD that some medieval practitioners used as an abortifacient, might have produced hallucinations that explain "flying" witches and other allegedly supernatural phenomena, but this remains speculative. Among many other achievements, the Jewish philosopher, physician, and rabbi Moses Maimonides (1135-1204) wrote a *Treatise on Poisons and Their Antidotes* (1198). During the Renaissance, the polymath Leonard da Vinci (1452-1519) conducted research on poisons, though he most assuredly was not the member of any secret societies, Dan Brown and *The Da Vinci Code* notwithstanding. His contemporary Paracelsus (1493-1541), who argued for the medicinal properties of minerals and researched toxicology, discovered that the size of the dose is what makes substances poison.

Later in the sixteenth century, Giambattista della Porta (c.1535-1615), authored a work titled *Magia Naturalis* in 1558 and continued expanding it until it reached 20 volumes in 1589. It deals with a variety of subjects that all had alchemical and occult associations at the time, though what connects them will not be immediately obvious to most modern readers. However, leaving aside geology, magnetism, and optics, what links cooking, cosmetics, gunpowder, medicine, metallurgy, perfume, and poisons is that all involve changing the state of substances through creating new chemical compounds or solutions, by the application of fire, and/or through the use of distillation. The sixteenth century regarded such changes, which we see as the product of scientific methodology, as alchemical or magical. Most of these processes also had in common the need for recipes, which at the time could be found in the same recipe books, and the intent of inducing change in others—heartier appetites from cooking, sexual attraction from cosmetics and perfume (a kind of love potion), wellness from medicine, and non-wellness from poison. Consider this: you can still buy cosmetics, perfume, and certain poisons at the drug store where you purchase medication. Incidentally, in Britain the pharmacist is known as a "chemist."

At the beginning of the same century, Pope Alexander VI (Rodrigo Borgia, born 1431, reigned 1492-1503) was both a notorious poisoner and a victim of poison, who favored cantarella (arsenic) for his own dirty work but died of poisoning himself in 1503, though his son (yes, his openly acknowledged son) Cesare, another poisoner, barely survived the same attempt to eliminate Borgia power, only to die fighting as a mercenary in Spain three years later. His sister Lucretia suffers from a reputation as a poisoner, too, though this appears to be guilt by association, as there is no evidence that she actually poisoned anyone. Speaking of Spain, the Spanish explorer Ponce de Leon (1474-1521)—who served as governor of Puerto Rico, explored and named Florida in 1513, and searched for the Fountain of Youth—on his last voyage in 1521 sustained an attack by Native Americans, who killed him with a poison arrow. Poison also killed pretty much everyone at the end of "The Black Seal," the sixth and final episode of the first season of *Blackadder* (1982), though it was funnier there.

Henry VIII of England (born 1491, reigned 1509-47) is best known for his marriages and divorces, but he also had a pathological fear of disease and poison. This was not entirely without foundation. Pope Clement VII (Giulio de Medici, born 1478, reigned 1523-34)—who denied Henry a divorce from Catherine of Aragon because he was essentially the prisoner of the English queen's nephew, Holy Roman Emperor Charles V—accidentally poisoned himself by eating Death Cap Mushrooms. Bishop John Fisher and Sir Thomas More were targets of attempted murder in 1531, along with several of Fisher's dinner guests, when someone poisoned the soup. Though Fisher and More opposed the divorce and eventually suffered execution in 1535, Henry was so incensed (and probably frightened) that he had the poor cook, Richard Roose (or Rice or Rouse) boiled alive as punishment. Notwithstanding the portrayal of this incident in Showtime's *The Tudors*, there is no evidence that the Boleyns put Roose up to it.

There is a much more humorous approach to the problem of poison in the film *Crossed Swords* (1977), one of the many cinematic versions of Mark Twain's *The Prince and the Pauper*. When a food taster tries the wine before the bogus "Prince Edward," i.e., the pauper Tom Canty, can drink it, Tom innocently inquires—in a line taken straight from the book—"If you think it may be poisoned, why don't you try it on dog. . . or a plumber?" (Twain evidently had some bad experiences with plumbers). There were a number of real plots to poison Elizabeth I during her long reign, but Shekhar Kapur's *Elizabeth* (1998) invents one involving a poison dress, which is quite dramatic but sounds more like something from a James Bond movie. William Shakespeare, reflecting contemporary fears of poison, used it as a plot device in both *Romeo and Juliet*, which ends with the tragic poisoning of both lovers, and *Hamlet*, which begins with Claudius poisoning Hamlet's father and ends with the poisoning of Gertrude, Hamlet, Laertes, and Claudius.

Of course not all murderers used poison. Ironically, Henri IV, the first Bourbon king of France (1589-1610) was deathly afraid of poison, given its prevalence at the French court during the French Wars of

Religion (1562-98) and the ascendancy of Catherine de Medici and her sons, the last three Valois kings: Francis II (1559-60), Charles IX (1560-74), and Henri III (1574-89). But though he was assassinated in 1610, his killer—Francois Ravaillac—stabbed him with a knife. Even earlier in 1584, William the Silent, Protestant leader in the Dutch Revolt, became the first major political figure to die at the hands of an assassin using a pistol, Balthasar Gerard. Because handguns were easy to conceal, they provided an alternative to poison for "up-close" attacks. However, poison continued to be a weapon.

In 1613 the English court was scandalized by the murder by poison of Thomas Overbury, a courtier, writer, and advisor to Robert Carr, the current favorite of James VI and I (born 1566, king of Scotland 1567-1625 and England 1603-25). Carr had an affair with Frances Howard, a member of the powerful Howard family and wife of Robert Devereux, 3rd Earl of Essex. Overbury, "the man behind the favorite," initially condoned the romance and even wrote Carr's love letters, but when Frances sought a divorce, Overbury changed his tune, fearing a loss of influence. This angered both Carr and the Howards, in addition to which his arrogance annoyed the king, who tried to send him abroad. When Overbury refused to leave, the king imprisoned him in the Tower, and Frances decided to poison him in collusion with apothecary James Franklin, Madame Anne Turner (who specialized in aphrodisiacs and poisons), and gaoler Richard Weston. However, the poisons merely caused Overbury great suffering for some three months but did not kill him. Frances became impatient, and on her orders the apothecary's assistant William Reeve gave Overbury a mercury enema, which killed him the next day (September 15). Frances married Carr, who became Earl of Somerset, but two years latter Reeve and the Lieutenant of the Tower, Gervase Halwyn, confessed. In a classic case of privileging the aristocracy, Franklin, Turner, and Weston suffered execution, while Carr and Frances were sentenced to death but had their sentences commuted to imprisonment.

Between 1675 and 1682 the court of Louis XIV (born 1638, reigned 1643-1715) was riveted by the Affair of the Poisons. The Marquise de Brinvilliers conspired with her lover Godin de Sainte-Croix to murder her father Antonine Dreux d'Aubray in 1666 and her brothers Antoine and Françoise in 1670 in order to get her hands on their estates. In 1675 she was arrested, convicted, beheaded, and her body burned. However, the case led to rumors and fears of attempted poisonings at court, with Louis XIV himself a potential target. In 1677, when Magdalaine de La Grange was arrested for forgery and murder, she appealed to the Secretary of State, the Marquis de Louivois, claiming to have information. Louvois reported this to Louis, who ordered an investigation by Paris Police Chief Gabriel-Nicolas de la Reynie, which led to numerous arrests of alchemists and fortunetellers who had been making prophetic predictions, holding séances, and selling aphrodisiacs and poisons. When tortured, they implicated others, including "La Voisin (Catherine Deshayes), who—though usually quite drunk—implicated several courtiers, including Olympe Mancini, Countess of Soissons, Marie Anne Mancini, Duchesse de Bouillon, and the Duke of Luxembourg. La Voisin even claimed that Louis' mistress, the Marquise de Montespan, bought aphrodisiacs and held black masses to keep the king's favor. In 1678, Eustache D'Auger de Cavoye, a disinherited noble who sold magical powders, disappeared. At one time he was thought to be the "Man in the Iron Mask," but actually his family imprisoned him. In 1680 La Voisin was burned as a witch and Luxembourg jailed, though the king's minister Jean Baptiste Colbert suppressed much of the story. Meanwhile, Reynie set up a Chamber Ardente ("burning chamber") that incinerated thirty-four witches between 1680 and 1682, after which the king abolished it.

Elsewhere, Holy Roman Emperor Charles VI died in 1640 after eating Death Cap Mushrooms. Rumors persist even today that the British poisoned Napoleon Bonaparte on St. Helena in 1621, though the arsenic in his system could have been medicinal, as he suffered from digestive ailments that arsenic was used to treat. American President Zachary Taylor's death in 1850 is variously attributed to cholera, a surfeit of cherries and milk, and poison. This led to the exhumation of his body in 1991, but though nothing was found, conspiracy theories continue. There have been a number of infamous poisoners whose victims were less exalted. Mary Ann Cotton (1832-73) used arsenic to poison four husbands, two lovers, and all of her children, adding up to at least twenty-one victims. Thomas Neill Cream "the Lambeth Poisoner" (1850-92) operated in Ontario, Chicago, and London, with five proven victims, though attempts to identify him as Jack the Ripper are fanciful. Vera Renczi (1903-60?) poisoned two husbands, a son, and many lovers, adding up to at least thirty-five. Nannie Doss "the Jolly Black Widow" (1905-65) poisoned at least eleven, including four of her five husbands, her mother, a sister, and a grandson, at least eleven in all. On the lighter side, John Cleese made a pre-Monty Python appearance on David Frost's *The Frost Report* (1966-67) for a sketch about a man attempting to buy rat poison to eliminate his wife.

Not surprisingly, in modern times poison has been both a weapon of war and an instrument of terrorism. In 1916, Russian aristocrats tried poisoning Grigory Rasputin, the favorite of Nicholas II and Alexandra, before drowning and then shooting him, poison gas made its horrific appearance in World War I, Adolf Hitler and the Nazis used Zyklon B to poison Jews and other victims during the Holocaust, and later committed suicide with cyanide in this bunker. Soviet leader Joseph Stalin (1878-1953), who is suspected of poisoning Lenin, supposedly uncovered the so-called Doctors Plot in 1953 shortly before his own death, though Nikita Krushchev's "Secret Speech" of 1956 cast doubt on the plot. In 1978, a total of 909 people at Jim Jones' Jonestown, Guyana compound committed mass suicide after Jones convinced them it was God's will. During the Iran-Iraq War (1980-88), Iraqi leader Saddam Hussein used poison gas against the enemy and to kill millions of his own population, with the actual work often falling to "Chemical Ali," Al Hassan al-Majid. In 1995 Shoko Asahara, founder of the religious cult Aum Shinrikyo, carried out an attack on the Tokyo subway system using Sarin gas, for which he remains on death row. Former KBG agent and defector Alexander Litvinenko died in London after being poisoned with Polonium 210. Al Qaeda is known to have plans for using biological toxins, poison in the food supply, Ricin, and poisoned perfume. And, on the lunatic fringe, Marshal Applewhite and the Heaven's Gate cult committed suicide in order to "meet" the Comet Hale-Bopp, which they believed to be a spacecraft sent by God.

As a holiday precaution, I urge you all to avoid eating spoiled salmon mousse, lest you end up accidentally poisoning yourselves like the unfortunate dinner guests who meet "Mister Death" at the end of Monty Python's *The Meaning of Life* (1983). But now, though Halloween is closer than Valentine's Day, let us turn to the more pleasant subject of love potions, as depicted, for example, in Evelyn de Morgan's painting, "Le Philtre d'Amour" (1903). As a favor to the guys in the audience, I am going to tell you how to make a love potion. Mix roses with Godiva chocolates, diamonds, and cash, and avoid being a jackass, and love is the likely result.

Having featured several scenes of potion making from the Harry Potter films in my pre-lecture film, I would be remiss to address the once prevalent allegations about the "poisonous" effects of J.K. Rowling's famous novels. Not long ago bookstores featured purported exposés of the "evil" influence of these books, such as Richard Abanes' *Harry Potter and the Bible: The Menace Behind the Magic* (2001), a book called *Harry Potter: Witchcraft Repackaged: Making Evil Look Innocent* (2001, with a DVD), and Steve Wohlberg's *Exposing Harry Potter and Witchcraft: The Menace Beneath the Magic* (2005). But from authors for whom rationality has replaced hysteria and who actually have read the books before commenting on them, we see titles like John Granger's *Looking for God in Harry Potter* (2007), Connie Neal's *The Gospel According to Harry Potter: The Spiritual Journey of the World's Greatest Seeker* (2006), and John Killinger's *God, the Devil, and Harry Potter: A Christian Minister's Defense of the Beloved Novels* (2002).

We should let this serve as an object lesson. Snoopy has more to do with Halloween than Satan does. Besides that, remember that Halloween is All Hallows' Eve, the day before All Saints Day, a day on which many Christians honor the saints, including Saint Michael the Archangel, who generally appears in artworks trampling upon the Devil. In truth, you can poison your mind with alcohol, drugs, ignorance, lies, and bigotry. But you will never poison it with knowledge, truth, or anything that is good. Or, for that matter, with candy. So, as we listen to Wayne Fontana and the Mindbenders performing "Love Potion Number 9," let me wish you a Happy Halloween, and please let me hear you say the magic words . . .

Suggestions for Further Reading

Deborah Blum, *The Poisoner's Handbook* (2010); John Emsley, *The Elements of Murder* (2005); Valerie Flint, *The Rise of Magic in the Early Middle Ages* (1991); Richard Kieckhefer, *Magic in the Middle Ages*, 2nd edition (2014); Brian Levack, *The Witch Hunt in Early Modern Europe*, 4th edition (2015); Mary Matossian, *Poisons of the Past: Molds, Epidemics, and History* (1991); Adrienne Mayor, *Greek Fire, Poison Arrows, and Scorpion Bombs* (2003) and *The Poison King: The Life and Legend of Mithridates, Rome's Deadliest Enemy* (2009), Lynn Wood Mollenauer, *Strange Revelations: Magic, Poison, and Sacrilege in Louis XIV's France* (2007), Anne Somerset, *The Affair of the Poisons: Murder, Infanticide, and Satanism at the Court of Louis XIV* (2004) and *Unnatural Murder: Poison at the Court of James I* (1998).

2012 THE ABORTED PREQUEL
BATTLING, BEDDING, BURNING, AND BEHEADING:
TRUE TALES OF TERROR FROM TUDOR TIMES

In a loss to Western Civilization perhaps equaled only by the burning of the ancient Library at Alexandria, the following script never became a film. First of all, I ran out of time. Secondly, my wife wisely advised me that it is too long. At the time I interpreted that as meaning "too stupid." Looking back at it now, I am certain that it was. But here is what you missed. Since it does not exist, you cannot watch it anywhere, thank God.

VOICE   Good afternoon, ladies and gentlemen, and welcome to the More-or-Less Annual Halloween Lecture, the concluding event in the 2012 Then and Now Fanfare History and Politics Lecture Series The subject of today's lecture is "Battling, Bedding, Burning, and Beheading: True Tales of Terror from Tudor Times." But first please watch the following exercise in shameless self-promotion by our sponsor.

SCREEN   Bill
BILL   Hello. I'm Bill Robison, and I approve of this ad.

SCREEN   Image of *The Tudors on Film and Television*
VOICE   This December will witness the publication of the most important book of the year, of the decade, of the twenty-first century, of the third millennium! McFarland Publishing presents the earth-shattering magnum opus, *The Tudors on Film and Television!*

SCREEEN   Pictures of Sue and her books
VOICE   One of the authors is Dr. Sue Parrill, retired Professor of English and Head of the Department of English at Southeastern Louisiana University and author of *Jane Austen on Film and Television* and *Nelson's Navy in Fiction and Film.* The other author is, well . . .

SCREEN   Footage of Frankenstein onstage, Preposterodamus' still, Henry VIII on the bike, Bill in the rubble, Santa, Satan,

VOICE   vampire, wizard
He once reanimated a dead body in front of a live audience. He constructed an alchemical apparatus to distill the quintessence known as the philosopher's stone. He raced around the world dressed as Henry VIII on a child's spider bike with flat tires. He survived Godzilla's destruction of Tokyo. He has impersonated both Santa Claus . . . and Satan. He is believed by many to be a vampire . . . or a wizard. He is the most interesting man in the world!

SCREEN   Bill at a table surrounded by women with a copy of the book

BILL   I don't always write about movies, but when I do, I write books like *The Tudors on Film and Television.* [Pause] Stay literate, my friend.

SCREEN   Footage from Harry Potter movies

VOICE   This holiday season you too can own this brilliant scholarly tome! Oh, sure, you could waste your time looking for some magically concealed Diagon Alley bookstore. You could buy the complete works of some pompous, self-aggrandizing, phony wizard. You could buy books that try to bite you, books in which demons literally leap from the pages, books possessed by a younger manifestation of the world's most powerful Dark Wizard, books full of deadly spells that let you cheat in Potions Class. But why bother when you can own the book that might have changed the history of the magical realm?

SCREEN   Harry Potter

HARRY   Is it true, Professor?

BILL   [As Dumbledore] That's right, Harry. The one thing Voldemort never could master is film studies. Oh, young Tom Riddle was a model student in every other respect, but he could never get more than a C in film class. Minerva McGonagall used to have Tudor Movie Night every Thursday and play Tudor Trivia afterward. Poor Tom never could keep straight all the actresses who played the wives in *The Private Life of Henry VIII.* Just think—if he had had this wonderful new book, *The Tudors on Film and Television*, all those years ago, he might have stayed in the game and never gone into the forbidden section of the library and learned about the spell to make a horcrux.

SCREEN   Image of *The Tudors on Film and Television*
VOICE   And, of course, if you do not have this book in your own Tudor film studies class, terrible things will happen.

SCREEN   Footage of Gandalf
GANDALF   You shall not pass!

SCREEN   Image of *The Tudors on Film and Television*
VOICE   So do what Bilbo did.

SCREEN   Footage of Bilbo
BILBO   I'm going to finish my book.

SCREEN   Image of *The Tudors on Film and Television*
VOICE   And, of course, the book that Bilbo finished reading was *The Tudors on Film and Television*. So do what Gandalf says.

SCREEN   Footage of Gandalf
GANDALF   Fly, you fools!

BILL   [As Gandalf] Actually, what I meant to say there was, buy, you fools. Buy. B-u-y. Buy *The Tudors on Film and Television*.

SCREEN   Footage from *The Hobbit* commercials and *The Tudors*
VOICE   That's right. Once you've seen *The Hobbit* fifteen or twenty times this December, you can make the switch from watching Bilbo, a short person from an imaginary race of humanoids, to reading about Jonathan Rhys Meyers, a short actor from an imaginary show about the Tudors.

SCREEN   Footage from Christmas commercials for jewelry, furs, etc.
VOICE   And don't waste your money on diamonds and furs or, for God's sake, electric razors. Books, writing, words—that is what is sexy this year.

SCREEN	Footage from *The Tudors*
A BOLEYN	Ravish me with your words. Seduce me.

SCREEN	Footage from *A Christmas Story* with dialogue dubbed
VOICE	Books are great for kids, too.
RALPHIE	What I really want for Christmas is *The Tudors on Film and Television*.

SCREEN	Footage of the South
VOICE	Books are great for country folk.
BILL	[As Willie Nelson] Hello, I'm Willie Nelson. When I'm riding around the big old state of Texas, getting stoned on the bus and avoiding the Internal Revenue Service, there's nothing I like better than watching movies about the Tudors. I just love all those redheaded kings and queens. That's why I can't wait for the publication of Sue Parrill and Bill Robison's new book, *The Tudors on Film and Television*. I'm buying copies for all my family and friends this Christmas, and I'm getting an autographed copy for my tax attorney.

SCREEN	A faux rap video
VOICE	Books are also great for urbanites.
MUSIC	If you want to know the truth about Henry and Liz
	You've got to read more than the dopes in showbiz
	There's sex and violence and murder and mystery
	But no soccer players in real Tudor history

Don't be a fool
Buy this book
It's better than school
Download it on a Nook
Read it on an iPad
Or even on a Kindle
It costs a lot of money
But it ain't no swindle

Hey there, fellows, if you want to get amorous
Women find hipster intellectuals glamorous
Ladies, don't settle for stupid and rude

When you can watch movies with a well-read dude

Don't be an ass
Get this book
Show a little class
Download it on a Nook
Read it on an iPad
Or even on a Kindle
If your partner won't buy it for you
Maybe a friend'll

Christmas is coming, and they're cheaper by the dozen
Give 'em to your mother and your brother and your cousin
Find out if Shakespeare really was the bard
Sellers will accept any major credit card

Don't be a Scrooge
Give this book
Don't be a stooge
Download it on a Nook
Read it on an iPad
Or even on a Kindle
Put it in your shopping cart
Or stuff it in a bindle

There's cinematic high art and television trash
So whip out your wallet and give up the cash
Now turn off your cell phone and get out your lighter
And sit up and listen 'cause here comes the writer

[Video ends, stage lights up, "Beautiful Day in the Neighborhood" plays, Bill changes capes]

[It is uncertain whether what follows should be considered part of the aborted prequel or an aborted part of the lecture.]

Hello, and welcome to the final installment of the 2012 Then and Now Fanfare History and Politics Lecture Series, also known as the More-or-Less Annual Halloween Lecture.

This year's lecture series, which as always is sponsored by the

Department of History and Political Science, is dedicated to Southeastern Louisiana University President Emeritus Dr. Randy Moffett.

I don't know if you've heard or not, but Sue Parrill and I have written a book called *The Tudors on Film and Television*. You can learn more about it at our website, www.tudorsonfilm.com, where we will continue to post new essays as new films come out in the future.

You probably haven't even thought of this, but with Christmas just around the corner, we remind you that books are the gift that you can open again and again, the gift that keeps on giving long after your Jelly-of-the-Month Club subscription has expired.

2012 LECTURE
BATTLING, BEDDING, BURNING, AND BEHEADING:
TRUE TALES OF TERROR FROM TUDOR TIMES

Hello, and welcome to the final installment of the 2012 Then and Now Fanfare History and Politics Lecture Series, also known as the More-or-Less Annual Halloween Lecture. The title of my lecture today is "Battling, Bedding, Burning, and Beheading: True Tales of Terror from Tudor Times." That, in fact, is a bit of a red herring. Today, after all, is Halloween, which means both treats and tricks, and I am nothing if not a trickster. So, if you came expecting extensive footage of battling, bedding, burning, and beheading, or if you have a pathological desire to be terrorized, you may be in for a disappointment. Yes, I enjoy a bit of irony now and then, and the truth is that I have had about enough doom and gloom for one year. We have had budget cuts, hurricanes, and attacks on American embassies. We have had a presidential campaign that has been going on for at least a millennium and that is saturated with Kool-Aid but short on civility and reason. For months I have prayed that it will end before I alienate all of my friends on both sides of the political aisle. So today—on Halloween, the eve of All Saints Day—I feel like having fun.

My colleague Sue Parrill and I have written a book called *The Tudors on Film and Television.* You can learn more about it at our website, www.tudorsonfilm.com, where we will continue to post new essays as new films come out in the future. With Christmas just around the corner, we remind you that books are the gift that you can open again and again, the gift that keeps on giving long after your Jelly-of-the-Month Club subscription has expired. In addition, I am editing a book of essays from some twenty top Tudor scholars called *History, Fiction, and 'The Tudors': Sex, Politics, Power, and the Showtime Television Series.* In any case, I want to share with you some stories about the Tudor period, many of which are addressed by films and television programs that we discuss in the book, and to show you some related film clips. Some do concern "battling, bedding, burning, and beheading" and might even be considered "serious," so let us get that out of the way first.

Tudor battles were, indeed, terrifying, not only because of battlefield brutality but because of the primitive state of Tudor medicine. Physicians in this period did not study anatomy, physiology, pharmacology, and so on; rather, they practiced grammar and rhetoric, never actually touching their patients. Barber-surgeons did much of the surgery, setting of bones, and sewing up of wounds. That is why the barber pole has a red stripe. And if that at first seems odd, consider that cutting hair is a form of amputation. The worst problems for soldiers, however, were boredom, hunger, and disease since much of the warfare in this period took the form of long sieges like the siege of Boulogne portrayed in *The Tudors*. The most famous battle in the Tudor period and the most terrifying for Englishmen was the attack of the Spanish Armada in 1588, which has featured in numerous films about Elizabeth I. During the Armada campaign, Elizabeth I delivered her famous inspirational speech at Tilbury. But her promise of reward to those who fought proved empty. The government lacked the funds to pay the sailors and soldiers who won this battle, and many of them starved to death or ended up gaoled as thieves or vagabonds.

If battling often led to terror, bedding—i.e., sex—seems like a less hazardous and more pleasant occupation. No doubt that usually was the case. But the pox (venereal disease) was rampant in the sixteenth century, especially syphilis, for which there was then no treatment. Bathing was uncommon; in fact, it was considered dangerous, so the olfactory aspect of intimacy was at best a mixed blessing. Most people had bad teeth, and those who survived smallpox often were horribly scarred. Infections that today would be susceptible to a simple application of antibiotics could last a lifetime. Henry VIII had an ulcer on his leg that never healed and that occasioned unfavorable comment by his later wives. Edward VI died of tuberculosis while still an adolescent, Mary Tudor experienced a false pregnancy that was probably the result of uterine cancer, and Elizabeth remained unmarried and quite possibly a genuine virgin, not least because of her fear of the horrors of childbirth.

Burning alive may be the most horrible way that one can die. But the application of this punishment in Tudor England is often misrepresented and misunderstood. The English did not burn witches, as the Inquisition did on the continent; rather, they hanged witches. Burning was restricted to three main offenses. One was heresy. Henry VII burned heretics, Henry VIII burned both Catholics and Protestants who were not in line with his vision of the true church, and "Bloody Mary" earned her nickname by sending some 300 victims to the stake. A second category was women who committed treason. For male traitors the punishment was hanging, drawing, and quartering. But Anne Boleyn, for example, could have been burned rather than beheaded because her alleged adultery was also legally treason, as it had the potential to affect the succession to the throne. The third category was petty treason, which included a woman killing her husband, a clergyman killing his bishop, and servant killing his master. Although there are numerous scenes of burning in Tudor films, I have elected not to show any. We have been having a good time here, and I do not wish to see that go up in smoke. I will simply remind you of what the bishop said to the heretic: "Repent, brother. Do not make an ash of yourself."

For the more bloodthirsty members of the audience, here is a bit about beheading instead from a *Saturday Night Live* skit about the death of Anne Boleyn. Beheading was the punishment meted out to traitors. Most crimes led to hanging. But in the case of traitors, beheading was usually a blessed release from the agonies that preceded it. Typically, a traitor was tied to a hurdle, dragged through the streets behind a horse, hanged until nearly unconscious, cut down, castrated, and disemboweled, with his testicles and entrails burned before his eyes. Once decapitated, his body was cut into quarters, each of which might be displayed in a different town as a warning to other would-be malefactors. Elizabeth has the reputation of being less savage than her predecessors, but she faced numerous plots—usually with the goal of deposing her and placing Mary Queen of Scots on the throne—and she sent a whole series of plotters to horrible deaths, as she did with any Roman Catholic priests who were caught in Protestant England. Though reluctant to do so, in the long run she even allowed the beheading of Mary Queen of Scots. [Bugs Bunny: "Oh, I'm dying" clip]

Of course those wishing to avoid some horrible fate might seek to discern the future by consulting an astrologer like the Elizabethan John Dee or even through the more sinister practice of necromancy. [Clip of Elizabeth, Dee, and Edward Kelly discussing necromancy] Don't try that at home. Or anywhere. In fact, let's lighten up the mood here. One of the fun things about doing a book on Tudor films and television is all the odd stuff we have stumbled upon. So, let us address the fact that Tudor terror can turn up in unexpected places, like a bookshop where inanimate objects come alive at the stroke of midnight. See you if you can spot the Tudor elements in the first part of this 1946 Looney Tunes cartoon called *Book Revue*. [Clip]

As you may have noticed, the first book to appear is *The Complete Works of Shakespeare*, the cover of which depicts an animated silhouette of the bard with the mechanical works of a clock inside. Shortly thereafter an Indian maiden begins a striptease on the cover of *Cherokee Strip*, eliciting catcalls and wolf whistles from various characters and causing Shakespeare to explode. Among those howling is Henry VIII, clearly based on Charles Laughton in *The Private Life of Henry VIII*. The king's outraged "mother" calls him from the cover of *The Aldrich Family*, a reference to the radio sit-com which opened with Henry Aldrich's mom calling out "Hen-reeeee" and the young teen answering, "Coming, Mother!" Mother is, in turn, smitten by "Frankie" Sinatra singing. This leads to a riotous series of songs and sight gags, culminating in a completely insane song-and-dance by Daffy Duck, but no further appearances by anyone from the Tudor era.

If you think that it is weird, check out this video for the song "Lorraine" by the British band Bad Manners, which features lead singer Buster Bloodvessel (Douglas Trendle) as Henry VIII. [Clip] That is terrifying in more ways than I even want to consider. But surely Henry VIII would never show up in a real horror movie? Well, consider. One of the most influential Tudor films of all time is *The Private Life of Henry VIII*, which appeared in 1933. In that movie, Elsa Lanchester portrayed Henry's fourth wife, Anne of Cleves. Two years later she played the title role in *The Bride of Frankenstein*. Did Henry come along? The evil Dr. Pretorius' experiments show the obscure actor "Pop" Bryan as the "Little King," who is obviously Henry even if not specifically identified as such.

But what about actors known mainly for horror movies who appear in Tudor films? Vincent Price is Sir Walter Raleigh in the Bette Davis/Errol Flynn classic, *The Private Lives of Elizabeth and Essex* (1939). I don't know about you, but seeing them together makes me nervous, and their costumes certainly fill me with terror. They are even more frightening than the most terrifying new Halloween costume I have seen in years, i.e., Slutty Big Bird. Is that what Mitt Romney was talking about in the debate? Speaking of bad costuming, look at Eric Bana as Henry VIII in *The Other Boleyn Girl* (2008). Look at this shoulders—they are more than twice as wide as those of the guy next to him. The ridiculously broad-shouldered Bana reminds me of another piece of more deliberate bad costuming. [Clip of Carol Burnett as Scarlet O'Hara with dress made from curtains] Tara, Terra, Terror—it's all the same to me.

In Tudor films, of course, we expect not Scarlet O'Hara, but witches. [Clip of the *Bewitched* episode at Henry VIII's court] Or, if there are no witches per se, then perhaps there might be a little magic. [*I Dream of Jeannie* clip with Henry] And, of course, when you think about the reign of Henry VIII, naturally you also think about sex, and you can get a whole movie's worth of silly sex in *Carry On Henry*, the film about a man who is good with this chopper.

Another form of horror for those of us who like Tudor films is bad casting. The most egregiously awful casting decision in Tudor film was the choice of Jonathan Rhys Meyers to play Henry VIII in *The Tudors*. But for now, let's look at another unfortunate decision from that series: Sebastian Armesto is unintentionally comical as Charles V, who evokes something other than imperial majesty in the following clip, the soundtrack for which I admittedly have modified to drive the point home. [Clip of Armesto with soundtrack from *The Princess Bride* with Inigo Montoya saying, "Hello, my name is Inigo Montoya. You killed my father. Prepare to die."]

Another unfortunate bit of casting is the entire cast of *Elizabeth I the Virgin Queen* (2005), a BBC mini-series that brought the once might *Masterpiece Theatre* to its knees. Tom Hardy—who can be excellent in certain roles, as he was in *Inception*—is a disaster as Robert Dudley, Earl of Leicester. Indeed, you might say he is the bane of the film, as this clip illustrates. [Clip of Hardy walking] Now what were they thinking? What inspired this terrible choice? Here is what I believe did it. [Same clip with substitute soundtrack featuring the Bee Gees' "Night Fever" from *Saturday Night Fever*]

Horror movies often feature characters who go through horrific physiological transformations. Look at what has happened to poor Henry VIII, his wives, and his courtiers here. [Clip of the Simpsons episode "Margical History Tour"] Another horror flick commonplace is the undead. Usually that means vampires or zombies, but what about a Tudor king who simply keeps living for 500 years and ends up in a house in the suburbs? [*Henry 8.0* clip from BBC website] A king who survived into modern times could find himself on a television show like *The Terrible Tudors*. [Clip] Another traditional trope in tales of terror is torture. Here we see the Elizabethan representative of the Black Adder Clan descendant, who has been kidnapped, being held in a filthy dungeon and forced to play charades with a psychopathic gaoler. [*Black Adder II* clip from the episode "Chains"]

Doctor Who's TARDIS, the Time and Relative Dimension in Space time machine and space craft disguised as a police telephone box, once brought the Doctor, Amy Pond, and Rory Williams back to the early Tudor era, where they found themselves under Henry VIII's bed. But time travel is a common, if generally unacknowledged element in Tudor films. Thomas Cromwell routinely goes back in time to have a job at the royal court in the 1520s. In reality he obtained a position under the king only after the death of Cardinal Thomas Wolsey, his predecessor as Henry's chief minister. The unfortunate 3rd Duke of Buckingham pops up all over the decade of the 1520s to have his head chopped off. Perhaps the champion, however, is composer and musician Thomas Tallis, who actually arrived at the royal court in 1543 and married a woman named Joan in 1552. But on *The Tudors* he turns up in 1519, and apparently has experienced a time-travel-induced change in sexual orientation, for on the show he is gay. Speaking of music, as you may have guessed, even the More-or-Less Annual Halloween is not over until the fat lady sings. [Clip of Donizetti] Gaetano Donizetti's opera *Anna Bolena* (1830) may terrify some rock and roll fans here today. But of course there are rock songs about Henry VIII, too. [Herman's Hermits clip, "I'm Henery the Eighth, I Am"] On second thought, that is just as terrifying to rock fans as opera. Perhaps I had better just throw candy. So what do you say?

Suggestions for Further Reading

John Bellamy, *The Tudor Law of Treason*, rprt. (2013); Susan Brigden, *New Worlds, Lost Worlds: The Rule of the Tudors 1485-1603* (2001); S.B. Chrimes, *Henry VII* (1992); Susan Doran and Thomas Freeman, eds, *Tudors and Stuarts on Film: Historical Perspectives* (2008); John Guy, *Queen of Scots: The True Life of Mary Stuart* (2004); Christopher Haigh, *English Reformations: Religion, Politics, and Society Under the Tudors* (1993); E.W. Ives, *Lady Jane Grey: A Tudor Mystery* (2009) and *The Life and Death of Anne Boleyn* (2004); David Loades, *Mary Tudor: A Life* (1990); Wallace MacCaffrey, *Elizabeth I* (1993); Colin Martin and Geoffrey Parker, *The Spanish Armada*, rev. ed. (2002); H.C.G. Matthew and Brian Harrison, eds., *Oxford Dictionary of National Biography*, 60 vols. (2004); Sue Parrill and William B. Robison, *The Tudors on Film and Television* (2013); William B. Robison, editor, *History, Fiction, and 'The Tudors': Sex, Politics, Power, and Artistic License in the Showtime Television Series* (2016); J.J. Scarisbrick, *Henry VIII* (1969); James Sharpe, *Instruments of Darkness: Witchcraft in Early Modern England* (1997); Nancy Siraisi, *Medieval and Early Renaissance Medicine: An Introduction to Knowledge and Practice* (1990); Chris Skidmore, *Edward VI: The Lost King of England* (2007); David Starkey, *Six Wives: The Queens of Henry VIII* (2004); Keith Thomas, *Religion and the Decline of Magic: Studies of Popular Beliefs in Sixteenth and Seventeenth Century England* (1971); Greg Walker, *The Private Life of Henry VIII: A British Film Guide* (2003); Benjamin Woolley, *The Queen's Conjurer: The Science and Magic of Dr. John Dee, Adviser to Queen Elizabeth I* (2002).

2013 PREQUEL
THE ORIGINAL TRICKY DICK

This video begins with a montage of images of Richard III, his recently discovered skeleton, actors who have played Richard in Shakespeare's play, excerpts of films and plays, various versions of James Weldon Johnson's "Dry Bones," and cartoons with skeletons. This segues into the song, "The Original Tricky Dick." Watch the video at https://myspace.com/headongoolah/videos and listen to the songs on the CD *Show Tunes* by Headongoolah (which is me before Impaired Faculties).

The Original Tricky Dick

He's the original tricky Dick
Malevolent evil on a stick
The king whose body time forgot
Till they dug it up in a parking lot

There for centuries it did fester
Beneath the ground in the town of Leicester
Six feet under plastic cones
Lay poor Richard's dead dry bones

With crooked frame and withered arm
He did the House of York some harm
Took the crown from nephew Ed
And pretty soon that kid was dead

With his little brother in the Tower
But uncle Richard's luck turned sour
Two years later that royal brooder
Lost the throne to Henry Tudor

But in his winter of discontent
He got no sleep in the royal tent
Troubled by weird premonitions
Kept awake by apparitions

Wide-eyed through the whole damn night
Maybe his helmet was on too tight

196

But while his wounded comrades squealed
He took it in the head at Bosworth Field.

His armor they stripped off, of course
And threw his body across a horse
Then took it into town to show
He wouldn't be coming back no mo'

In Grey Friars priory two days later
They buried the great manipulator
But when Henry VIII broke with Rome
They dug him up and lost his bones

Bad luck, fate, or maybe karma
Avengers all like Chicken Shawarma
Richard I might have died in a war zone
But they never lost his dead dry bones

Richard II got dethroned
But at least his corpse has got a home
Richard III had a hump, they say
So guess what day it is today

The cat, the rat, and Lovel our dog
Ruled all England under the hog
Summer's glorious sun of York
Had another slice of government pork

Sow's ear in a silken purse
Said my kingdom for a hearse
Souvenirs and plastic crap
Pave paradise, put up a tourist trap

2013 LECTURE
MY KINGDOM FOR A HEARSE:
THE LIFE, DEATH, AND ABANDONED BONES
OF KING RICHARD III

Hello. Excuse me just a moment. Hey, Richard. Hey, Richard. Hey, Richard. Hey, Richard. Guess what day it is? Okay, just had to get that out of my system [a reference to the famous GEICO camel commercial about "Hump Day"].

And so welcome to the final installment of the 2013 Then and Now Fanfare History and Politics Lecture series, which is also the More-or-Less Annual Halloween Lecture, which this year I am presenting on the day before Halloween, which is Wednesday, which is hump day. As you may know, "Halloween" is short for All Hallows Eve, and hump day is short for hump day. Halloween is so called because October 31 falls the day before All Saints Day, which at times used to be called All Hallows Day. Hump day is so called because it is Wednesday, and after that you are over the hump of the week. Richard III supposedly had a hump back, but more on that later. Since the 'een' at the end of Halloween means 'even' or 'the evening before,' you could call today, October 30, "Halloweeneen" and yesterday, October 29, "Halloweeneeneen," and so on. However, I do not recommend that, as it would be even more irritating than Humphrey the Hump Day Camel and might incite some humorless person to do to you what Henry VII did to Richard III at Bosworth Field, which was less a treat than a fairly unpleasant trick and which occurred on Saturday, August 22, 1485, which was neither Halloween nor hump day but an important occasion nonetheless.

That brings me to the fittingly macabre subject of today's Fanfare More-or-Less Annual Halloweeneen Hump Day Lecture, which involves bastardy and blood, intrigue and insurrection, legends and lies, myths and mysteries, skeletons and skulls, grave accusations and accusational graves, and which—rather sinisterly—is titled "My Kingdom for a Hearse: The Life, Death, and Abandoned Bones of Richard III." So, who was Richard III? And how did he go from looking like this [the late sixteenth century portrait in the National portrait gallery] or perhaps like this [the Paston portrait, c.1520 from a lost original], though not really quite like this [a still of Laurence Olivier from *Richard III*, 1955] and certainly not like this [Ian McKellen from the "1930's" *Richard III*, 1995], to looking like this [Richard's skeleton in the Leicester car park grave] or—once they cleaned him up a bit—like this [Richard's skull and skeleton]? To answer that question, we will look at six interrelated topics: (1) the dynastic strife that culminated in the Wars of the Roses, (2) Richard's own life and reign, (3) accusations against him and mysteries surrounding his life and death, (4) opinion pro and con over the last five centuries, (5) the depiction of Richard in drama, fiction, and film, and (6) the recent, spectacular recovery of his abandoned bones.

The traditional dates of the Wars of the Roses are 1455-1485. But one might as easily say that the conflict began in 1399, and it certainly had its roots in the reign of Edward III. This civil war—one of several in English history—pitted the House of Lancaster (signified by the red rose) against the House of York (signified by the white rose) and eventually led to the rise of the House of Tudor (which combined the two). However, all three dynasties stemmed from the House of Plantagenet. Edward III could trace his lineage to the first Plantagenet, Henry II. Edward began the Hundred Years War and fathered five sons. The eldest was Edward the Black Prince, who died before his father. Thus the throne went to the Black Prince's son, Richard II, who had a troubled reign and was deposed in 1399.

Thereupon, the House of Lancaster came to power, proceeding from Edward III's third son, John of Gaunt. He was Duke of Lancaster; hence, the name of the dynasty that began with his son, Henry IV, who deposed Richard II. Subsequently the crown went to his son, Henry V, a brilliant soldier and administrator who revived the Hundred Years War, defeated the French at Agincourt in 1415, and secured his family's claim to the French throne. By the 1420 Treaty of Troyes he married the French king's daughter Catherine, who later remarried to a courtier named Owen Tudor. Meanwhile, she gave the king a son, Henry VI, who came the throne as an infant and whose long reign saw a series of crises, which led to Wars of the Roses in 1455. Henry VI married the formidable Margaret of Anjou, who functioned as the Lancastrian leader during his bouts of illness and insanity. She also bore him a son named Edward of Westminster, who was killed in battle in 1471.

Meanwhile, Henry and Margaret faced opposition from the House of York. The Yorkist line proceeded from Edward III through his second son, Lionel of Antwerp, Duke of Clarence and his fourth son, Edmund of Langley, Duke of York. Clarence's granddaughter, Anne Mortimer, and York's grandson Richard, Earl of Cambridge, married and had a son, Richard, who inherited the title of Duke of York and married Cecily Neville, who gave him four sons: Edward, Edmund, George, and Richard. York believed his descent from Edward III's second son, Clarence, gave him a better claim to the throne than Henry VI, though he bided his time for the moment. He had a powerful ally in Richard Neville, 16th Earl of Warwick, who later was known as the Kingmaker and was mentor to York's youngest son, Richard.

Henry VI fell ill in 1453, and the ensuing crisis led in 1455 to the 1st Battle of St Albans, at which the Yorkists were temporarily victorious. Fighting resumed in 1459 with another Yorkist success at the Battle of Blore Heath. However, the Lancastrians won at Ludford Bridge, forcing York into exile. He returned, won the Battle of Northampton, but failed to take the throne, and at the Battlefield of Wakefield was killed. His eldest son Edward won the Battle of Mortimer's Cross in 1461 and, despite the Lancastrian victory at the 2nd Battle of St Albans, he took the throne, which he successfully defended at the bloody Battle of Towton. Edward had a strong, though not indisputable, claim to the throne and enjoyed considerable support. In 1464 he married Elizabeth Woodville. Though this was controversial, as she was a widow and a commoner, she gave him ten children. Edward secured his position with victories in 1464 at the Battle of Hedgeley Moor and the Battle of Hexham.

However, Warwick turned against him, and he lost the Battle of Edgecote in 1469. Despite winning the Battle of Lose-coat Field, he was forced to flee England in 1470, and Henry VI briefly returned to the throne. However, Edward came back in 1471, won the Battle of Barnet, in which Warwick died, won the battle of Tewkesbury, in which the Lancastrian Prince Edward died, and arranged for Henry VI to die in captivity. Edward IV's second reign was successful. His brother Edmund, Earl of Rutland, had died years earlier at Wakefield, but Edward had to deal with plots involving his brother George, Duke of Clarence, whom he finally executed for treason in 1478. Edward died young in 1483 and was succeeded by his twelve-year-old son, Edward V. Richard assumed the title of Lord Protector and put the young king and his younger brother in the Tower of London. They were never seen again.

Richard—last surviving son of the old Duke of York—usurped the throne and ruled for the next two years as Richard III. Though Richard is Shakespeare's archetypal villain, he has defenders in the English Richard III Society and the American Friends of Richard III, who regard him as unfairly maligned by Tudor propaganda. Though the Tudor depiction contains a significant element of truth, Richard differed from his contemporaries only in degree. As historian Charles Ross noted in his biography, *Richard III*, "the later fifteenth century in England is now seen as a ruthless and violent age as concerns the upper ranks of society, full of private feuds, intimidation, land hunger, and litigiousness, and consideration of Richard's life and career against this background has tended to remove him from the lonely pinnacle of Villainy Incarnate on which Shakespeare had placed him." He was twice exiled as a child, his father was killed in battle, his brother Edmund murdered, his brother George executed, and many of his acquaintances died violently. If he was brutal, it was because he learned well the lessons his society taught him. Moreover, if his method of becoming king was hardly laudable, he was a competent monarch nonetheless.

Richard was born on October 2, 1452 at Fotheringay Castle in Northamptonshire. In 1459 his father York and brother Edmund fled to Ireland, his brother Edward and Warwick went to Calais, and Henry placed young Richard, his mother, and his bother George in the Duchess of Buckingham's custody. But after Edward and Warwick captured Henry in 1460, they moved to London. When York died, his wife sent George and Richard to Philip the Good, Duke of Burgundy. But soon Edward IV called them home, made them Knights of the Bath, gave them land, and made George Duke of Clarence and Richard Duke of Gloucester. The next few years of Richard's life are obscure, but by late 1465 he entered Warwick's household, where he remained until 1468 or 1469. Edward endowed Clarence with vast estates and responsibilities in the 1460s but was less generous with Richard, who became a Knight of the Garter in 1466 and obtained a handful of offices over the next few years.

Richard opposed Warwick's treason, joined Edward in exile, helped reconcile him with Clarence, and fought at Barnet and Tewkesbury. Afterward he received Warwick's former lands and built a powerful northern affinity. He married Warwick's daughter Ann, whose sister Isabel was married to Clarence. In 1473 Ann gave birth to a son, Edward, who was briefly Prince of Wales when his father became king. Richard accompanied Edward IV on his French campaign in 1475 and became lord admiral in 1478 and lieutenant general in 1480. In 1482 Edward attempted to oust James III of Scotland in favor of his brother, Alexander, Duke of Albany. Though this failed, Richard—commanding the English forces—captured the castle of Berwick.

When Edward IV died on April 9, 1483, a power struggle ensued between Richard and the Woodvilles, including Earl Rivers. Richard and the Duke of Buckingham arrested Rivers, took custody of Edward V, and escorted him to London on May 4. Edward IV's widow Elizabeth fled to sanctuary at Westminster with her daughters and younger son, the Duke of York. Richard rescheduled the coronation for June 22, summoned a

Parliament for June 25, and moved Edward V to the Tower of London. By June 10 he claimed a Woodville conspiracy against him was afoot and summoned forces from York. On June 13 he arrested his former ally, William Lord Hastings, who was immediately executed without trial, and Elizabeth Shore, who allegedly had attacked him with sorcery. He also persuaded Elizabeth to send the little Duke of York from sanctuary to the Tower.

By June 20 Richard had decided to take the throne. On June 22 Ralph Shaw preached in his favor at St. Paul's Cross, and on June 24 Buckingham spoke on his behalf at the London Guildhall. Though he cancelled Parliament, an assembly of lords recognized him as king on June 25, and he began his reign on the 26th. By then he had executed Rivers, Lord Grey, and Sir Thomas Vaughan at Pontefract without trial. Crowned on July 6 at Westminster, he soon embarked on a lengthy progress through his realm.

Richard's usurpation and the belief that he had murdered his nephews led to rebellion in October. Southern magnates, including former members of Edward IV's household, instigated the plot, which for some reason Buckingham joined. They contacted Henry Tudor, who planned to invade England in conjunction with an insurrection on October 18 and take the throne. However, Richard foiled the plot, executed the leaders, and had parliament pass an act of attainder against 100 rebels. Remaining alert, he persuaded his nieces to leave sanctuary and considered marrying the eldest, Elizabeth, whom Tudor had promised to wed. He called on the bishops to attack immorality, probably trying to bolster his image. His heir died in April.

Richard persuaded the Duke of Brittany to withdraw protection from Henry Tudor, but the latter fled to France, where he obtained Charles VIII's support. Early in 1485 Richard learned that Henry was planning an invasion and incurred further unpopularity by levying a forced loan to strengthen his defenses. Richard had recognized Clarence's son, Edward, Earl of Warwick as royal heir, but now replaced him with his sister's son, John de la Pole, earl of Lincoln. Henry landed near Milford Haven on August 7 and marched to Bosworth. Wearing his crown into battle, a demoralized Richard met Henry on August 23. Hampered by the terrain, Lord Stanley's desertion, and the Earl of Northumberland's failure to join the fray, Richard tried to engage Henry in personal combat, but was killed before reaching him. His naked body was thrown over a horse, taken to Leicester, and displayed for two days before he was buried at Grey Friars. Though Henry VII built a tomb for him, it was destroyed during the

Reformation, and until recently Richard was the only English monarch since the Norman Conquest without a suitable burial place.

Henry VII, as Tudor now became, was a "Lancastrian." His grandfather Owen married Henry V's widow Catherine, and thus his uncle, Jasper, Duke of Bedford and his father Edmund were half-brothers of Henry VI. More important, his mother, Margaret Beaufort, was descended from John of Gaunt and plotted with Elizabeth Woodville to overthrow Richard III. Henry thus had Lancastrian connections on both sides, but he also shrewdly courted the Yorkists. In 1486 he married Elizabeth of York, thereby uniting the two lines.

What sort of man was Richard? One of the strongest points in his favor is his loyalty to Edward IV, in spite of the fact that he received substantially less reward than Clarence prior to the latter's death. Richard built his affinity in Edward IV's interests and associated membership therein with service to the crown. More generally Richard was devoted to the Yorkist cause, and even his usurpation of the throne and arbitrary use of power can be seen as an attempt to maintain Yorkist control of the realm and continuity with Edward's regime. Prior to the October 1483 rising he employed many members of Edward's household and many of the same local officials.

As duke and king, Richard demonstrated the good lordship expected of medieval magnates. He skillfully built influence in the north, where he assumed leadership of the Kingmaker's affinity and won the loyalty of other noblemen, including the powerful Northumberland. He established lesser affinities in East Anglia, Wales, and elsewhere. Richard displayed considerable ability as a soldier. It is often overlooked that he deserves credit for suppressing "Buckingham's rebellion" and that he came near to winning the Battle of Bosworth. Had he done so, Henry Tudor would merit small attention in history books, and Richard—given more time—might have erased his negative image. After all, Edward IV and Henry VII were usurpers, too.

Richard worked hard at governing. His one Parliament is best known for attainting rebels, but it also ratified his title and passed legislation regulating landholding, uses, and the cloth trade, increasing protection for defendants in felony cases, and outlawing benevolences, arbitrary taxes levied by Edward IV. He also created the Council of the North as a counterpart to Edward's Council for Wales. Richard was genuinely pious, patronized religious institutions, founded numerous chantries and collegiate establishments, and planned a college at York. He showed real interest in scholarship, the new humanism, and music.

Certainly he deserves approbation for giving Henry VI a decent tomb. His success in foreign policy was limited by lack of money and the use of Tudor as a diplomatic pawn by Brittany and France.

Richard's most prominent critics are all Tudor propagandists. Polydore Vergil, author of the *Anglica historia*, was an Italian who served Henry VII and clearly favored the Tudor position. Thomas More, who wrote *The History of King Richard III*, was Henry VIII's closest friend prior to their split over the king's divorce and break from Rome. William Shakespeare, author of *The Tragedy of King Richard the Third, containing his treacherous plot against his brother Clarence; the pitiful murder of his innocent nephews; his tyrannical usurpation; with the whole course of his detested life and most deserved death* (c.1592), enjoyed the patronage of Elizabeth I. All had an agenda.

Many of the crimes imputed to Richard are unproven. Reportedly he suggested killing the recorder of York when that city obstructed Edward IV's return in 1471. It is alleged that he and Clarence murdered Edward, the Prince of Wales, at Tewkesbury and that Richard murdered Henry VI in the Tower. Though neither is impossible, it is unlikely that Richard would have acted without orders from Edward IV. The charge that Richard murdered Thomas, the bastard of Fauconberg, in 1471 is false and so almost certainly is the rumor that he murdered his wife in 1484. His alleged role in Clarence's death is discounted even by his implacable critic, More. However, it says something that contemporaries believed such stories, and there is an element of poetic justice in Richard's treatment by Tudor propagandists, since he was, as Ross notes, "the first English king to use character-assassination as a deliberate instrument of policy."

Many allegations against Richard are real enough. He shared responsibility for executing the duke of Somerset and other Lancastrians in 1471, though this must be viewed in the context of war. In 1474 he and Clarence deprived their mother-in-law of any right in the Warwick inheritance. Particularly difficult to excuse are the summary executions without trial of Hastings, Rivers, and others and his mistreatment of Mistress Shore, whose patient endurance of punishment won her considerable sympathy. His resort to a forced loan compromised his legislation against benevolences. Most damning is that Richard usurped the throne and murdered his nephews. He claimed the crown on dubious grounds, first alleging that Edward IV was a bastard, then charging that his marriage to Elizabeth Woodville was invalid and his children illegitimate. There is little reason to doubt that he had his nephews murdered. This created a vicious circle that ultimately led to Bosworth. It cost Richard the loyalty of Edward IV's servants. Following the 1483 rebellion, he had to rely on his own affinity, and the intrusion of his northern followers into southern shires created further disaffection, including the risings in the fall of 1484. As Richard gave more authority and rewards to a shrinking group of dependable servants, other magnates concluded that they had no future under him and threw their support to Henry Tudor.

To some extent, Richard's supporters and opponents in the artistic community break down by genre. A great many novelists have used imagination and speculation to fill the gaps in our knowledge about his reign, and often they conclude that he was innocent of the death of his nephews. The most prominent of these is Josephine Tey, whose novel *The Daughter of Time* (1951) will repay reading by even the most skeptical of Richard's critics, though its source-based argument has not convinced many historians. In drama, of course, Shakespeare dominates the field where Richard is concerned, and far people are likely to base their opinion of the last Yorkist king on the play than on recent scholarship. Shakespeare's hunchbacked Richard is self-consciously evil, his physical deformity reflecting his inner state. The play remains one of Shakespeare's most popular works, and theatre companies perform it regularly. Beyond that, it has been filmed many times, first in 1908, most recently in 2008. By far the most famous versions are Laurence Olivier's from 1955 and Ian McKellen's from 1995, but even those films—aesthetically brilliant though they are—have serious problems. First, the original play is not history. Secondly, Olivier's version omits a substantial amount of the play, and McKellen's leaves out even more. Third, McKellen's version is actually reset in an imaginary fascist state in Britain in the 1930s. Obviously, there is little historical insight to be had there!

What then can we learn from abandoned bones? This is a question that actually applies to two great mysteries that have long surrounded Richard III. The first concerns the location of the Battle of Bosworth Field. That is not as simple as it might sound. We know that it was somewhere near Bosworth in Leicestershire, but our only written source is a poem. For decades scholars have believed that the battle took place on Ambion Hill, but they long have puzzled over the lack of archaeological evidence there. However, the discovery of a treasure trove of artifacts offers conclusive proof that it actually occurred about a mile-and-a-half southwest of Ambion Hill.

For centuries scholars had little hope of solving the other great mystery, the location of Richard's long-missing body. Last year, however, screenwriter Philip Langley spearheaded an effort that involved historian Michael Jones, a team of scholars at the University of Leicester, the

Leicester City Council, and the Richard III Society to look for the demolished Grey Friars Church and the body of the missing king under a parking lot in Leicester. In September 2012 they announced that they had found both. DNA testing confirmed that the body they unearthed is Richard. Osteo-archaeologist Jo Appleby has shown that Richard did, indeed, suffer from a crooked back in the form of scoliosis and that he died from an extraordinarily high number of wounds. A further, far less romantic discovery is that Richard apparently was infested with roundworms at the time of his death, which probably was not unusual at the time. Perhaps not surprisingly, there is now a huge controversy over where the body should be buried. Both prestige and tourist dollars are at stake. Of course, all of this fails to take account of by far the most controversial account of Richard's demise and the disposition of his body, and it would be irresponsible of me not to share it with you. That is found in an episode of *The Black Adder*, "The Foretelling" (1983), which humorously suggests that Edmund Blackadder killed Richard III, who initially was succeeded by "Richard IV".

Whatever your opinion of this last theory, it is clear that Richard III remains an intriguing subject for historians and an inspiration to writers of fiction. He also provides us with the opportunity to conclude the More-or-Less Annual Halloween Lecture as I always do. So, what are the magic words?

Suggestions for Further Reading

David Baldwin, *Richard III* (2015); Annette Carson, *Richard III: The Maligned King* (2009); S. B. Chrimes, *Henry VII* (1999); Sean Cunningham, *Richard III: A Royal Enigma* (2003); Keith Dockray and Peter Hammond, *Richard III from Contemporary Chronicles, Letters, and Records* (2015); Glenn Foard and Anne Curry, *Bosworth 1485: A Battle Rediscovered* (2013); Michael Hicks, *The Family of Richard III* (2015) and *Richard III* (2001); John Ashdown Hill, *The Mythology of Richard III* (2015); David Hipshon, *Richard III* (2010); Rosemary Horrox, *Richard III: A Study in Service* (1991); David Horspool, *Richard III: A Ruler and His Reputation* (2015); Michael Jones, *Bosworth: The Battle That Transformed England* (2015); Paul Murray Kendall, *Richard III* (1955); Philippa Langley and Michael Jones, *The King's Grave: The Discovery of Richard III's Lost Burial Place and the Clues It Holds* (2013); V. B. Lamb and Peter Hammond, *The Betrayal of Richard III: An Introduction to the Controversy* (2015); Amy License, *Anne Neville: Richard III's Tragic Queen* (2013) and *Richard III: The Road to Leicester* (2014); Thomas More, *The History of King Richard III*, ed. Simon Webb (2015); A. J. Pollard, *Richard III and the Princes in the Tower*

(1997); Charles Ross, *Edward IV* (1974) and *Richard III* (1983); Desmond Seward, *Richard III: England's Black Legend* (1984); William Shakespeare, *Richard III*, ed. Barbara Mowat for the Folger Shakespeare Library (2004); Josephine Tey, *The Daughter of Time* (the highly influential novel, 1951); Polydore Vergil, *Anglica historia*, ed. Henry Ellis (1846); Horace Walpole and Thomas More, *Richard III: The Great Debate*, ed. Paul Murray Kendall (1992).

2014 PREQUEL
DOCTOR WHO'S ON FIRST

This one is pretty simple. It takes the classic routine, "Who's on First" as Bud Abbott and Lou Costello performed it on the May 15, 1953 episode of *The Abbot and Costello Show*, "The Actor's Home," and inserts a picture of Doctor Who (rotating all thirteen doctors from William Hartnell through Peter Capaldi) each time either says the word "who." Who can watch it? You can watch it at https://myspace.com/headongoolah/videos.

2014 LECTURE
DOCTOR WHODAT HATCHES A HALLOWEEN
DOCTOR WHO HAPLESS HORTONLESS HISTORY LESSON

[Each of the silly questions and silly answers in the lengthy series below is accompanied by appropriate images onscreen and film clips for the detailed examples.]

Hello, whoever you are.

Now, who is Doctor Who?

Doctor Who is a Time Lord from Gallifrey.

What is Gallifrey?

Gallifrey is the planet of the Time Lords.

What are Time Lords?

Time Lords are a humanoid species with a non-linear perception of time and the capability for time travel and regeneration.

Like who?

Naturally!

So Doctor Who is not hu-man?

No. He has two hearts.

Now what is a hoo?

A hoo is a ship burial site like the one in Sutton Hoo, Suffolk, England.

What (not who) is a Who?

A Who is a citizen of Whoville.

Who hears Who's?

Horton hears Who's.

What is a Who's Who?

A Who's Who is a scam created to sell you an expensive *Who's Who in Whatever* volume with your name in it, a reminder of P.T. Barnum's famous dictum, "There's a sucker born every minute."

What are Hooters?

Get your mind out of the gutter. I am talking about owls.

Who is Wat?

Wat Tyler was the leader of the Peasant Revolt of 1381.

Who said "wot wot"?

King George III said "wot wot."

What is a watt?

A watt is a derived unit of power named for James Watt.

What is a Hiwatt?

A Hiwatt is a guitar amplifier.
What is the Who?
The Who is a British rock band.
Who in the Who used a Hiwatt?
Pete Townsend used a Hiwatt.
How many watts are in a Hiwatt?
There are 100 watts in a Hiwatt?
Who is Thufir Hawatt?
Thufir Hawatt is a mentat.
What is a mentat?
A mentat is a human computer in Frank Herbert's novel and movie
Dune.

What is a Whodat?
Originally a Whodat was a gag in a minstrel show, as in "Whodat
say whodat when I say whodat?"
Whodat is Doctor Whodat?
Naturally!
Who is Hoover?
It could be former President Herbert Hoover or former FBI
Director J. Edgar Hoover.
What is a Hoover?
A Hoover is a vacuum cleaner.
What is the Tardis?
The Tardis is a Time and Relative Dimension in Space time
machine and space ship.
How is the Tardis?
The Tardis is bigger on the inside.
Who is the Tardis?
She is [picture of humanoid manifestation of the Tardis].
Is there a Tidy Bowl Tardis?
Apparently there is a Tidy Bowl Tardis near Bristol [a telephone
box with a toilet and lavatory].
Does Doctor Who Hoover the Tardis?
Probably not.
What is a hoodoo?
A hoodoo is a form of folk magic.
What is voodoo?
Voodoo is a syncretic religion.
How does Who do that voodoo that Who do so well?
He's a Time Lord.

Who are Who's ho's?

The Who's ho's are his companions [Clara observes onscreen, "That is just wrong." The crowd booed.]

Who's the greatest woman of Doctor Who?

Rose is the greatest woman of Doctor Who, according to a 2012 BBC survey that took place before the arrival of Clara [Clara observes onscreen, "That is wrong, too."]

Who has a hose and ho ho ho's?

Santa Claus with a hose.

Which Who is he who is not Who and why?

Peter Cushing is the un-canonical 1960s movie Doctor from *Dr. Who & the Daleks* (1965) and *Invasion Earth* (1966).

Where does Who go and when?

Wherever and whenever he wants to go.

Who are Who's top ten enemies?

These guys: (10) the Silence, (9) Sontarans, (8) Zygons, (7) Ice Warriors, (6) Autons, (5) Silurians, (4) Weeping Angels, (3) Cybermen, (2) the Master, (1) Daleks.

What does Doctor Who have to do with history and how?

Screenwriters cannot resist having time travelers visit historical characters.

Now, of course, Doctor Who is not real, and we do not know his name. Doctor WhoDat [me] is real, though his real name is something else. Cybermen, Daleks, and their ilk are not real. However, historical characters, events, and situations in *Doctor Who* are real even if their depiction may not be. So let us have a look at them. I will mention all of the historical episodes, though I will draw illustrative clips from episodes dealing with the Tudor period, given that I am a Tudor historian.

With the First Doctor (William Hartnell, 1963-66), the series devoted a lot of episodes to historical figures, including Episodes 1:2-4 (i.e., Season 1, Episodes 2, 3, and 4) to a trip to the dawn of history c.100,000 BC and the discovery of fire; 1:14-20 to Marco Polo and Kublai Khan in the thirteenth century; 1:27-30 to the Aztecs in the sixteenth;1:37-45 to the French Revolution in the eighteenth; 2:12-15 to ancient Rome; 2:22-25 to the Third Crusade, Richard I, and Saladin in the late thirteenth; 2:30-35 to a nineteenth century sailing ship, the twentieth century Empire State Building, plus the Beatles, Dracula, Frankenstein, Elizabeth I, and William Shakespeare; 2:36-39 to the Norman Conquest in 1066; 3:6-9 to the Trojan War in the thirteenth century BC; 3:18 to ancient Egypt; 3:22-25 to Huguenots and the St. Bartholomew's Day Massacre in 1572; 3:34-37 to

Wyatt Earp and his fellow gunfighters at the OK Corral in nineteenth century America; and 4:1-4 to Cornwall in the seventeenth century.

Episode 2:30, "The Executioners," is the first in a six-part sequence collectively known as *The Chase*. Not surprisingly, it is Daleks who are doing the chasing. Meanwhile, in the TARDIS, the Doctor is working on a device called a Time-Space Visualizer that allows users to view specific events in history. Between Ian watching Abraham Lincoln's Gettysburg Address and Vicki watching the Beatles in 1965, Barbara Wright selects the court of Elizabeth I, and they see Francis Bacon conducting William Shakespeare into the presence of the queen, who questions him sharply about the resemblance of his character Falstaff to the traitor Sir John Oldcastle. Shakespeare admits it, Elizabeth suggests that he write about Falstaff in love (a reference to The Merry Wives of Windsor), and Bacon recommends the subject of Prince Hamlet of Denmark, which the bard rejects before reconsidering. This is all very playful and obviously fictitious, though it requires that the audience know something of Elizabeth, Bacon, and Shakespeare in order to get the joke.

With the Second Doctor (Patrick Troughton, 1966-69), the series devoted Episodes 4:15-18 to Scotland in 1746 after the Battle of Culloden; 4:19-22 to a dubiously "historical" visit to Atlantis; 4:38 to England in the nineteenth century; 5:11-16 to the Ice Age; and 6:35-44 to the American Revolution, World War I, and other times and places.

With the Third Doctor (John Pertwee, 1970-74), the series devoted none of Seasons 7 and 8 to historical episodes, Episodes 9:24-26 to another visit to Atlantis, 10:5-8 to the 1920s; and none of Season 11.

With the Fourth Doctor (Tom Baker, 1974-81), the series devoted none of Season 12 to historical episodes; Episodes 13:9-12 to 1911; 14:1-4 to Italy in the fifteenth century; 14:21-26 to Victorian London; none of Seasons 15-16; 17:7 to Florence in 1505; and none of Season 18.

With the Fifth Doctor (Peter Davison, 1981-84), the series devoted Episodes 19:17-18 to England in 1925, 20:21-22 to King John and Magna Carta in 1215, and none of the earlier portion of Season 21 to historical episodes.

With the Sixth Doctor (Colin Baker, 1984-86), the series devoted none of the later portion of Season 21 to historical episodes, Episodes 22:5-6 to the nineteenth century, and none of Season 23.

With the Seventh Doctor (Sylvester McCoy (1987-89), the series devoted Episodes 24:9-11 to Disneyland in 1959, 25:1-4 to 1963 (though it concerned the Daleks), 25:8-10 to a seventeenth century witch in modern times, 26:5-7 to a haunted house in 1883, and 26:8-11 to World War II.

With the Eighth Doctor (Paul McGann, 1996), there was only a made-for-television movie that did not involve history.

How and why are there so many Who's?

Because the Doctor regenerates [clips of all regenerations, including that from Matt Smith to Peter Capaldi].

Does Doctor Whodat regenerate?

No, he degenerates [clip with funny pictures of Doctor Whodat]

With the Ninth Doctor (Christopher Eccleston, 2005), the series devoted Episode 1:3 to Charles Dickens in nineteenth century London, and 1:9-10 to London during early World War II in 1941.

With the Tenth Doctor (David Tennant, 2005-10), the series devoted Episode 2:2 to Queen Victoria in nineteenth century Scotland, 2:4 to Madame de Pompadour in eighteenth century Versailles, 2:7 to London in the 1950s, 3:2 to William Shakespeare in London in 1599 [clip] 3:5 to Manhattan in the 1930s, 3:8-9 to England 3:8-9, 3:10 to various times and places with Sally Sparrow (Carey Mulligan, possibly the best one-off character ever to appear on the show, in the episode that introduces the Weeping Angels), 4:2 to Pompeii in 79 (an episode that featured in another role the future Doctor Peter Capaldi), and 4:7 to Agatha Christie in the 1920s.

By the time the Tenth Doctor visits Shakespeare—in person, not via a Time-Space Visualizer—the show has come a long way in terms of plotting and special effects. In New Series Episode 3:2, the Doctor takes his new companion Martha Jones back to 1599 to see Love's Labour's Lost at the Globe Theatre. There three witchlike aliens called Carrionites, who will remind viewers of Macbeth, are plotting to bring their entire banished race to Earth. The episode is full of jokes in which the Doctor suggests lines from Shakespeare to Shakespeare and of others referring to the Harry Potter films, in which David Tennant (the Doctor) recently had appeared as the evil Barty Crouch (Harry Potter and the Goblet of Fire, 2005). In the end, the Doctor and Martha save the day, but Queen Elizabeth I appears and is furious with the Doctor. Later, in the two-part episode, "The End of Time," it turns out that the Doctor was once married to Elizabeth (for more on that, see below).

With the Eleventh Doctor (Matt Smith, 2010-13), the series devoted Episode 5:3 to Winston Churchill in World War II, 5:6 to Venice in the sixteenth century, 5:10 to Vincent Van Gogh in 1890, 5:12-13 to the ancient Roman Empire, 6:1-2 to Richard Nixon in 1969 and Charles II in the seventeenth century, 6:3 to a pirate ship in the seventeenth, 6:8 to Berlin in the 1930s, 6:13 to Churchill and the stoppage of time, 7:0 to

213

London in 1938 and Dorset in 1941, 7:2 to Nefertiti in the fourteenth century BC and to dinosaurs in prehistory, 7:3 to the Old West in nineteenth century America, 7:6 to London in 1892, 7:9 to a Cold War era Soviet submarine, 7:10 to England in 1974, 7:12 to Yorkshire in the nineteenth century, the Fiftieth Anniversary Special, "Day of the Doctor," to Elizabeth I in sixteenth century England. Here the Tenth Doctor reveals to the Eleventh that he was once married to Elizabeth, who appears rather smitten and silly.

[With the Twelfth Doctor (Peter Capaldi, 2014)—or is he the Thirteenth, given the introduction of John Hurt's Doctor in 7:13 and "The Day of the Doctor"—only 8:3 thus far has featured a quasi-historical episode involved a robot version of Robin Hood, presumably in the twelfth century.]

And, finally, how do Who do Halloween?

Like this! Happy Halloween!

[And much candy is redistributed.]

Suggestions for Further Reading

BBC, *Doctor Who: The Essential Guide to 50 Years of Doctor Who* (2013); Graeme Burk and Robert Smith, *The Doctors Are In: The Essential and Unofficial Guide to Doctor Who's Greatest Time Lord* (2015); Mark Campbell, *Doctor Who: The Complete Guide* (2013); Annabel Gibson and Moray Laing, *Doctor Who: Character Encyclopedia* (2013, updated without attribution in 2014); Marcus Heam, *Doctor Who: The Vault: Treasures from the First 50 Years* (2013); Jason Loborik, *Doctor Who: The Visual Dictionary* (2014); Stephen Nicholas and Mike Tucker, *Doctor Who: Impossible Worlds: A 50-Year Treasury of Art and Design* (2015); Justin Richards, *Doctor Who: The Secret Lives of Monsters* (2014); Gary Russell, *Doctor Who: The Encyclopedia* (2011); Cavan Scott and Mark Wright, *Doctor Who: Who-ology* (2014), Steve Tribe and James Goss, *Doctor Who: A History of the Universe in 100 Objects* (2012).

2015 PREQUEL
CHEAP AND CHEESY SHAMELESS SELF-PROMOTION

The following "public service message" appeared just prior to the 2015 lecture but also at the end of an hour that featured a Festival of Fanfare Films, in which I showed every film that I have made as a prequel to previous Fanfare lectures—each for only the second time in public—interspersed with cheap and cheesy shamelessly self-promoting videos about Impaired Faculties' new twenty-song double CD, *Lipstick and Whiskey*, and this book. The films in question are *A Witch, A Wizard, An Apple, and the Devil* (2002); *Preposterodamus: The Forgotten Seer* (2003); *Mr. Robison's Spooky Neighborhood* (2004); *Monster Matinee* (2005); *It's A Live Onstage Reanimation* (2006); *It's a War . . . A War on Christmas!* (2007); *Heartbreak of Tudoriasis* (2008); *Reality Television* (2009); *Who Killed the Great Pumpkin?* (2010); *It's Poison!* (2011); *The Original Tricky Dick* (2013); and *Doctor Who's On First* (2014). You can watch this announcement at https://myspace.com/headongoolah/videos.

SCREEN	A solemn looking Bill Robison.
BILL	Hello, my name is Bill Robison. Today, as we conclude the 2015 Then and Now Fanfare History and Politics Lecture Series, I want to share something very personal with you. For years I have suffered from a serious and hitherto incurable medical condition known as . . .
SCREEN	*Caseumitis non erubescebanthymia*
BILL	. . . *Caseumitis non erubescebanthymia*, or to render it in vernacular English,
SCREEN	*Caseumitis non erubescebanthymia* Utter Shamelessness complicated by Extreme Cheesiness.
BILL	. . . Utter Shamelessness complicated by Extreme Cheesiness.
SCREEN	Images of More-or-Less Annual Halloween Prequels
BILL	If you have been in this auditorium at any time during the last hour and have seen any of the movies I have made since 2001 as prequels to my More-or-Less Annual Halloween Lectures, you will know that during all that time—for the entirety of the new century, indeed, the

entirety of the new millennium—I have had no shame while being afflicted with an excess of cheesiness.

SCREEN BILL	Images of the More-or-Less Annual Halloween Lectures If you have been in this auditorium at any time during the last fifteen years and have seen any of the presentations I have given since 2001 as my More-or-Less Annual Halloween Lectures, you will know that during all that time—for the entirety of the new century, indeed, the entirety of the new millennium—I have had no shame while being afflicted with an excess of cheesiness.
SCREEN BILL	Images of the More-or-Less Annual Halloween Flyers If you have been on this campus at any time during the last fifteen years and have seen any of the posters I have made since 2001 to advertise my More-or-Less Annual Halloween Lectures, you will know that during all that time—for the entirety of the new century, indeed, the entirety of the new millennium—I have had no shame while being afflicted with an excess of cheesiness.
SCREEN BILL	Eureka! A cure! Today, however, I am extremely pleased to announce that I have discovered a cure for the dread malady known as Caseumitis non erubescebanthymia, or to render it in vernacular English, Utter Shamelessness complicated by Extreme Cheesiness,
SCRREN BILL	Obviously skeptical person looking at Bill from behind . . . and that you see before you this very minute the first beneficiary of this revolutionary breakthrough, for I have been completely cured.
SCREEN BILL	Obviously skeptical people rolling their eyes behind Bill Yes, rather than experiment on helpless animals or hapless humans, I courageously took the risk of trying on myself this new medical miracle, which I funded entirely on my own, exhausting my personal fortune and selling all my possessions. It was I who ingested the first capsule of . . .

SCREEN BILL	Bottle of Le Dommage Sans Fromage . . . Le Dommage Sans Fromage, or to render it in vernacular English . . .
SCREEN BILL	Shame Without Cheese . . . Shame Without Cheese.
SCREEN BILL	Person behind Bill holding sign that reads "He's lying" Yes, I have become a new, more serious and solemn citizen of academe, a more worthy representative of the sober and wise professoriate whom I hitherto have left aghast with my perennial gimmicks and stunts, a more austere avatar of the *dignitas* and *gravitas* that have characterized the great figures of civilization, untarnished by shenanigans and tomfoolery.
SCREEN BILL	Image of book with headline, "Buy My New Book!" Yes, friends, there will be no more silly Halloween hats, no more cavorting onstage with witches and devils in a wizard outfit, no more absurd pretense of being Preposterodamus the illegitimate half-brother of Nostradamus, no more posing as host of Mr. Robison's Neighborhood, no more masquerades as a vampire, no more facades as Frankenstein, no more Christmas rap videos.
SCREEN BILL	Image of CD with headline, "Buy My New CD?" Yes, indeed, there will be no more bogus Tudor rock operas, no more unreal reality television programs, no more phony documentaries investigating the murder of the Great Pumpkin, no more dissimulation about poisons and potions, no more deceitful promises of Tudor ghost stories, no more hip-hop requiems for Richard III, no more sham glamour as Doctor Whodat.
SCREEN VOICE	Scrolling "warning" of the text below. Le Dommage Sans Fromage is available in Regular Strength or new Maximum Strength for Politicians, Preachers, and Pundits. This product has not been FDA-approved. May cause anxiety, bloating, constipation, diarrhea, eczema, flatulence, gout, hives, indigestion, kidney stone, lycanthropy, myopia, neuralgia, obesity, psoriasis, quacking,

rabies, schizophrenia, tumescence, ulcers, vampirism, warts, xerostomia, yeast infection, and zombification. Stop taking and call your doctor immediately if you see aliens in your broom closet, develop an uncontrollable urge to bark like a dog, experience explosive incontinence on a ski-lift, suffer from delusions that you are a sentient pumpkin targeted for surveillance by the National Security Agency, or become obsessed with real world workforce readiness.

SCREEN   Bill with headline, "Hire Me For Lectures and Music!"
BILL   From now on there shall be only the antithesis of asinine antics, the bane of bogus behavior, the confounder of capering clowns, the doyen of decorous deportment, the epitome of elegant erudition, the foe of fatuous frivolity, the goad of gratuitous goofiness, the hinderer of harebrained hijinks, the impediment of inane idiocy, the judge of jejune jests, the knocker of knucklehead knowledge, the lash of ludicrous lunacy, the muter of meat-headed monkeyshines, the nullifier of naughty nonsense, the opponent of opprobrious obnoxiousness, the proper purveyor of prudence, the reserved raconteur of the recondite, the stately sage on the stage, the terror of tendentious titillation, the unction of uncouth utes, the voider of vacuous vaudeville, the warden of wankerish wastrels, the x-terminator of x-uberant x-cess, the yoke of yodeling yoyos , the zapper of zealous zaniness.

SCREEN   Bill
BILL   I shall proceed with pride and propriety . . .

SCREEN   Bill with a trombone
BILL   . . . and a trombone.

218

2015 LECTURE
A FEAST OF FAMOUS FIFTEENS
IN FACT, FICTION, AND FILM

Hello, and thank you for coming to my lecture, "A Feast of Famous Fifteens in Fact, Fiction, and Film." Now you may be wondering what on earth this lecture actually will address, why I am giving it, and what it has to do with Halloween. Perhaps you came here today out of curiosity about those very questions. Or it could be you came seeking extra credit in a class for which a night of debauchery instead of studying yielded a less than satisfactory test score. Or possibly you came because you know I throw candy to the audience, and there are still three more days before you can put on your costume and go from house to house collecting treats from your neighbors [this lecture was delivered on October 28]. Or maybe you wandered in here thinking this was a trombone recital. If so, this is your lucky day, for that is part of the program.

First, though, let me answer your questions. I chose "Famous Fifteens" for this year's lecture topic because 2015 is the fifteenth anniversary of the Then and Now Fanfare History and Politics Lecture Series sponsored each year by the Department of History and Political Science and of the More-or-Less-Annual Halloween Lecture that so far I have given each year. It is also the thirtieth anniversary of Fanfare, which is two-times-fifteen. For 363 days this year—until December 30—I will continue to be sixty, which is four-times-fifteen. It is also the centennial or multi-centennial of numerous very important events in history. I will discuss fifteen such centennial or multi-centennial years that yielded such events, and I will link every one of them to Halloween, even if it is a stretch in some cases. No doubt many of you will get extra credit for being here, and if you stick around to the end, I will throw candy your way. Finally, I will do something momentarily with the trombone.

But why the trombone, you ask? Though nothing links it to a year ending in "15," there were seventy-six trombones that led the big parade in *The Music Man*, which is five-times-fifteen plus one, and everyone loves having a plus-one. Additionally, the instrument was invented in the fifteenth century. It initially was known as the sackbut, from the French sacqueboute, which presumably means that early trombonists were called sackbutists or perhaps sackbutters or sackbuttons. Perhaps this accounts for the trombone's somewhat ambiguous reputation. True, the nineteenth century French Romantic composer Hector Berlioz asserted, "The trombone is the true head of the family of wind instruments, which I have named the "epic" one. It possesses nobility and grandeur to the highest degree; it has all the serious and powerful tones of sublime musical poetry, from religious, calm and imposing accents to savage, orgiastic outburst." However, not everyone shares his enthusiasm.

Mark Twain opined: "If it please your neighbor to break the sacred calm of the night with the snorting of an unholy trombone, it is your duty to put with his wretched music and your privilege to pity him for the unhappy instinct that movies him to delight in such discordant sounds." George Bernard Shaw observed: "My father destroyed his domestic peace by immoderate indulgence in the trombone." Sigmund Freud commented: "I'm not sure why, but trombones make me very uncomfortable" (though sometimes a trombone is just a trombone). Even trombonists have reservations. Samuel Jay Keyser notes: "Some men womanize. Some take to drink. Some play the trombone." Roswell Rudd points out: "You blow in this one end and a sound comes out the other end that disrupts the universe." Delfeayo Marsallis reveals: "When I first saw a trombone, it looked like the instrument no sane person would want to play, so I immediately found my niche." But what the heck, here goes. [Trombone interlude] Now was that not worth the price of admission? Okay, so you got in free. Everybody is so technical.

So why the trombone? To be perfectly honest, it is a cheap and cheesy excuse for me to indulge in a little shameless self-promotion by pointing that I now mostly play the guitar instead of the trombone and do so with the band Impaired Faculties, whose brand new twenty-song double CD, *Lipstick and Whiskey*, you can purchase in the lobby after the lecture and get it autographed by the band. While you are at it, you also can pick up a copy of my new book from Happy Pigg Publishing, *The Halloween Lectures: Fifteen Fiendish Years of Vampires, Werewolves, Witches, Wizards, Monsters, Movies, Tudors, Tricks, and Treats 2001-2015*, which includes links to all the Fanfare prequel movies that I showed at noon today. It also comes with a free DVD of *Preposterodamus: The Forgotten Seer* and a free CD called *Show Tunes* by my pre-Impaired Faculties music project, Headongoolah, which contains all the music from the aforementioned films. Later, three pieces of the Halloween candy I throw to the audience will be wrapped in coupons good in one case for a free copy of the CD, in a second for a free Impaired Faculties t-shirt, and in a third for a free copy of *The Halloween Lectures*. I also urge you to check out my colleague, friend, band mate, and fellow Fanfare lecturer Joe Burns' new solo CD, *Rock and Roll Loser*, which you can download free of charge by following the link on the Impaired Faculties Facebook page. Thank you for listening to this commercial message. We now return you to your regularly scheduled programming.

There have been only twenty years in history that have the potential to be Famous Fifteens, that is, years in which something famous happened and that have centennial or multi-centennial anniversaries in 2015. They start with AD 15 and end with AD 1915. Of course you might ask, what about 15 BC, 115 BC, and so on? But none of those years have centennial anniversaries this year, e.g., 15 BC was 2,030 years ago. In addition, not every "Anno Domini fifteen" witnessed a sufficiently notorious occurrence to qualify. That is really more information than you need about my entirely arbitrary concept for this lecture, is it not? But there it is.

The most noteworthy occurrence in AD 15 was that new Roman Emperor Tiberius transferred election of public officials from popular assemblies to the Senate. But how many of you knew that? So that year is nor a contender. AD 115 brought the beginning of the Kitos War, part of the Jewish-Roman Wars, but the most famous event in that conflict, the Siege of Masada, had happened forty years earlier. About the best thing that year was that the Emperor's name was Trajan, which was just one vowel away from making him the subject of two millennia of condom jokes. Still not good enough. AD 215 is the traditional year associated with the Apostolic Tradition of Hippolytus, a crucial source for the early Christian liturgy containing a forerunner of the Apostles' Creed. But the dating on that could be off by two centuries. No cigar.

AD 315 is a more solid date for early Church history and provides our first Famous Fifteen. That year Emperor Constantine abolished crucifixion for executing certain criminals, and Christians began using the Lamb of God (Agnus Dei) as a symbol for Jesus Christ. What links those two occurrences is that in 313 Constantine issued the Edict of Milan ending the persecution of Christians in the Roman Empire. So what is the tie to Halloween? Until the end of the Roman persecution of Christians, the early Church honored martyrs put to death by non-Christian Emperors rather than the saints whose lives it later celebrated. But after the persecutions ended, there ceased to be a steady supply of new martyrs, and the Church increasingly turned its attention to a new crop of saints. By the eighth century, the Church had an annual festival for honoring the saints, and though at first different countries observed it on various dates, eventually all adopted the common date of November 1 for All Saints Day or All Hallows. The day before, October 31, is All Hallows Eve or Halloween.

A century later our second Famous Fifteen finds the uncomfortable shoe of persecution on the other martyred foot (a metaphor as tortured as the persecuted victims). AD 415 saw a mob of angry Christians murder the female mathematician and Neoplatonist philosopher Hypatia of Alexandria, whom modern scientists revere, whom Second Wave feminists have adopted as one of their own, and who has been the focus of serious scholarly study and a fictionalized character is a host of novels, plays, films, and television shows, including the *Doctor Who* episode, "Time and the Rani," in which she is one of several kidnapped philosophers. What is the link to Halloween? Although Hypatia enjoyed the esteem of contemporary Christian author Socrates Scholasticus, by the seventh century the Coptic Bishop John Nikiû accused her of performing Satanic magic, and in 1843 German scholars Gottlieb Soldan and Heinrich Heppe argued that Hypatia was the first prominent victim of a Christian witch-hunt. Additionally, in the fifteenth century the Renaissance brought a revival of Neoplatonism, which linked external physical deformity to inner imperfection or evil and became the theoretical justification for identifying "ugly" men and women as potential witches during the Great Witch Hunt c.1450-1650. Although Halloween has nothing to do with the Devil and witches save as costume material, disassociating them now is a losing battle.

After Hypatia we hit another dry spell. The best AD 515 can offer is that the Emperor Anastasius I defeated the revolt of Vitalian with a sulfurous substance that resembled Greek Fire but was not, as the Byzantine Empire did not get around to inventing that napalm-like incendiary weapon until 672. Sulfur is redolent of hellfire, but that is just not enough. In 615 the still-pagan Slavs were busy overrunning the Balkans and earning a devilish reputation among Greek Orthodox Christians, but they had started earlier and were not finished, so that does not count.

AD 715 is another story, providing our third Famous Fifteen, as Charles Martel became de facto ruler of the Franks as major domo, or mayor of the palace, to the Merovingian kings. Subsequently he defeated the Moors at the Battle of Tours in 732, thereby preventing the Muslim conquest of the Franks. He also aided the Anglo-Saxon St. Boniface, who established a parish structure for the Frankish church and built numerous monasteries in the kingdom before being murdered in 754 by Frisian pagans angry with him for felling a gigantic tree known as Thor's oak. Charles Martel's son, Pepin the Short, deposed the last of the Merovingian kings in 751 and took the throne in his own right—with papal support—as the first Carolingian king. His son, in turn, was the mighty Charlemagne, who established the Carolingian Empire with a royal court at Aachen, where scholars preserved much of the learning of the classical world. But can we link Charles Martel to Halloween? Oh, yes. For one thing, the rather oblique allusion to Thor above conjures up his legendary hammer Mjölnir and, by implication, the lyrical reference to the "Hammer of the Gods" in "Immigrant Song" by the allegedly Satanic Led Zeppelin. But more the point is that Charles' nickname "Martel" means "Hammer," as in "Hammer of the Moors." Early on Greek Christians mistook Islam for a Christian heresy, but by the eighth century Western Christians were inclined to see Moors as infidels in a league with the Devil (the feeling was mutual, though both sides were wrong). Furthermore, Hammer Films made some of the scariest movies of the 1950s and 60s, as Kate Bush reminds us in her song, "Hammer Horror." How is that for an eclectic, multivalent reference?

AD 815 is our fourth Famous Fifteen due to the discovery of Iceland, which made possible various Viking sagas, important World War II Allied naval bases, and the eccentrically dressed musician Björk. Iceland is known for its volcanoes, which medieval Christians understandably regarded as gates to Hell. Similarly, they saw Vikings as diabolical, including the phrase "God protect us from the Northmen" in their daily prayers. This, of course, is long before Vikings became spokesmen for Capital One. What's in your wallet?

AD 915, by contrast, offers nothing about Vikings or anybody else. But in 1015 we find the fifth Famous Fifteen. The Viking king of Denmark, Cnut the Great, invaded England, setting the stage for his takeover of the kingdom the following year, exactly half a century before William the Conqueror, a descendant of Vikings in Normandy, did the same thing with a longer lasting legacy. Incidentally, the earlier, Danish king's name is not pronounced—as one of my students once mistakenly rendered it—"See-Nut." The real risk, of course, is not with mispronunciation but with misspelling by accidentally rearranging the letters. I spent twenty-five years waiting for this to happen—as students instead wrote about the Prince of "Whales" with an "h"—without a single instance, and then a few years ago a particularly industrious student did it three times in one paragraph. At any rate, Cnut—which cowards spell "Canute" or "Knut"—established a North Sea Empire based in Denmark, Norway, and England that had as good a chance of surviving as William I's Anglo-Norman Empire if only the former had produced capable heirs. That Cnut's sons Harold Harefoot and Harthacnut were less capable than William's sons Robert Curthose, William II, and Henry I is a reminder of the role played in history by contingency, which some might call luck or fortune. That evokes the pagan goddess Fortuna and the pagan Fates. And, of course, in the present both Christian fundamentalists and neo-pagans link paganism, rightly or wrongly, to Halloween.

By the way, having already witnessed the lengths to which I will go to link events to Halloween, you may be wondering, does this guy ever play 'Six Degrees of Kevin Bacon'? Well, yes, in fact, I do. I am two degrees away from Mr. Bacon, for my wife Bibbet and sister-in-law Tasha were both extras in the movie *JFK* (1991), which Oliver Stone filmed in New Orleans and in which Bacon played the fictional character Willie O'Keefe. Incidentally, bacon—the pork product, not the actor—is shunned by both Jews and Muslims, whom some medieval Christians rather uncharitably regarded as minions of the Devil (again, it was mutual). Sadly, no one in my neighborhood hands out bacon during Trick or Treat, or I might mask up and hit the streets.

Our sixth Famous Fifteen gives us two for the price of one. In 1115 St. Bernard founded the Abbey of Clairvaux in northeastern France, giving an enormous boost to the Cistercian Order of monks, which had broken away from the Cluniac Order in 1098 and became one of the most important contributors to the monastic reforms of the High Middle Ages. Bernard later became the namesake of a large and loveable species of dog. Also in 1115, Peter Abelard—a well-known, if controversial, Scholastic theologian—moved to Paris, where he became master of Notre Dame and canon of Sens, moved into the house of the secular canon Fulbert, and began an affair with the latter's niece Héloïse. Their letters and the tragic end of their liaison have made this one of the most famous love matches in history. After Héloïse became pregnant, Abelard sent her to a nunnery, and Fulbert hired a group of men to break into his room and castrate him.

Subsequently, Abelard entered the monastery at St. Denis and wrote the famous theological treatise, *Sic et Non* (*Yes and No*) and other influential works that, because of their allegedly excessive rationalism, led to charges of heresy, conflict with Bernard, and excommunication by Pope Innocent II. Fortunately, Peter the Venerable, Abbot of Cluny, patched things up between Abelard and Bernard and got Innocent to lift the excommunication, and Abelard died a respected theologian. Héloïse became a well-known thinker in her own right, and modern feminists now claim her as they do Hypatia. Both Abelard and Héloïse also wrote music. So did Jean-Jacques Rousseau, who c.1742 invented a new but unsuccessful system of musical notation and in 1761 published a best-selling novel, *Julie, or the New Héloïse*, which the Catholic Church promptly listed on the Index of books prohibited as heretical.

Now how do we connect all this to Halloween? Certainly Abelard was even more unlucky than Charlie Brown, whose unrewarding efforts at

Trick or Treating got him nothing him but rocks in his sack. I sense those of you with your minds in the gutter waiting for me to make an obvious joke here, but I assure you that I would not dream of it. Instead, let us turn to Bernard, who in 1128 played a major role in creating the Rule of the Knights Templar, a crusading order later at the heart of some of the most ridiculous conspiracy theories anyone has ever conceived and a couple of highly improbable films starring Nicholas Cage, who now makes witch movies. In no small part this is because in 1307 the French King Philip IV destroyed the order on trumped-up charges of heresy and Satanism. Meanwhile, Bernard also emphasized the intercessory role of the Virgin Mary, which Protestants in the sixteenth century rejected along with the veneration of the saints, the observance of All Saints Day, and Halloween. He also preached the disastrous Second Crusade (1145-49). Despite that, in 1174 he was canonized, becoming the first Cistercian saint, and Catholics still honor him on All Saints Day.

AD 1215, Famous Fifteen number seven, is particularly important, not only because seven is a magic number but also because the English barons, assembled at Runnymede, forced the infamous King John to agree to the Magna Carta. Even though the devious John soon repudiated the document and died the following year facing armed revolt, subsequent kings reissued the Great Charter, and it has had enormous influence on the subsequent development of parliamentary government in Britain and its offshoots in America and the Commonwealth. At the time the barons intended only to protect their own interests, but Magna Carta established several important constitutional and legal precedents that have expanded over the centuries to include all citizens. One is the right to trial by a jury of one's peers. Another is due process of law, enshrined in the writ of habeas corpus in the British Habeas Corpus Act of 1679 and the United States Constitution, Article One, Section 9, Clause 2. Magna Carta also stipulates that there are limits on the power of monarchy or, more broadly speaking, on government in general. Initially it specifically required the king to seek his tenants-in-chiefs' approval before requesting feudal aids beyond those that vassals traditionally owed their lord under the principles of English feudalism. In other words, he must obtain the nobility's approval before levying new taxes. On the basis of this requirement, subsequent kings began summoning the nobility periodically to councils where they would redress the nobles' grievances in return for revenue. Eventually, kings began including prosperous commoners in this process, which gave birth to Parliament, an institution that takes its name from the French verb "parler," to talk.

Given the importance of Magna Carta, the sophisticated thinking required to fully understand its principles, and its general lack of sexiness, it is perhaps inevitable that the film industry has dealt with it in a less than historically accurate fashion. Let us take, for example, the most recent Robin Hood film (2010), starring Russell Crowe, which—like all Robin Hood films—is fictitious and—like most of them—makes John a bumbling villain. In it we "learn" that the actual author of Magna Carta was Robin of Locksley's father (along with the discovery that in the late twelfth century the French invaded the English coast using Higgins boats). But even films with John as the main character tend to misrepresent him and Magna Carta, including the problematic recent film, *Ironclad* (2011).

But what allows us to connect John to Halloween? On one hand, there is a good deal of masking in the Robin Hood films, and the gang from Sherwood Forest play quite a few tricks and collect no shortage of treats. Beyond that, the well-known Disney *Robin Hood* (1973) makes John a lion and gives him as his principal advisor a snake named Sir Hiss. Traditionally, Christianity associates the snake with temptation and the Devil on the basis of the *Book of Genesis*, and some modern folk then erroneously relate the Biblical serpent to Halloween. Actually the serpent in *Genesis* is never identified as the Devil, and Halloween in reality has nothing to do with Satan, but if we want to stretch the point (and we do), then Sir Hiss is a rather elastic reptile. But, not to settle for one stretch when two are twice as much fun, there is also a legend that associates John's name with the privy—not the Privy Council, which did not exist in his day, but the outhouse. And during the heyday of outdoor plumbing in nineteenth and early twentieth century America, a favorite prank of Halloween tricksters was to tip over outhouses, preferably while occupied. So there you go.

AD 1315, the eighth Famous—and frigid—Fifteen, witnessed the beginning of the Great Famine of 1315-22 in England and the rest of Europe as the result of the very real global cooling that occurred in the fourteenth century in the so-called "Little Ice Age," leading to a series of poor harvests and widespread starvation. The famine was part of a more generalized demographic crisis that was in turn part of what historians call the General Crisis of the Fourteenth Century. The crisis also brought the Black Death to Europe in 1347-51, during which it wiped out about one-third of the entire population, disappeared for a time, and then reappeared periodically for the remainder of the century and beyond. Monty Python satirized the collection of multiplying dead bodies by carters with the worst job in town in *Monty Python and the Holy Grail* (1975), but the pervasiveness of death was no joke. The devastating pandemic left survivors obsessed with death and led to a proliferation of artworks featuring the *dans macabre*, with dancing skeletons and corpses in various stages of decomposition. Going house-to-house collecting corpses sounds like a very bizarre analogue to Trick or Treating, while the connection of dancing skeletons to Halloween really should require no explanation. For good measure, people at the time looked for scapegoats, and those who did not blame the Jews often attributed the plague to witchcraft.

In another two-fer, AD 1315 also witnessed the Battle of Morgarten, in which the Swiss Confederation won its independence from Leopold I, Duke of Austria. Among the Swiss who fought in this conflict was William Tell, who—according to legend—in 1307 defied the Habsburg representative Gessler's demand that he bow to a pole on which he had placed his hat. As punishment, Gessler required him to shoot an apple off the head of his son Walter with a crossbow. This made Tell into a Swiss national hero and earned him the starring role in a nineteenth century opera by Gioachino Rossini, the overture to which my generation knows as the theme song for *The Lone Ranger*, the hero of which is a man wearing a mask. Need I say more? If so, let me add that we no longer encourage parents to shoot apples off the heads of their children with crossbows, but we have a safer—if slightly messy—Halloween sport that involves bobbing for apples. This, of course, entails its own risks, as Lucy van Pelt will tell you.

AD 1415, our ninth Famous Fifteen, brought the most famous victory of Henry V, the great warrior king of England. At the Battle of Agincourt, Henry and his yeoman archers defeated a supposedly superior French army. In the process it wiped out a substantial portion of the French nobility, who prior to the battle were unable to conceive of defeat at the hands of their social inferiors, the merely bourgeois English yeomanry. Thus, in a sense, Agincourt turned the world upside down, just as carnivalesque festivals like Halloween and Mardi Gras temporarily do. Moreover, in William Shakespeare's play, *Henry V*, the English king masks himself in a cloak on the eve of battle in order to circulate among his troops and get a sense of their mood, though he collects no treats. The battle was not on Halloween, but famously it occurred on October 25, the feast day of St. Crispin, another of those saints revered a week later on All Saints Day. There are two excellent film versions of Shakespeare's play, directed by and starring Laurence Olivier and Kenneth Branagh, respectively.

AD 1515, Famous Fifteen number ten, saw a major setback for

Henry VIII, who idolized Henry V, studied his Agincourt campaign, and dreamed of completing the earlier king's project of making himself King of France as well as England. Henry VIII already had fought one war against France as the ally of his father-in-law, Ferdinand of Aragon, and had captured Thérouanne and Tournai following the 1513 Battle of Guinegate or the Battle of the Spurs, as the English called it because the French cavalry retreated in such haste. Henry forced peace on the elderly Louis XII; however, the French king died in 1515, and his successor was Francis I, a man just as ambitious, talented, and youthful as Henry. Later that year, Francis won a huge victory in the Habsburg-Valois Wars in Italy, defeating the purportedly invincible Swiss mercenary pikemen in the pay of the Emperor Maximilian I. For the moment this made Francis the dominant figure in Europe, much to the envious Henry's dismay. It only got worse the following year, when Ferdinand of Aragon died and was succeed as King of Aragon and Castile by his grandson, Charles I, who was similarly ambitious, capable, and young. In 1519, after Maximilian also died, the Spanish king also became Holy Roman Emperor Charles V in an imperial election in which the electors chose him over both Francis and Henry. He consolidated his position as new dominant figure with a victory over Francis at the Battle of Pavia in 1525.

Adding insult to injury for Henry was that both Charles and Francis had no trouble producing male heirs, while the English king's only surviving child with his first wife, Catherine of Aragon, was a daughter Mary. By the mid-1520s Henry was attempting to divorce Catherine, with whom he believed himself to be living in sin based on the statement in the Old Testament Book of Leviticus that a man who "uncovers the nakedness of his brother's wife shall be childless." Desperate for a son to inherit his throne, Henry planned to marry Anne Boleyn, who he was certain would give him a surviving male child. When Pope Clement VII refused to grant his approval, Henry broke away from Roman Church and collaborated with Parliament to make himself Supreme Head of the Church of England. Henry, who met Anne during a masque—a theatrical production in which all participants were masked—was extremely fond of dressing in costumes and, as his later girth attests, of treats. However, after the break with Rome, saints fell out of favor in England and thus so did Halloween. After a subsequent generation of Catholic radicals attempted to kill the Protestant King James I, the nobility, and the bishops by blowing up Parliament in the Gunpowder Plot of November 5, 1605, annual celebrations of their failure on Gunpowder Day or Guy Fawkes Day replaced Halloween as the main fall festival in England.

AD 1615 is Famous Fifteen number eleven thanks to Johannes Kepler, one of the giants of the First Scientific Revolution along with his predecessor Nicolas Copernicus, his former employer Tycho Brahe, his contemporaries Francis Bacon, Rene Descartes, and Galileo Galilei, and the eminent successor he so greatly influenced, Isaac Newton. In 1615 Kepler published the first volume of his three-part *Epitome of Copernican Astronomy*, which explicated his law of planetary motion, whereby the same mathematical formula describes the elliptical orbits of the six innermost planets of our solar system. This is one of the first scientific laws that, along with the work of Galileo and Newton, led to the Enlightenment-era idea of a mechanistic universe in which God is the Great Clockmaker.

Like all astronomers in his day, Kepler was also an astrologer and thus the practitioner of an extraordinarily sophisticated, if ultimately fallacious, pseudo-science with occult overtones that often associate its moons, stars, and mysteries with Halloween in popular culture. But the best link between Kepler and Halloween is that in 1615 a woman named Ursula Reingold accused his mother Katherina of poisoning her with a witch's brew, charges that she made formal in 1617, landing Katherina in prison for fourteen months in 1620-21, though she ultimately was exonerated. This is a useful reminder that every generation has one foot in the scientific future and one in the superstitious past.

AD 1715, the twelfth Famous Fifteen, gives us a trifecta. First of all, it witnessed the death of the long-reigning absolutist monarchy and namesake of our home state, Louis XIV of France. Between 1677 and 1682 his reign witnessed the notorious Affair of the Poisons, which led to thirty-six people—including members of his own inner circle—being executed on charges on poisoning and witchcraft. Secondly, it brought the failed rebellion of the Jacobites in Britain known as the "Fifteen," in which supporters of the Catholic Stuart line sought to replace the Protestant Hanoverian King George I with the son of the Catholic King James II deposed in the Glorious Revolution of 1688, i.e., James Edward the "Old Pretender" or "James III" as he styled himself. The Jacobites tried again in 1745 with James Edward's son Charles Edward the "Young Pretender," who was also known as "Bonnie Prince Charlie" and is the subject of the song "My Bonnie Lies Over the Ocean." Bonnie Prince Charlie had to escape from Scotland after his failed invasion by masking, i.e., disguising himself as a woman. Finally, 1715 saw the sinking of a Spanish treasure fleet off the coast of what is now Vero Beach, Florida, where subsequently it was partially salvaged by pirates. As we all know, pirates fly a flag with a skull and crossbones, deal with occult figures in films like the *Pirate of the*

Caribbean series, drink rum and sing as many people do on Halloween, are important characters in "Garfield's Halloween Adventure" (1985), and are the source for one of the essential Halloween costumes, though ultimately pirate outfits are less popular than the Slutty Nurse get-up.

AD 1815 is Famous Fifteen number thirteen—another famously occult number—and offers not three but four events of significance. First, the year began with the Battle of New Orleans in which forces led by General Andrew Jackson and Jean Lafitte—ahem, a pirate—defeated the British, whose leader General Pakenham was killed and sent home in a barrel of—yes, you guessed it—rum. We do not know for certain if Lafitte wore a mask before the victory led to his pardon, but we do know that he never allowed himself to be painted, as he did not wish to be recognized. The famous portrait of Lafitte is an artist's conception. As the home of haunted houses, vampire authors, voodoo queens, and virtually year-round processions in which participants collect goodies, New Orleans' affinity with Halloween is obvious. The same year also brought the final defeat of Napoleon at the Battle of Waterloo by forces under the Duke of Wellington and the Prussian General Gebhard Leberecht von Blücher, who shares a surname with the terrifying Frau Blücher of the movie *Young Frankenstein* (1974).

Then came the Congress of Vienna, which redrew the map of Europe and sought to restore peace and order to post-Napoleonic Europe. Halloween is not a German holiday, though Martinstag on November 11 involves costumes and a lantern-lit procession that resembles Trick or Treating. However, Catholics in Vienna do observe All Saints Day, the Austrian city is home to a number of haunted sites, including the distinctly spooky Cemetery of the Nameless, and the nearby town of Retz holds an annual fall pumpkin festival. Finally, 1815 brought the eruption of Mt. Tambora in Indonesia, one of the most powerful volcanoes in history and the explosive power of which surpassed that of Krakatoa in 1883. Not only did Tambora seem like a gate to Hell, it appeared to unleash Hell in this world, where the cloud of ash spread across the Earth and remained airborne for so long that it is known as the Year Without a Summer. Spooky enough.

The fourteenth Famous Fifteen is 1915, which offers a plethora of memorable and frequently scary events. It began with Harry Houdini escaping from a strait jacket on New Year's Day, was the first full year of World War I (which involved much wearing of gas masks), the U.S. House of Representatives rejected a bill to give women the right to vote five months before Denmark and Iceland adopted women's suffrage (which should have had Congress hiding behind masks), an earthquake in Italy registered 6.8 on the Richter scale and killed 30,000, German zeppelins bombed England for the first time, the British Navy sank the German *SMS Blücher*, Typhoid Mary wound up quarantined after infecting numerous people, D.W. Griffith premiered *Birth of a Nation* (which featured some unpleasant fellows in "ghost" costumes), Percival Lowell photographed Pluto (named for the Roman god of the Netherworld) though it was not until 1930 that Clyde Tombaugh recognized it as a planet, Germany became the first country to use poison gas on a large-scale basis, the Armenian Genocide began, the failed Gallipoli campaign in Turkey nearly destroyed Winston Churchill's political career, Italy defected to the Allies from the Triple Alliance, John McCrae wrote the poem "In Flanders Fields," Babe Ruth hit his first home run as a member of the Boston Red Sox, a German U-boat sank the *Lusitania*, the worst rail disaster in British history occurred in Quintinshill in Scotland, Lassen Peak erupted in California (the last volcanic eruption in the forty-eight contiguous states prior the Mt. St. Helens in 1980), an unnamed hurricane devastated Galveston and New Orleans, the British tested the first armored tank, William Simmons revived the Ku Klux Klan at Stone Mountain in Georgia, and Albert Einstein developed his theory of general relativity.

Can I relate all these events to Halloween? You bet, but you will have to take it on faith unless you want to be here another couple of hours. Instead, let me do this. I will point out that Einstein undermined the safe reality of Newtonian physics and reintroduced uncertainty into the universe, which is the spookiest thing I have ever heard. Appropriately, then, you may be wondering what has become of Famous Fifteen Fifteen. Has it vanished beyond the event horizon into a black hole?

Or could it be this year? I must point out that historians have yet fully to assess 2015, though we already recognize that on the negative side it has given us a premature presidential campaign featuring a host of really scary candidates in both parties of whom most of us already are well and truly sick. That sounds more like infamy than fame. Ah, but on the positive side, 2015 has given you the opportunity—in case I have not mentioned it—to acquire the brand new Impaired Faculties CD, *Lipstick and Whiskey*, and a copy of *The Halloween Lectures*, a book that even includes the lecture I am concluding now. Now that is a famous opportunity indeed!

Finally, let's have a little test. If you fail, I will play the trombone some more. But if you know the magic words, I will stop talking and throw candy. So . . .

Suggestions for Further Reading

Alessandro Barbero, *Charlemagne: Father of a Continent* (2004); Jeremy Black, *The Battle of Waterloo* (2010); Mary T. Boatwright, et. al., *The Romans: From Village to Empire: A History of Rome from Earliest Times to the End of the Western Empire*, 2nd edition (2011); James Burge, *Héloïse and Abelard: A New Biography* (2004); Jesse Byock, *Medieval Iceland: Society, Sagas and Power* (1988); James A. Connor, *Kepler's Witch* (2009); Anne Curry, *Agincourt: A New History* (2005); Maria Dzielska, *Hypatia of Alexandria* (1996); Gillian Evans, *Bernard of Clairvaux* (2000); Martin Gilbert, *The First World War: A Complete History* (2004); Randolph C. Head, "William Tell and His Comrades: Association and Fraternity in the Propaganda of Fifteenth- and Sixteenth-Century Switzerland," *The Journal of Modern History* 67.3 (1995): 527–557; Trevor Herbert, *The Trombone* (2006); Walter Isaacson, *Albert Einstein: His Life and Universe* (2008); William Chester Jordan, *The Great Famine* (1997); R.J. Knecht, *Francis I* (1984); M.K. Lawson, *Cnut: England's Viking King* (2011); Sinclair McKay, *A Thing Unspeakable Horror: The History of Hammer Films* (2007); Diarmaid MacCulloch, *Christianity: The First Three Thousand Years* (2011); Lynn Wood Mollenauer, *Strange Revelations: Magic, Poison, and Sacrilege in Louis XIV's France* (2007); David Potter, *Constantine the Emperor* (2015); Robert Remini, *The Battle of New Orleans: Andrew Jackson and America's First Military Victory* (2001); Nicholas Rogers, *Halloween: From Pagan Ritual to Party Night* (2002); J.J. Scarisbrick, *Henry VIII* (1997); Daniel Szechi, *1715: The Great Jacobite Rebellion* (2006); Ralph Turner, *Magna Carta Through the Ages* (2003); Brian E. Vick, *The Congress of Vienna: Power and Politics After Napoleon* (2014); Timothy R. Walton, *The Spanish Treasure Fleets* (2002); Gillen D'Arcy Wood, *Tambora: The Eruption That Changed the World* (2014).

ABOUT THE AUTHOR

William B. (Bill) Robison is native of Lecompte, Louisiana, where he grew up working in and later managed a successful family-owned hardware store. He attended Louisiana State University at Alexandria (1973-75) and LSU-Baton Rouge (1975-83) on a National Merit Scholarship and other scholarships but otherwise paid for his education by working as a graduate assistant, carpenter, furniture mover, and house painter. He earned the PhD in History at LSU in 1983 and has been a faculty member in the Department of History and Political Science at Southeastern Louisiana University (Hammond) ever since. He served as coordinator of the Master's program in History from 1992 to 1998, achieved the rank of Professor of History in 1993, served as an assistant to the Provost in 1998-99, became Department Head in 1999, and has steadfastly resisted attempts to move him into administration and out of the classroom. He teaches undergraduate and graduate courses on British and Early Modern European History, received the President's Award for Excellence in Teaching in 1996, and held the Fay Warren Reimers Distinguished Teaching Professorship in the Humanities in 1996-99.

Robison is already at work on a sequel to *The Halloween Lectures* called *More Lectures About Everything*. He is editor of *History, Fiction, and 'The Tudors': Sex, Politics, Power, and Artistic License in the Showtime Television Series* (2016), which features essays from twenty leading historians of the Tudor era; co-author with Sue Parrill of *The Tudors on Film and Television* (McFarland, 2013) and maintains the associated interactive website www.tudorsonfilm.com; co-editor with Ronald H. Fritze of the *Historical Dictionary of Stuart England* (1996) and *Historical Dictionary of Late Medieval England* (2002); author of numerous articles on early modern England, film history, popular culture, and music; currently is doing research on the intersection of national and local politics during the English Reformation, particularly in Surrey, and on Mark Twain and the Tudors; is director of the film *Louisiana During World War II*; and is a published poet.

Robison's outreach activities include administration of the department's Cultural Resources Management, Public History, and Political Science internship programs; coordination of the department-sponsored Constitution Day Lecture, Then and Now Fanfare History and Politics Lecture Series, Veterans Day Lecture, Black History Month Lecture Series, Women's History Month Lecture Series, Holocaust Remembrance Day Lecture, and Deep Delta Civil War Symposium; and service as the academic coordinator for two $1 million Teaching American History

Grants held in partnership with the Tangipahoa Parish School District (2004-11), which provided thousands of hours of Continuing Learning Units to area teachers, enabled over 100 to become highly qualified under No Child Left Behind, allowed about twenty to earn Master's degrees in History, and contributed to significant improvement in standardized test scores by students in participating teachers' classes.

Robison plays guitar with a band of colleagues called Impaired Faculties, which also includes Joe Burns, Dan McCarthy, Randy Settoon, and Ralph Wood. The band has just released its first full-length recording, a twenty-song double CD called *Lipstick and Whiskey*, in addition to which Burns has a solo CD called *Rock and Roll Loser*. Follow them on Facebook!

Robison is available for a wide variety of lectures and six-week library programs, which are detailed at length at www.tudorsonfilm.com.

Made in the USA
Lexington, KY
16 June 2018